Capital, Exploitation and Economic Crisis

Imperative reading for those engaged in Marx's political economy and its application to contemporary capitalism.

Prof. Ben Fine, *School of Oriental and African Studies (SOAS), UK*

The first edition of *Capital, Exploitation and Economic Crisis* was the best critical introduction to Marxist economic theory. John Weeks has now restated and strengthened his original argument, in particular by engaging in detail with more mainstream neoclassical and Keynesian economics, and has brought it up to date with a final chapter on the global economic and financial crisis that started in 2007. An indispensable book for anyone trying to understand Marx and capitalism.

Prof. Alex Callinicos, *King's College London, UK*

In 2008 the capitalist world was swept by the severest crisis since the Great Depression of the 1930s. Mainstream economics neither anticipated nor could account for this disastrous financial crisis, which required massive state intervention throughout the capitalist world. Karl Marx did anticipate this type of financial collapse, arguing that it was derivative from the "fetishism of commodities" inherent in the capitalist mode of production. This book substantiates the foregoing claim by a journey from Marx's analysis of commodities to the capitalist crisis of the twenty-first century.

The book demonstrates that Marx's framework (1) demonstrates that capitalism is but one historical form of class society among many, (2) explains the transition from precapitalist to capitalist society, (3) reveals the concrete operation of a capitalist economy and (4) shows why others would explain the capitalist economy in alternative theoretical frameworks. The central element in his framework from which all else derives is "the theory of value". This book is not an exercise in the history of thought. It is an attempt to analyze the nature of contemporary capitalist society. While Marx's analysis of capitalism has implications for political action, these need not lead one to embrace revolution in place of reform, though it can and has provided the analytical foundation for both. Marx's analysis of capitalism is a coherent whole, and meaningful insights cannot be obtained by extracting elements from it.

Weeks starts out by looking at the nature of capitalism and an analysis circulation, money and credit unfold from the theory of value. The nature and inherent necessity of competition are demonstrated in Chapter 8. A consequence of competition, expressed in the movement of capital, is technical change, the contradictory impact of which is explained in Chapter 9. This is brought together with the other elements of value theory (money, credit and competition) in Chapter 10, where economic crises are treated in detail. The final chapter applies the theory of crisis to the extreme financial disturbances of the 2000s.

This book should be of interest to students and researchers of economics, politics and sociology.

John Weeks is Professor Emeritus of Economics at the University of London, UK.

Routledge frontiers of political economy

1 **Equilibrium Versus Understanding**
Towards the rehumanization of economics within social theory
Mark Addleson

2 **Evolution, Order and Complexity**
Edited by Elias L. Khalil and Kenneth E. Boulding

3 **Interactions in Political Economy**
Malvern after ten years
Edited by Steven Pressman

4 **The End of Economics**
Michael Perelman

5 **Probability in Economics**
Omar F. Hamouda and Robin Rowley

6 **Capital Controversy, Post Keynesian Economics and the History of Economics**
Essays in honour of Geoff Harcourt, volume one
Edited by Philip Arestis, Gabriel Palma and Malcolm Sawyer

7 **Markets, Unemployment and Economic Policy**
Essays in honour of Geoff Harcourt, volume two
Edited by Philip Arestis, Gabriel Palma and Malcolm Sawyer

8 **Social Economy**
The logic of capitalist development
Clark Everling

9 **New Keynesian Economics/ Post Keynesian Alternatives**
Edited by Roy J. Rotheim

10 **The Representative Agent in Macroeconomics**
James E. Hartley

11 **Borderlands of Economics**
Essays in honour of Daniel R. Fusfeld
Edited by Nahid Aslanbeigui and Young Back Choi

12 **Value, Distribution and Capital**
Essays in honour of Pierangelo Garegnani
Edited by Gary Mongiovi and Fabio Petri

13 **The Economics of Science**
Methodology and epistemology as if economics really mattered
James R. Wible

14 **Competitiveness, Localised Learning and Regional Development**
Specialisation and prosperity in small open economies
Peter Maskell, Heikki Eskelinen, Ingjaldur Hannibalsson, Anders Malmberg and Eirik Vatne

15 **Labour Market Theory**
A constructive reassessment
Ben J. Fine

16 **Women and European Employment**
Jill Rubery, Mark Smith, Colette Fagan and Damian Grimshaw

17 **Explorations in Economic Methodology**
From Lakatos to empirical philosophy of science
Roger Backhouse

18 **Subjectivity in Political Economy**
Essays on wanting and choosing
David P. Levine

19 **The Political Economy of Middle East Peace**
The impact of competing trade agendas
Edited by J.W. Wright, Jnr

20 **The Active Consumer**
Novelty and surprise in consumer choice
Edited by Marina Bianchi

21 **Subjectivism and Economic Analysis**
Essays in memory of Ludwig Lachmann
Edited by Roger Koppl and Gary Mongiovi

22 **Themes in Post-Keynesian Economics**
Essays in honour of Geoff Harcourt, volume three
Edited by Claudio Sardoni and Peter Kriesler

23 **The Dynamics of Technological Knowledge**
Cristiano Antonelli

24 **The Political Economy of Diet, Health and Food Policy**
Ben J. Fine

25 **The End of Finance**
Capital market inflation, financial derivatives and pension fund capitalism
Jan Toporowski

26 **Political Economy and the New Capitalism**
Edited by Jan Toporowski

27 **Growth Theory**
A philosophical perspective
Patricia Northover

28 **The Political Economy of the Small Firm**
Edited by Charlie Dannreuther

29 **Hahn and Economic Methodology**
Edited by Thomas Boylan and Paschal F. O'Gorman

30 **Gender, Growth and Trade**
The miracle economies of the postwar years
David Kucera

31 **Normative Political Economy**
Subjective freedom, the market and the state
David Levine

32 **Economist with a Public Purpose**
Essays in honour of John Kenneth Galbraith
Edited by Michael Keaney

33 **Involuntary Unemployment**
The elusive quest for a theory
Michel De Vroey

34 **The Fundamental Institutions of Capitalism**
Ernesto Screpanti

35 **Transcending Transaction**
The search for self-generating markets
Alan Shipman

36 **Power in Business and the State**
An historical analysis of its concentration
Frank Bealey

37 **Editing Economics**
Essays in honour of Mark Perlman
Edited by Hank Lim, Ungsuh K. Park and Geoff Harcourt

38 **Money, Macroeconomics and Keynes**
Essays in honour of Victoria Chick, volume one
Edited by Philip Arestis, Meghnad Desai and Sheila Dow

39 **Methodology, Microeconomics and Keynes**
Essays in honour of Victoria Chick, volume two
Edited by Philip Arestis, Meghnad Desai and Sheila Dow

40 **Market Drive and Governance**
Reexamining the rules for economic and commercial contest
Ralf Boscheck

41 **The Value of Marx**
Political economy for contemporary capitalism
Alfredo Saad-Filho

42 **Issues in Positive Political Economy**
S. Mansoob Murshed

43 **The Enigma of Globalisation**
A journey to a new stage of capitalism
Robert Went

44 **The Market**
Equilibrium, stability, mythology
S.N. Afriat

45 **The Political Economy of Rule Evasion and Policy Reform**
Jim Leitzel

46 **Unpaid Work and the Economy**
Edited by Antonella Picchio

47 **Distributional Justice**
Theory and measurement
Hilde Bojer

48 **Cognitive Developments in Economics**
Edited by Salvatore Rizzello

49 **Social Foundations of Markets, Money and Credit**
Costas Lapavitsas

50 **Rethinking Capitalist Development**
Essays on the economics of Josef Steindl
Edited by Tracy Mott and Nina Shapiro

51 **An Evolutionary Approach to Social Welfare**
Christian Sartorius

52 **Kalecki's Economics Today**
Edited by Zdzislaw L. Sadowski and Adam Szeworski

53 **Fiscal Policy from Reagan to Blair**
The left veers right
Ravi K. Roy and Arthur T. Denzau

54 **The Cognitive Mechanics of Economic Development and Institutional Change**
Bertin Martens

55 **Individualism and the Social Order**
The social element in liberal thought
Charles R. McCann, Jnr

56 **Affirmative Action in the United States and India**
A comparative perspective
Thomas E. Weisskopf

57 **Global Political Economy and the Wealth of Nations**
Performance, institutions, problems and policies
Edited by Phillip Anthony O'Hara

58 **Structural Economics**
Thijs ten Raa

59 **Macroeconomic Theory and Economic Policy**
Essays in honour of Jean-Paul Fitoussi
Edited by K. Vela Velupillai

60 **The Struggle over Work**
The "end of work" and employment alternatives in post-industrial societies
Shaun Wilson

61 **The Political Economy of Global Sporting Organisations**
John Forster and Nigel Pope

62 **The Flawed Foundations of General Equilibrium Theory**
Critical essays on economic theory
Frank Ackerman and Alejandro Nadal

63 **Uncertainty in Economic Theory**
Essays in honor of David Schmeidler's 65th birthday
Edited by Itzhak Gilboa

64 **The New Institutional Economics of Corruption**
Edited by Johann Graf Lambsdorff, Markus Taube and Matthias Schramm

65 **The Price Index and its Extension**
A chapter in economic measurement
S.N. Afriat

66 **Reduction, Rationality and Game Theory in Marxian Economics**
Bruce Philp

67 **Culture and Politics in Economic Development**
Volker Bornschier

68 **Modern Applications of Austrian Thought**
Edited by Jürgen G. Backhaus

69 **Ordinary Choices**
Individuals, incommensurability, and democracy
Robert Urquhart

70 **Labour Theory of Value**
Peter C. Dooley

71 **Capitalism**
Victor D. Lippit

72 **Macroeconomic Foundations of Macroeconomics**
Alvaro Cencini

73 **Marx for the 21st Century**
Edited by Hiroshi Uchida

74 **Growth and Development in the Global Political Economy**
Social structures of accumulation and modes of regulation
Phillip Anthony O'Hara

75 **The New Economy and Macroeconomic Stability**
A neo-modern perspective drawing on the complexity approach and Keynesian economics
Teodoro Dario Togati

76 **The Future of Social Security Policy**
Women, work and a citizens' basic income
Ailsa McKay

77 **Clinton and Blair**
The political economy of the third way
Flavio Romano

78 **Marxian Reproduction Schema**
Money and aggregate demand in a capitalist economy
A.B. Trigg

79 **The Core Theory in Economics**
Problems and solutions
Lester G. Telser

80 **Economics, Ethics and the Market**
Introduction and applications
Johan J. Graafland

81 **Social Costs and Public Action in Modern Capitalism**
Essays inspired by Karl William Kapp's theory of social costs
Edited by Wolfram Elsner, Pietro Frigato and Paolo Ramazzotti

82 **Globalization and the Myths of Free Trade**
History, theory and empirical evidence
Edited by Anwar Shaikh

83 **Equilibrium in Economics**
Scope and limits
Edited by Valeria Mosini

84 **Globalization**
State of the art and perspectives
Edited by Stefan A. Schirm

85 **Neoliberalism**
National and regional experiments with global ideas
Edited by Ravi K. Roy, Arthur T. Denzau and Thomas D. Willett

86 **Post-Keynesian Macroeconomics**
Essays in honour of Ingrid Rima
Edited by Mathew Forstater, Gary Mongiovi and Steven Pressman

87 **Consumer Capitalism**
Anastasios S. Korkotsides

88 **Remapping Gender in the New Global Order**
Edited by Marjorie Griffin Cohen and Janine Brodie

89 **Hayek and Natural Law**
Eric Angner

90 **Race and Economic Opportunity in the Twenty-First Century**
Edited by Marlene Kim

91 **Renaissance in Behavioural Economics**
Harvey Leibenstein's impact on contemporary economic analysis
Edited by Roger Frantz

92 **Human Ecology Economics**
A new framework for global sustainability
Edited by Roy E. Allen

93 **Imagining Economics Otherwise**
Encounters with identity/difference
Nitasha Kaul

94 **Reigniting the Labor Movement**
Restoring means to ends in a democratic labor movement
Gerald Friedman

95 **The Spatial Model of Politics**
Norman Schofield

96 **The Economics of American Judaism**
Carmel Ullman Chiswick

97 **Critical Political Economy**
Christian Arnsperger

98 **Culture and Economic Explanation**
Economics in the US and Japan
Donald W. Katzner

99 **Feminism, Economics and Utopia**
Time travelling through paradigms
Karin Schönpflug

100 **Risk in International Finance**
Vikash Yadav

101 **Economic Policy and Performance in Industrial Democracies**
Party governments, central banks and the fiscal–monetary policy mix
Takayuki Sakamoto

102 **Advances on Income Inequality and Concentration Measures**
Edited by Gianni Betti and Achille Lemmi

103 **Economic Representations**
Academic and everyday
Edited by David F. Ruccio

104 **Mathematical Economics and the Dynamics of Capitalism**
Goodwin's legacy continued
Edited by Peter Flaschel and Michael Landesmann

105 **The Keynesian Multiplier**
Edited by Claude Gnos and Louis-Philippe Rochon

106 **Money, Enterprise and Income Distribution**
Towards a macroeconomic theory of capitalism
John Smithin

107 **Fiscal Decentralization and Local Public Finance in Japan**
Nobuki Mochida

108 **The "Uncertain" Foundations of Post-Keynesian Economics**
Essays in exploration
Stephen P. Dunn

109 **Karl Marx's *Grundrisse***
Foundations of the critique of political economy 150 years later
Edited by Marcello Musto

110 **Economics and the Price Index**
S.N. Afriat and Carlo Milana

111 **Sublime Economy**
On the intersection of art and economics
Edited by Jack Amariglio, Joseph W. Childers and Stephen E. Cullenberg

112 **Popper, Hayek and the Open Society**
Calvin Hayes

113 **The Political Economy of Work**
David Spencer

114 **Institutional Economics**
Bernard Chavance

115 **Religion, Economics and Demography**
The effects of religion on education, work, and the family
Evelyn L. Lehrer

116 **Economics, Rational Choice and Normative Philosophy**
Edited by Thomas A. Boylan and Ruvin Gekker

117 **Economics Versus Human Rights**
Manuel Couret Branco

118 **Hayek Versus Marx and Today's Challenges**
Eric Aarons

119 **Work Time Regulation as Sustainable Full Employment Policy**
Robert LaJeunesse

120 **Equilibrium, Welfare and Uncertainty**
Mukul Majumdar

121 **Capitalism, Institutions and Economic Development**
Michael Heller

122 **Economic Pluralism**
Robert Garnett, Erik Olsen and Martha Starr

123 **Dialectics of Class Struggle in the Global Economy**
Clark Everling

124 **Political Economy and Globalization**
Richard Westra

125 **Full-Spectrum Economics**
Toward an inclusive and emancipatory social science
Christian Arnsperger

126 **Computable, Constructive and Behavioural Economic Dynamics**
Essays in honour of Kumaraswamy (Vela) Velupillai
Stefano Zambelli

127 **Monetary Macrodynamics**
Toichiro Asada, Carl Chiarella, Peter Flaschel and Reiner Franke

128 **Rationality and Explanation in Economics**
Maurice Lagueux

129 **The Market, Happiness, and Solidarity**
A Christian perspective
Johan J. Graafland

130 **Economic Complexity and Equilibrium Illusion**
Essays on market instability and macro vitality
Ping Chen

131 **Economic Theory and Social Change**
Problems and revisions
Hasse Ekstedt and Angelo Fusari

132 **The Practices of Happiness**
Political economy, religion and wellbeing
Edited by John Atherton, Elaine Graham and Ian Steedman

133 **The Measurement of Individual Well-Being and Group Inequalities**
Essays
in memory of Z.M Berrebi
Edited by Joseph Deutsch and Jacques Silber

134 **Wage Policy, Income Distribution, and Democratic Theory**
Oren M. Levin-Waldman

135 **The Political Economy of Bureaucracy**
Steven O. Richardson

136 **The Moral Rhetoric of Political Economy**
Justice and modern economic thought
Paul Turpin

137 **Macroeconomic Regimes in Western Industrial Countries**
Hansjörg Herr and Milka Kazandziska

138 **The Political Economy of the Environment**
Edited by Simon Dietz, Jonathan Michie and Christine Oughton

139 **Business Ethics and the Austrian Tradition in Economics**
Hardy Bouillon

140 **Inequality and Power**
The economics of class
Eric A. Schutz

141 **Capital as a Social Kind**
Definitions and transformations in the critique of political economy
Howard Engelskirchen

142 **Happiness, Ethics and Economics**
Johannes Hirata

143 **Capital, Exploitation and Economic Crisis**
John Weeks

Capital, Exploitation and Economic Crisis

John Weeks

Routledge
Taylor & Francis Group
LONDON AND NEW YORK

First published 2010
by Routledge
2 Park Square, Milton Park, Abingdon, Oxon OX14 4RN

Simultaneously published in the USA and Canada
by Routledge
711 Third Avenue, New York, NY 10017

Routledge is an imprint of the Taylor & Francis Group, an informa business

British Library Cataloguing in Publication Data
A catalogue record for this book is available from the British Library

Library of Congress Cataloging in Publication Data
A catalog record for this book has been requested

ISBN: 978-0-415-61055-1 (hbk)
ISBN: 978-0-203-82839-7 (ebk)

Typeset in Times New Roman
by Wearset Ltd, Boldon, Tyne and Wear

Contents

Preface

A brief statement of what I consider the most important points in this book might aid the potential reader in deciding whether to go beyond this preface. The points all derive from the defining characteristic of capitalism: products are produced to be sold; they are commodities. Commodities have a dual nature, value in use and value in exchange. This dual nature creates the obfuscations and illusions that make understanding capital and capitalism so difficult. Marx summarized these illusions and obfuscations in the term "the fetishism of commodities", in which commodity exchange obscures the relations of production. Each of the most important points is a revelation of the reality underlying an illusion created by relations of exchange.[1]

First, that the limits to capitalism are set by capital itself, which implies that economic crises are the outcome of the strength and vigor of capitalism, not from its weaknesses. The accumulation of wealth in capitalist society generates grotesque inequality, sanctions anti-social behavior and generates appalling waste, most notably unemployment. These are not manifestations of weakness, they are the inherent by-products of the strength of capitalist relations.

Second, and contrary to almost all treatments of capitalist economies by both Marxists and non-Marxists, aggregate production should be analyzed as the circulation of total commodity value. Reducing the aggregate economy and aggregate capital to the mainstream categories of value added and national income yields misleading conclusions arising from internal inconsistencies.

Third, money in all its forms is based on a money commodity, unusually gold. This is likely to be the most controversial single argument in the book. When first I read *Capital*, I gave little thought to Marx's unambiguous argument that a commodity is the basis of all forms of money, including credit. I suspect that like others I dismissed his argument as an anachronism of little modern relevance. To paraphrase Samuel Clements, I first read Marx's writings on money in the 1970s, and with each rereading I have been amazed by how much Marx had learned in the interim.[2] I hope this book demonstrates that Karl Marx was without exception the greatest monetary theorist.

These points are made in a book that is a complete rewrite of *Capital and Exploitation*, which was published in 1981.[3] I was prompted to return to it almost three decades later at the urging of Alfredo Saad-Filho, whose *The Value of*

Marx is the best book on Marxian economic theory during that interim. My initial purpose was to make a few corrections, up-date the references and eliminate the glaring errors and anachronistic references to the current events of the late 1970s.

For several reasons the "revision" quickly became a complete rewriting of the text. First, in the thirty years since I wrote the book my knowledge of both Marxist and non-Marxist economic analysis increased substantially, especially with regard to the neoclassical treatment of money. Central to my increased understanding was the research done for *A Critique of Neoclassical Macroeconomics*, published in 1989, and now suffering its own rewrite under the title *False Paradigm: The Internal Inconsistencies of Neoclassical Macroeconomics*. I embarked on *A Critique* with the belief that one could not understand the profundity of Marx's contribution without a prior understanding of the dominant alternative framework.

If I can compare the mundane to the sublime, *A Critique* and its reincarnation as *False Paradigm* served for me the role that *Theories of Surplus Value* played for Marx. I once thought that neoclassical economics so polluted the mind that one could better understand Marx never having encountered it. That was wrong and failed to appreciate the role played by the critique of Smith and Ricardo and others in Marx's intellectual development. However, I still believe that neoclassical economics is a potential virus that can corrupt rational thought.

For those who might have read *Capital and Exploitation*, its differences with this book are on every page, but the most obvious are the following. First, the editorial aspect of the rewriting is total: hardly a sentence remains unchanged. The writing style in *Capital and Exploitation* was unnecessarily verbose and prone to arcane terminology that was relevant in the nineteenth century and has subsequently fallen from use.

In the new book I have retained all the conceptual terms and notations Marx used, with two exceptions. I use "aggregate rate of profit" for Marx's "average rate of profit", because the latter might suggest to some that it arises from an averaging process, which it does not. Second, after some thought I abandoned the universally used notation for the circuit of capital, M-C-M′. This notation has a serious ambiguity for my purposes, because it does not let one distinguish between "minus", as in ($M' - M = \Delta M$), and "changes into", as in money into commodities. In place of the familiar notation I use, $M \rightarrow C \rightarrow M'$, makes the meaning of ($M' - M$) unambiguous.

Second, at many points in *Capital and Exploitation* I made reference to or actively engaged in polemical language that I now believe to be a barrier to understanding Marx's contribution. Marx was the greatest economist of the nineteenth century. It is unnecessary to be a revolutionary to understand the importance of his contribution. Understanding his contribution need not make one a revolutionary. With this principle to guide the rewriting, I eliminated almost all references and discussion whose purpose was to demonstrate the shortcomings of other writers. The only major exception is the discussion of Engels, because it proved impossible to rewrite Chapter 1 and the annex to Chapters 1 and 2 without explicit reference to Marx's great collaborator and friend. However, in the spirit of focusing on issues rather than people, I discarded the appendix on Stalin's analysis of the economics of socialism.

Along with the editorial rewriting and changes in tone of presentation, *Capital, Exploitation and Economic Crisis* has substantial additions. First, the analysis in *Capital and Exploitation* moved directly from the production of surplus value to consider money (Chapters 3 and 4), which was a serious analytical and presentational mistake. In this book the exposition of surplus value is followed by a new chapter on the circuit of capital, which makes the rest of the book easier to write and easier to follow by the readers. Second, the analysis of money in *Capital and Exploitation* was inadequate, more suggestive of Marx's contribution than an explanation of it. The discussion of money and credit was reorganized and lengthened into three chapters, which made it possible in the new final chapter to consider in a serious manner the financial crisis of 2008–2009.

The chapter on competition in *Capital and Exploitation* had the conclusions I wished to reach, but these were not related in sufficient detail to non-Marxist treatments of the subject. Of all the myths of capitalism perhaps the most ideologically powerful is the almost universal acceptance that competition is a good thing, that it brings benefits to all, including the poor. To deconstruct this myth and reveal it as analytically unfounded and practical rubbish required substantial additions to the analysis of competition.

In the process of rewriting the chapter on fixed capital it became clear that *Capital and Exploitation* had been vulnerable to misinterpretation on the role of aggregate demand in the circuit of capital. Several people questioned whether in my presentation of crises I denied the existence of failures of demand. This confusion about my meaning led two new Appendices, to Chapter 4 and to Chapter 9, which directly relate Marx's macroeconomic categories to those of the neoclassicals and Keynesians. In the almost thirty years since *Capital and Exploitation* was published I became increasingly impressed by the insights of J.M. Keynes. As a result I was tempted to expand the Appendix to Chapter 9 to treat aspects of his theory that complement Marx. I resisted because this would substantially repeat what can be found in *A Critique* and *False Paradigm*.

Completely new is the final chapter, on the financial crisis which was current when the rewriting was in process. Central to writing this final chapter were discussions with Jan Toporowski, whose book on "financial disturbances" is outstanding (Toporowski 2005). The crisis demonstrated the power of Marx's critique of capitalism. Despite repeated financial disturbances during the 1990s and 2000, in Mexico, Asia, Russia, throughout Latin America, deep into the 2000s, mainstream writers and some radicals assured us that in the "new economy" major financial convulsions would not occur. Marx taught me not to believe that, and he was right.

Introduction

In 2008 the capitalist world was swept by the severest crisis since the Great Depression of the 1930s, which took the form of a collapse of financial assets, many of which were arcane and incomprehensible even to experts. Mainstream economics neither anticipated nor could account for this disastrous collapse of assets, which required massive state intervention throughout the capitalist world. Karl Marx did anticipate this type of financial collapse, arguing that it was derivative from the "fetishism of commodities" inherent in the capitalist mode of production. This book substantiates the foregoing claim by a journey from Marx's analysis of commodities to the capitalist crisis of the twenty-first century.

Karl Marx provided an analytical framework to explain (1) that capitalism is one form of exploitative (class) society among many through history, (2) the historical transition from precapitalist to capitalist society, (3) the concrete operation of a capitalist economy and (4) why others would explain the capitalist economy in alternative theoretical frameworks. The central element in his framework from which all else derives is his analysis of the value of commodities, "the theory of value".

This book is not an exercise in the history of thought. It is an attempt to analyze the nature of contemporary capitalist society. If I make Marx's writings more understandable, but that provides no insight to capitalist society in the latter part of the twentieth century, the book has failed in its purpose. While Marx's analysis of capitalism has implications for political action, these need not lead one to embrace revolution in place of reform, though it can and has provided the analytical foundation for both. Marx's analysis of capitalism is a coherent whole, and meaningful insights cannot be obtained by extracting elements from it. However, the coherent whole does not lead inevitably to the necessity for revolution and the "dictatorship of the proletariat". It leads inevitably to a better understanding of capitalism.

Whatever political message one extracts from the analysis in *Capital*, Marx's theory is not a critique of the *abuses* of capitalism. While *Capital*, particularly Volume I, contains descriptions of the horrors of the Industrial Revolution and capitalist abuses of the masses in Great Britain and elsewhere, Marx considered capitalism to be progressive compared to previous social systems. Marx's critique demonstrated that capitalism was and is but one historically specific mode of social reproduction, and one with its own limits. The purpose of his analysis, and the purpose of this book, is not to expose the abuses of capitalism, which were and are obvious, but to reveal the contradictory nature of capitalism, which necessarily sets limits to its development.

The key to unlocking the inner nature of capitalism is the labor theory of value. This theory is the theoretical core from which all other analysis unfolds. That value theory is the theory of capitalist society and is reflected in the organization of this book. I begin with three chapters on value theory and its implications, in which it is demonstrated that the general production of useful objects for exchange necessarily implies a capitalist society, which is a society based on exploitation, the appropriation by the capitalist class of unpaid labor performed by the working class. Marx used the word "exploitation" in a strict, technical sense: exploitation occurs when part of the production someone generates is taken from him or her by a non-producer. The means by which that part is appropriated by the non-producer defines a mode of production. These chapters demonstrate the central role in capitalist society of the process of value formation, which includes the necessarily disruptive process by which technical changes generate uneven development among capitalist producers. This disruptive process manifests itself in the movement of relative prices.

While capitalism is but one form of exploitative society, it is the only form in which the products of labor circulate in general in money form. The analysis of circulation, money and credit (Chapters 4 through 7) unfolds from the theory of value, as logical extensions of the contradictions arising from the process of value formation. The process of value formation, brought about by the movement of money capital, involves intra-class struggle, competition among capitalist enterprises. The nature and inherent necessity of competition are demonstrated in Chapter 8. A consequence of competition, expressed in the movement of capital, is technical change. Technical change is the central motive force of economic crises, giving rise to the famous "law of the tendency for the rate of profit to fall". The contradictory impact of technical change is explained in Chapter 9, and is brought together with the other elements of value theory (money, credit and competition) in Chapter 10, where economic crises are treated in detail. The final chapter applies the theory of crisis presented in Chapter 10 to the extreme financial disturbances of the 2000s.

The obfuscating nature of capitalist production will be a repeated theme of this book. These obfuscations arise not from any conspiracy, though capitalists may conspire, but from the nature of capitalist society itself, in which the class relations of that society appear as relations between commodities. Value theory is not primarily a theory of exchange or allocation. It is primarily a theory that reveals the class relations underlying a commodity-producing society. As a result, the analysis begins with the value relation, the *differentia specifica* of capitalism. Perhaps the central message of value theory, certainly not exploitation which Marx was not the first to recognize, may seem disarmingly simple: in capitalism things are not as they appear. The profoundness and depth of this insight cannot be stressed too much.

1 Value as embodied labor

Introduction

For almost all the people in the world, life is maintained through the purchase of commodities, products and services that feed, clothe, house and provide pleasure. The prices of commodities are their exchange values expressed in the money of the country or territory in which people live. The prices of commodities and, therefore, their exchange values, fluctuate through time. For at least 250 years, social theorists and commentators, as well as the public, have sought to determine whether exchange values fluctuate systematically and, if they do, what might be the underlying determinant of the exchange values observed in markets.

All theories of capitalist economies recognize the difference between the market price of a commodity and an underlying mechanism that determines price. Theorists, Marxist and non-Marxist use the word "value" to refer to that which determines market prices. How this value is determined, its composition and the units in which it can be measured define the major schools of economic and social thought. To state the theoretical issue succinctly, prices fluctuate with demand and supply. These fluctuations occur around some center of gravity. Theories differ in their analysis of that center of gravity.[1]

A coherent theory of value is essential in a capitalist society because it is the first society characterized by the general circulation of commodities. In capitalist society, production results in circulation of outputs as commodities within a social division of labor that appears to have no conscious regulation. This mediating role of exchange in capitalist society requires the analysis of the quantitative aspect of exchange, since it is the exchange ratios among commodities which determine the social survival of buyers and sellers. For private producers the quantities in which their products exchange against other products determines the conditions for repeating the production and circulation process.

The quantities in which commodities exchange and the underlying social relations determining exchange correspond to what Marx, in his unique writing style, called "exoteric" and "esoteric" phenomena. Exoteric refers to the appearance of things, in the case of commodities their exchange value. Esoteric refers to what is not observed, what determines the appearance of things, the value of commodities. The role of theory is to explain the exoteric by revealing the esoteric.

Relating exchange value to its underlying value is a subtle and difficult intellectual process. To demonstrate the importance of understanding the essentially esoteric nature of Marx's scientific investigation of value I first consider analytical attempts to move directly from exchange value to the nature and measurement of value. Considering such attempts reveals confusion and contradictions arising when a theory of value is developed at the level of appearances.

Engels' formulation of the law of value

The analytical power of Marx's theory of value derives from the *form of value* being the basis of his consideration of the magnitude of value (exchange value). In the terminology of Marx, "form of value" refers to the form taken by the social distribution of products, which can be summarized in a question that is the subject of the next chapter: why does the value of commodities take the form of exchange value, or, why do commodities exchange? Answering this question is the purpose of Marx's theory of the form of value.

Consideration of magnitude without attention to why products are commodities, "form of value" in Marx's sense, characterizes the value theory of David Ricardo, Sraffa and Sraffians.[2] Treatment of the labor theory of value[3] primarily as theory of the magnitude of value is common among those who consider themselves Marxists, and they can find support for their approach in an authority no less illustrious than Friedrich Engels. Engels played a central role in both the socialist and communist movements in Europe, and by doing so earned the respect of subsequent generations of progressives and revolutionaries. He was not only Marx's friend and benefactor but also a revolutionary theorist of great importance. Recognition of Engels' contributions does not, however, make his work immune to criticism. The following discussion, which demonstrates his basic disagreements with Marx, does not deny his major contributions to the development of socialist thought and practice.

His role in the debate over the theory of value arises from a commentary he appended to the end of Volume III of *Capital*, "Law of Value and Rate of Profit". In this annex he sought to provide a brief explanation of Marx's value theory, partly in response to critics of Marx. Because of the close personal and professional association of Marx and Engels, this commentary came to have major influence on subsequent Marxists. In his defense of Marx, Engels begins by considering the interpretation of Marx's theory of value by Werner Sombart, a nineteenth century German economist who argued that value is not an empirical category, but a mental construct (Marx 1971a: 817–18).[4] Sombart argued that in a capitalist economy commodity value does not exist independently of one conceiving it; it is a concept created in order to explain reality. Engels agreed with this,[5] but objected that "it by no means exhausts the entire significance of the law of value for the economic stages of society's development dominated by the law" (ibid.: 894).

Engels went on to argue that the law of value ruled exchange for the entire history of the circulation of products as commodities:

> The Marxian law of value holds generally, as far as economic laws are valid at all, for the whole period of simple commodity-production, that is, up to the time when the latter suffers a modification through the appearance of the capitalist form of production.... [T]hus the law of value has prevailed during a period of from five to seven thousand years.
>
> (ibid.: 899–900)

This conclusion leaps off the page, especially since the upper limit of the estimate, 7000 years, reaches to the beginning of recorded society. The assertion has two closely related parts: first, that "the law of value holds generally" for all periods of commodity circulation; and second, that it holds *up to* the appearance of capitalism, when it undergoes a "modification". More important than the particular time span is the view that the value form is not specific to capitalism. Engels suggests that it persists in modified form under capitalism, and in precapitalist society assumed its pure form. These two related aspects of Engels' theory of value result from his method of analysis.

Engels develops his theory of why products are commodities (the form of value) on the basis of surplus of products arising in "more or less communistic communities" (ibid.: 895). It is unclear if this is a general surplus above subsistence production, or surpluses of specific products. The ambiguity is important, for the former implies a class society. A general surplus can exist as an objective phenomenon only if it is appropriated from the direct producer. In the absence of specific reference to classes, there can be no analysis of the appropriation of the surplus product from a producing class to a non-producing class. Without classes, no part of society's production appears as a surplus. In such circumstances, a surplus product must be deduced on the basis of some physical (subsistence) definition of surplus, which an observer imposes analytically on the society. Thus, a general surplus product either is an objective phenomenon of exploitation, an observable, material aspect of society manifesting itself in the accumulation of wealth by a dominant group; or it is arbitrarily and subjectively defined by an external observer.

If Engels did not mean a general surplus, but surpluses of specific products, then he implies a division of labor, such that the surpluses reflect the anticipation of the producers to exchange one product for another. This presupposes a process by which individual producers or groups of producers decide to specialize. In either case, a general or specific surplus, we have the presupposition of social relations upon which exchange is predicated. The question, why is there exchange, the form of value, is not considered.

On the basis of these surpluses, exchange develops between communities first, Engels wrote, "but later also prevails within the community" (ibid.: 895). Exchange exists because individuals specialize and as a result of specialization produce more than they and their households can use. Exchange progressively provokes the dissolution of the primitive communities, so that the exchange of products becomes the motive force for changes in social relations among producers. The exchange is carried out by "family heads", who have the ownership right to the product of their labor (ibid.: 895). As the argument develops, a picture of the society emerges, which endured for 5000 to 7000 years according to Engels: independent, exchanging producers ("working peasants … with … their own farmsteads"), specializing within a social division of labor, with property rights to what they produced. It is unclear how such a society would include the dominant classes that characterized most of human history, since the appropriation of the surplus product of the direct producers is the basis of a dominant class.

Engels considered exchange as marginal to the reproduction of the producing families, referring to "the little that such a family had to obtain by barter or buy" (ibid.: 897). Explicit is the presumption that the methods of manufacture of the products entering exchange are known by the exchanging parties, not just by the producer of each product. In this presumption Engels gives an explanation for the division of labor that the exchange process presupposes:

> [Exchange] consisted principally of the objects of handicraft production, that is, such things the nature of whose manufacture was by no means unknown to the peasant, and which he did not produce only because he lacked the raw material or because the purchased article was much better or very much cheaper.
>
> (ibid.: 897)

The argument by Engels implies that specialization, division of labor, derives from a process akin to what Ricardo and neoclassical economists call "comparative advantage". The choice of what to produce is individually determined based on resource endowments and abilities. Explicit is the presumption that those in the exchange process meet each other in the marketplace as equals: "the peasants, as well as the people from whom they bought, were themselves workers; the exchanged products were each one's own products" (ibid.: 897). This sentence makes clear that the exchange process is not in a class system in which the surplus products are appropriated by a ruling class, but a society of equals, exchanging the products of their labor.

From the logic of Engels one can infer a possible answer to the question, why is there exchange (the analysis of the form of value): at some point in history individual producers achieved a level of productivity such that their output exceeded their needs, which led to individual decisions to specialize, creating a social division of labor, and to exchange. The analysis of the magnitude of value, quantities at which products exchange, follows directly from this analysis of the form of value.

> Hence the peasant of the Middle Ages knew fairly accurately the labor time required for the manufacture of the article obtained by him in barter. What had they expended in making these products? Labor and labor alone….

> [H]ow then could they exchange these products of theirs for those of other laboring producers otherwise than in *the ratio of the labor expended on them?* Not only was the labor-time spent on these products the only suitable measure for the quantitative determination of the values to be exchanged; no other was possible.
>
> (ibid.: 897)

Engels encapsulates his argument with a rhetorical question appealing to the native intelligence of the peasant and craftsman, "Or is it believed that the peasant and the artisan were so stupid as to give up the product of ten hours labor of one person for that of a single hour's labor of another?"[6]

We can summarize Engels' theory of value as follows: exchange occurs because of the production of a technologically available surplus, and specialization results from producers achieving quality or cost advantages based on access to raw materials or individual abilities. The magnitude of value is determined by the knowledge or perception that the exchanging parties have of the labor time required in production; and this knowledge is obtained from direct observation. Further, this system of exchange is based upon each independent producer possessing the right to the full product of her or his labor. Two aspects of this analysis require stress. First, the labor time it takes to produce a product is the underlying basis of value, and it is overtly manifested and known by individual observation. There is nothing esoteric about the role of value in determining exchange value. Second, members in society consider the working time of all producers to be equal. This is a society in which all producers are formally equal, what Marx called "bourgeois right" (treated in the next chapter).

Engels then argues that the law of value, defined as the law of exchange values, undergoes a major modification with the introduction of money ("metallic money" is Engels' term). The exchange of products according to their labor content operates in its purest form when exchanges are barter.[7] With the introduction of a money commodity, "value" in the sense of embodied labor becomes obscured. The obfuscation is of a particular type: that which before was directly observed can no longer be observed. With the introduction of money,

> [T]he peasant and artisan were partly unable to estimate approximately the labor employed therein ... From the practical point of view, money became the decisive measure of value.... [T]he more [commodities] came from distant countries, and the less, therefore, the labor-time necessary for their production could be checked.
>
> (ibid.: 899)

It is not obvious why money should play an obfuscating role. By hypothesis peasants and artisans have direct knowledge of the concrete labor time expended in production of commodities, and exchange is based on this knowledge. The introduction of money only requires the seller to keep in mind how much of her/his labor time is exchanged against a given quantity of money when she/he becomes a buyer of a commodity whose embodied labor time he knows. In other words, if labor times are known, they are known whether or not exchanges involve money.[8] Engels deals with this inconsistency by writing, "[C]onsciousness [on the part of peasants and artisans] of the value-measuring property of labor had been fairly well dimmed by the habit of reckoning with money; in the popular mind money began to represent absolute value" (ibid.: 899).

Whether or not one thinks that consciousness and habit play a decisive role in the quantitative determination of exchange, this position would seem to be inconsistent with Engels' rhetorical question about the intelligence of peasants and artisans. One could ask, "is it believed that the peasant and artisan, having direct knowledge of embodied labor times, were so stupid as to forget this knowledge with the introduction of money?" Given that the theory is based on perception, the key to the obfuscation of embodied labor time would have to be that commodities begin to come "from distant countries", so that embodied labor cannot be directly known. Money in such a theory plays no role except as a convenient unit of account; it is only a means of circulation.[9] Its use in exchange does not affect Engels' theory so long as exchange is between individual direct producers, his comments to the contrary notwithstanding (ibid.: 899).[10]

After presenting his theory of value, which is explicitly formulated for non-capitalist relations of productions, Engels considered the relevance of value to capitalism. Analysis of capitalism requires the introduction of a concept of profit. Engels begins with merchant's capital, a form of capital that pre-dated industrial capital. Here his argument parallels his earlier one. Merchants, like artisans and peasants, know each other's costs, and on the basis of these perceptions, "the merchant's efforts are deliberately and consciously aimed at making this rate of profit equal for all participants" (ibid.: 901–2). Thus, in precapitalist times, products exchanged as commodities according to embodied labor time and rates of profit on merchant capital tended to equalize.[11] Both of these tendencies were the result of direct knowledge and perception of labor times and costs.

However, profit by merchants contradicts exchange at embodied labor time. By definition merchant's capital operates only in circulation, not production ("pinned in circulation", Marx wrote). It follows that its profit must arise from unequal exchange, buying below embodied labor value and selling above. Engels points this out and suggests that the precapitalist world was characterized by equal exchange domestically (between individual producers) and unequal exchange internationally (under merchant's capital). In this context he makes the observation that the opposite holds in the "present-day world" (Marx 1971a: 902), which implies a fundamental difference between capitalist and precapitalist exchange based on the geographical character of exchange, though he does not pursue this reversal in exchange.

From this theory of value derives a particular view of the transition to capitalism. The transition Engels describes in his essay at the end of Volume III of *Capital* is substantially the same as that in *Anti-Duhring*, where he summarizes by writing, "The entire process [of the development of capitalism] is explained by *purely economic* causes, without the necessity for recourse *even in a single* instance to robbery, the state, or political interference *of any kind*" (Engels 1976: 208, emphasis added).

While the transition to capitalism in some countries may have involved force, one can understand it by abstracting from force, the state, and "political influence of any kind", and treat it in purely economic terms. Since the development of capitalism involves the separation of labor from the means of production, it must be the case that this separation can be explained by purely economic causes with no reference to force.[12] In specific, the precapitalist society in which Engels' law of value operates is one in which rural and urban producers have control or ownership of their tools and land (in the case of farmers). This arrangement cannot be the basis of capitalist production, because under capitalist production relations the capitalist monopolizes the means of production, with the result that the vast majority of the laboring population must of necessity hire itself out to the capitalist. Engels hypothesized that this fundamental change was achieved without force, which is consistent with his general view that exchange generates changes in social relations.

Another rhetorical question is used to explain the separation of producers from their means of production that created capitalists and capitalism (Marx 1971a: 905): "Now what could induce the merchant to take on the extra business of a contractor?" That is, to take control of the production process, which is viewed as something the proto-capitalist must be induced into doing. The dissolution of feudal relations, the separation of labor from the means of production, will be explained by the motivations of individuals. By taking this approach, Engels anticipates the argument of Sweezy in the 1950s debate over the transition to capitalism (Hilton 1976).[13]

The answer to the question is obvious to Engels: only the anticipation of an increased profit would induce the merchant to become a "contractor" (Marx 1971a: 905). The question remains of the source of the increased profit. Since the artisan is assumed to have the right to the full product of his labor, no increased profit can be made without a change in the social relations of production. By some means the merchant must appropriate part of the artisan's labor. Engels argues that the artisan voluntarily accepts the appropriation and exploitation that profit making requires: "By thus *guaranteeing the weaver regular employment*, [the merchants] could depress the weaver's wage to such a degree that a part of the labor-time furnished remained unpaid for" (ibid.: 905, emphasis added).

The transition from individual private property with the artisan owning her or his own means of production and the farmer having title to her or his land, to capitalist exploitation and the separation of labor from the means of production is achieved through a voluntary agreement, a social contract in which independent producers choose wage slavery and merchants choose greater profit. Artisans and independent farmers surrender their means of production to merchants in return for a guarantee of regular employment. At the very least this was an assessment of the stability of capitalist employment in conflict with the reality of the society in which Engels lived. He attempts to give verisimilitude to this theory of the transition to capitalism with a numerical example involving "the certainly very modest surplus value rate of 25 percent" (ibid.: 905). Once this voluntary pact between exploited and exploiter is in operation, the "merchant-contractor" is able to undersell her/his competitors, and these "will also gradually be converted into contractors", presumably by seeking out more artisans willing to trade part of their independence for regular employment. As this process develops, the epoch of the production of surplus value begins. The motive force for capitalist expansion is the advance of the productive forces associated with large-scale industry, which renders the remaining craftsmen, who stubbornly refuse to treat with the merchants-cum-contractor, unviable because of higher costs.

Engels establishes his theory of the rate of profit in capitalist production without employing what is perhaps Marx's most important conceptual contribution, the value of labor power (see Chapter 3). In the analysis of Engels, profit arises from a change in the distribution of the net product of labor, and the rate of profit is determined separately in each production unit, depending upon the bargain struck between exploiter and exploited. In Engels' analysis the transition to capitalism is a purely economic process, induced by the prospect of higher profit, with merchant capitalists becoming contractors. Profit is obtained through a voluntary agreement of artisans to surrender their independent status and accept lower "wages", implying that profit arises in distribution, not production. Finally, the process is generalized by the development of the productive forces, which makes capitalistically produced commodities progressively cheaper.

The purpose of dissecting the analysis of Engels has been to provide insight into the nature of capitalism. The first insight Engels provides is that beginning with the question, what determines the amount of one product that exchanges for another, results in treating exchanges as characterizing all societies and, therefore, seeking an explanation general enough to cover all societies. Second, because that question focuses on buyers and sellers, and because exchanges appear voluntary, it must treat the parties to the exchanges as equals.

These two insights combine into a third: capitalist society reproduces itself on the basis of exchanges that appear equal and between equals, while it is a society divided into classes based on exploitation. This is the contradiction between the exoteric (equality in exchange) and the esoteric (class-based exploitation) that Marx analytically resolved in the first volume of *Capital*. Before turning to Marx's revelation of the nature of capitalism, a further ingredient into the analytical puzzle is required, competition.

Value and competition

For those who felt that the concept of value should not have its theoretical basis in individual perception, Ronald Meek provided an alternative interpretation that maintained much of the analysis and the conclusions of Engels, while demonstrating the regulating role of value as objective, rather than subjective (Meek 1977). Like Engels, Meek argued that Marx's value analysis applied to a range of "commodity producing systems", and capitalism is "first and foremost ... a *particular form of the system of commodity production*" (ibid.: 128).

Meek argued that Marx believed value ruled exchange before capitalism, because he (Marx) spent most of Volume I of *Capital* considering the exchange of commodities at their embodied labor times. Since we know that commodities do not exchange in such proportions under capitalist relations,[14] why would Marx begin with exchange under such a rule unless he thought it had actually occurred historically? Pursuing this line of reasoning, Meek concludes that commodities exchanged at value (embodied labor) before capitalism, then exchanged at prices of production after capitalism developed. He used "prices of production" to mean exchange values (prices) consistent with an equal rate of profit across sectors of an economy (see Chapter 3).

> Marx's *logical* analysis of commodities, money, and value, I believe, and in particular his analysis of the transformation of values into prices, *was* envisaged by him as a kind of "corrected reflection" of a real development which had taken place in history...
>
> In its "classical form" as Marx conceived it, simple or petty production is a state of affairs ... in which a significant minority of products is produced as commodities, under fairly competitive conditions, by independent artisans and peasants who own their own means of production and who therefore think of their net receipts as a reward for their labor.
>
> (ibid.: 143)

Meek's position is quite close to that of Engels': they postulate a precapitalist society of independent producers united with their means of production, exchanging their products according to embodied labor time. In Meek's analysis this exchange according to embodied labor is achieved not by knowledge or perception, but by competition, and he sought to establish historical evidence for it.[15]

On close inspection, Engels' argument implies competition among producers, though he did not state this explicitly. Knowledge of embodied labor time is useful only if it can be acted upon (Morishima and Catephores 1975, 1978). If, for example, urban artisans produce within guilds that control membership and output levels, then monopoly pricing by the guilds could force peasants to accept exchange ratios above those implied by embodied labor times. Mobility of workers between crafts and occupations is a necessary condition to equalize rates of remuneration per unit of labor time (Morishima and Catephores 1978: 184). If there were excess demand for a commodity, attempts by the buyer to obtain it at its embodied labor time either would be unsuccessful or leave some buyers unsatisfied, which would push up the market price of the commodity, and it would no longer exchange at its embodied labor time. A barter in which a peasant surrendered, say, "ten hours of labor time for a single hour's labor of another" (to use Engels' example) would reflect not stupidity, but market conditions.

Meek's competitive mechanism would seem a necessary component of theory of value proposed by Engels in Volume III of *Capital*. We can summarize the amended analysis as follows: prior to the capitalist epoch, there existed for a considerable period of time societies of commodity producers with the right to the product of their labor, exchange in such societies tended to be at embodied labor times and this rule of exchange was generated by competition among producers, including mobility between occupations. The explicit addition of competition into the putative society of independent producers provides a further insight: it appears as a process that generates an equilibrium among equal buyers and sellers, yet capitalism in practice is periodically beset with crises during which competition becomes a destructive force. As with exchange, Marx would resolve this apparent contradiction and in doing so reveal the inner nature of capitalism.

2 Value as a social relation

Concrete and abstract labor

Chapter 1 demonstrated that moving directly from exchange value to value yields unmanageable analytical contradictions. The contradictions result from the incomplete specification of commodities themselves. Everything that is bought and sold has a value in exchange, its price, and also a value in use, which is the reason people want to buy it. Introduction of this additional concept, the use value of a commodity, provides the key to the nature of the underlying value that determines exchange value.[1]

Exchange value guided the analysis to the dual nature of commodities, which itself immediately implies a further concept, abstract labor. As use values, commodities are non-comparable, possessing different objective characteristics. When they exchange, they are comparable (and compared), in a process that abstracts from their differences, from their use values. When considered as exchangeable articles, the commodities represent abstract labor as well as useful labor. At this point in the analysis, "abstract labor" is a definitional concept, being the type of labor which commodities have in common as a result of exchange: when commodities exchange they are equivalent by definition and represent the same quantity of abstract labor.

Introducing the term abstract labor does not alter the non-comparability of the use value of the commodities, and comparability of commodities does not result from them being products of human labor. The use values were qualitatively different because the laboring capacities that produced them were qualitatively different. The work of a carpenter is qualitatively different from that of a farmer, just as a chair is different from an ear of corn. That both commodities required an expenditure of human effort for some quantity of time no more indicates the exchange value of the commodities than that they both occupying a certain amount of space. Marx makes this point with a rhetorical question of his own (1970a: 56): "Because trade may, for example, consist in the exchange of the labor of a shoemaker, miner, spinner, painter and so on, is therefore the labor of the painter the best measure of the value of shoes?"

The mistake of using observed (concrete) labor time as a measure of value is shown by considering another characteristic of commodities, their weight.

No one would suggest that commodities exchange proportionally to their weight. While knowing the weight of each commodity is useful for some purposes, determining their exchange value is not among them. What one observes (working time) requires a mediation process by which it is transubstantiated into exchange value. Marx explicitly warned against "confusing the labor which is materialized in the exchange value of commodities and measured in time units with the direct physical activity of individuals" (ibid.: 54), which is confusing abstract labor with concrete labor.

The value of commodities (abstract labor) cannot be directly observed, and knowledge of the labor time required to produce them (concrete labor) is irrelevant to the determination of exchange values. If one knows the time a shoemaker spends making a shoe, this provides no more information for determining the exchange value of the shoes than knowing shoes that are being made rather than a coat. The distinction between abstract and concrete labor reveals the irrelevance of perception of working time, and shall also reveal that it is incorrect to think that competition among independent producers who own their own means of production results in exchanges determined by actual working time. These points imply that value systematically rules exchange only under capitalist relations of production.

Private labor and social labor

Engels and others before and after him took the determination of the quantitative aspect of exchange as the central problem of value theory.[2] Over 100 years later this approach continues, frequently in the form of the belief that "proving Marx right" requires proving that "labor time determines prices". The important analytical problem is much broader: how to analyze a society characterized by the general production and circulation of the products of labor as commodities.

The central characteristic of the capitalist mode of production, from which all others follow, is that the private labor of individuals is not directly social. It must be rendered social by the exchange of products as commodities. Labor is directly social when the status of the worker, the product he/she produces and its subsequent distribution are determined prior to production and distribution. In all societies individuals labor, but within capitalist relations of production this labor is carried out in production units that are socially isolated.[3] Producers discover through the exchange of their products whether their individual production decisions conform to the requirement that society as a whole be reproduced in a sustained manner. This reproduction occurs via the interaction of commodity producers, in which individual labor must be integrated into a social whole. The labor theory of value is the analysis of how individual labor becomes socialized and explains this process through an analysis of how concrete, specific labor is rendered abstract.[4]

In capitalist society, the relations of production dictate specific laws of exchange. The direct producer, for example the worker on the shop floor, has been separated from the means of production and can only be reunited with them via exchange. This exchange which reunites workers and the means by which they can produce commodities occurs when the capitalist advances money to hire workers (labor power) and other ingredients of production (the means of production).

In all societies concrete labor is expended in a labor process to create products that feed, clothe and house the population. This concrete expenditure of labor power provides the material basis for the circulation of commodities. However, different commodity producers may expend different quantities of labor time in the production of the same product. Exchange itself does not imply a standard or normal expenditure of concrete labor time in production; on the contrary, the exchange can create a superficial equality that conceals differences in concrete labor.

Exchange itself renders commodities commensurate. Specifically, exchange renders the same commodity commensurate among its producers. The analytical task is to explain whether and how there should be a tendency for those producers of the same commodity to operate with similar efficiency.[5] It should be obvious that by some mechanism the social interaction of commodity producers establishes a norm in efficiency to which all gravitate. One could immediately invoke the word "competition", and assert "competition creates the tendency/pressure for the equalization of efficiency among producers". However, this assertion says no more than unequal things become equal by a process named "competition". Competition itself requires explanation, and has no explanatory value without specification of the social relations within which it operates. Specification of these social relations implies specification of the class relations underlying competition.

Consider first the case of individual producers that own their means of production. For simplicity, assume that the inputs used in production are produced within a self-contained labor process without exchange. A credible example might be a subsistence farmer selling a portion of his product. In this case, only the final product of the labor process is a commodity. The means of production, both equipment and current inputs, are produced by each producer and do not directly face the discipline of competition. There is no social mechanism for bringing about a normal expenditure of labor time for the means of production. In such a case, the limited function of competition is to impose a uniform selling price in a market place. Price is a "merely formal moment for the exchange of use values".[6]

This hypothetical example is not commodity production. Exchange does not appear until the end of the process, when all aspects of the labor process have been determined independently of exchange. Because the means of production are not exchanged, the producer faces no direct necessity to expend any specific amount of labor time on them. The only objective necessity is that his or her total labor expenditure (and that of the family) on use values produced, exchanged and not exchanged, be sufficient to allow for the sustained survival of the household. Should some producers be able to deliver their commodities with less expenditure of effort than others, these producers will enjoy a higher standard of living. This higher standard of living of some exerts no pressure on the less efficient to raise efficiency. As envious as the less efficient producers may be, the differences in concrete labor time expended may be beyond the ability of producers to change, due to differences in soil fertility, size of family and other factors.

Comparing concrete labor times in this hypothetical case has little meaning even were the laboring activities identical. Because inputs are not exchanged, there is no objective distinction in the process of the reproduction of the household between labor performed for exchange and labor performed directly for household consumption. In the context of household production relations, where exchange is marginal, any division between labor that is economic (for exchange) and labor that is not, is arbitrary. The household unit in this hypothetical case is involved in production for use, a part of which is exchanged. However wily and avaricious the individual producers may be, they are constrained by their social relations of production in their ability to rationalize their production, because they have no monetary costs. Without monetary costs, there is no vehicle to provide the information to adjust production along economic lines. Certainly all producers, in all circumstances, seek to economize on time, to expend less effort rather than more. This applies to the entire process of household reproduction, not specifically to production for exchange. Marx makes this point in the *Grundrisse*, when he writes of precapitalist exchange,

> Economy of time, to this all economy ultimately reduces itself. Society likewise has to distribute its time in a purposeful way, in order to achieve a production adequate to its overall needs.... Thus, economy of time, along with the planned distribution of labor time among the branches of production, remains the first economic law on the basis of communal production ... However, *this is essentially different from a measurement of exchange values (labor or products) by labor* time. The labor of individuals in *the same branch of work*, and the various kinds of work, are different from one another *not only quantitatively but also qualitatively.*
>
> (1973: 173, emphasis added)

A distinction can be drawn between the law of the economy of concrete labor time, applicable in all societies with or without exchange, and the law of the minimization of commercialized labor time. The exchange of products does not in and of itself impose a social standard in production, even if the family production unit specializes and produces a product that is exchanged in its entirety. As long as inputs are use values and not commodities, no mechanism exists to impose a standard through a market.

A special case of the argument that exchange by itself implies normalization in production can be found in neoclassical theory, the concept of "opportunity cost". It is argued that individuals survey the opportunities before them, then impute a value to their time based upon the most advantageous alternative. As we shall see, Marx's theory of value turns not upon the perception of individuals, but upon forces external to them, which are reflected in the consciousness of individuals.

Consider the next logical case, in which the means of production are monetized. Once a portion of the means of production must be bought, cycle of production and exchange changes. It becomes an extended cycle of exchange–production–exchange. Because money has been advanced prior to production for the ingredients of production, those means of production must be replaced in money form before they can be replaced in material form. Production to exchange did not require this condition in the first hypothetical case, that the price of the production must cover at least the money advanced for inputs.

As the producer buys more of the ingredients for production, that the sale price should cover money costs becomes an objective necessity. Costs do not reflect the subjective assessment of the producer of his or her expended effort, but an external necessity imposed by the interaction of many sellers. The use value emerging from the labor process becomes a commodity in its essence as well as its form. Above in the first case, exchange had a quantitative indeterminacy, because the part of the concrete labor of each producer appeared only as her or his own labor. In the second case, the means of production are presented to the producer as something separate from her or him, the product of social labor, the labor of others.[7]

Marx suggested that the one of the first major monetizations of the means of production came with the requirement that peasants pay money rent, rather than in kind:

> The transformation of rent in kind into money-rent, taking place first sporadically and then on a more or less national scale, presupposes a considerable development of commerce, of urban industry, of commodity-production in general, and thereby money circulation. It furthermore assumes a market-price for products and *that they be sold at prices roughly approximating their values, which need not at all be the case under earlier forms.*
>
> (1971b: 797)

Whether or not this is factually accurate, Marx's argument is clear: commodities do not exchange at value before rents take money form, a relatively late historical development in his view; then they do so only as a rough approximation. As long as money costs are few and represent a small part of the means of production, the producer is under no compulsion to enter into monetary exchange. If exchange is quantitatively unfavorable, the producer can withdraw to subsistence production except for essential items that must be obtained through exchange. Further, as the means of production increasingly take the form of commodities, the product of the labor process must be exchanged. A commodity per se is a product that not only is exchangeable but must be exchanged (Marx 1970b: 105). The producer must consider the product's exchangeability prior to production; i.e. must treat the product *as a commodity* from the outset.[8]

Products of labor become commodities not in the isolated act of exchange, but as part of a general process of the monetization of social relations. They are stamped as commodities in the production process. It is not their subsequent sale that makes them commodities. They are commodities before their sale, which is one moment of several in general commodity circulation. As explained below, the moment of circulation derives from the moment of production.[9] When one observes a fully developed commodity-producing society, it appears that products become commodities by being exchanged. This is one of many obfuscations of commodity-producing society, the illusion that exchange is both the defining and the final moment of commodity circulation. This illusion explains why people might believe the exchange of products in precapitalist societies to be commodity production, all the more because exchange obscures the social relations underlying exchange.[10]

Engels considered the value of commodities to be something directly observed, and that the general use of money obscures the ability to observe value. The opposite proves to be true. One perceives concrete labor, the actual activity of producing. The transformation of this concrete labor into abstract, value-producing labor is not directly observable. Perception plays no important role in the determination of prices (exchange values), so its role cannot be obscured by money. The introduction of money forces the producer to consider market costs as a socially imposed norm, which he or she must recover through sale or be unable to repeat production, whatever the perceptions might be. In this process money reveals value as price in exchange.

When production is carried out by independent producers, exchange reflects incomplete monetization even if all the means of production are commodities. A portion of the labor time expended in commodities remains concrete labor which has undergone no abstraction, passing through no market process by which it would become socially commensurate. The currently expended ("living") labor of the proprietor and family is not monetized, and, therefore, not normalized by exchange. This labor remains private; it does not directly enter exchange and become social labor.

The producer must replace the inputs into production by money by their specific market-dictated prices, because the labor in those inputs has been exchanged. There is no necessity that the living labor be replaced by money in its entirety, because it never assumed money form prior to production. Indeed, since the laboring time of the producer remains concrete, not abstract labor, "in its entirety has no objective meaning". Were we dealing with wage labor, capitalist relations of production, failure to sell the commodity at a price covering the wages advanced and the means of production would leave the capitalist unable to re-initiate production at the same level. Failure to realize a profit would mean that the capitalist would lack the money for expansion. The production unit using family labor does not face these necessities. Marx summarizes the behavior of the independent producer as follows:

> For the peasant owning a parcel, the [lower] limit of exploitation is not set by the average profit of capital, in so far as he is a small capitalist; nor, on

> the other hand, by the necessity of rent, in so far as he is a landlord. The absolute limit for him as a small capitalist is no more than the wages he pays to himself, after deducting costs. So long as the price of the product covers these wages, he will cultivate his land and *often at wages down to a physical minimum.*
>
> (1971b: 805–6, emphasis added)

This type of exchange is not completely ruled by monetary cost, even if the peasant exchanges in a society that is predominantly capitalist. Again, from Marx,

> For the peasant parcel holder to cultivate his land, or to buy land for cultivation, it is therefore not necessary, as under the normal capitalist mode of production, that the market-price of the agricultural products rise high enough to afford him the average profit, and still less a fixed excess above this average profit in the form of rent. It *is not necessary, therefore, that the market-price rise, either up to the value or the price of production of his product.*
>
> (ibid.: 806, emphasis added)

Because the living labor of the independent producer is not monetized, "the regulating market-price of the product will reach its value *only under extraordinary circumstances*" (ibid.: 806). The peasant with unusually good land will have expended less working time in producing a given amount of maize, for example, than a less fortunately endowed peasant. As a consequence, the labor of the first peasant is worth more in exchange.[11] That a significant portion of the labor required to produce wheat is not monetized means there is indeterminacy in the regulation of price.

Value acts as a regulator of price once the entire product, all inputs, are monetized; until this occurs, the product is not a commodity in its entirety and all the concrete labor time expended on it need not be replaced by money. This occurs only with the development of capitalist production.[12] It is important not to become entangled in semantics. "Value" regulates price under capitalist relations and can be used as a tool of analysis only in capitalist society.

Subjective and objective value

The value of a commodity is determined objectively, independently of the perception or knowledge of exchanging parties, and this objectification of labor time is achieved through the monetization of the elements of production, labor and non-labor. Personal judgments as to what portion of a producer's laboring time or the laboring time of others is necessary for production are no more than that, subjective judgments that may or may not be accurate.[13]

In all societies exchange is a part of the general process of social reproduction and governed by the necessity that the class relations society must be reproduced.

When exchange is marginal and few inputs are monetized, prices are regulated by the condition that the exchange of use values cannot be on terms so unfavorable to the exchanging parties that it leaves those on one side of the exchange unable to satisfy their subsistence needs. If this requirement is not met, one side must cease exchanging and retreat from market relations. Such a very general law of exchange allows for considerable indeterminacy in exchange ratios, an indeterminacy resolved in practice by the relative power of the exchanging parties. When exchange is infrequent and the means of production unmonetized, it is ruled by the "law of subsistence".

Once the means of production assume money form, the indeterminacy is reduced. Exchange becomes increasingly ruled by the "law of monetary costs and subsistence". If the current input of labor is not monetized, value does not determine exchange value, except as an externally, idealistically imposed benchmark; it would be an anachronism to apply the value category.[14] When under capitalist relations of production labor power becomes a commodity, value assumes full application and the indeterminacy of exchange disappears. At this point, exchange is ruled by the law of value, a law that has two clauses. These two aspects are the "law of socially necessary labor time" and the "law of the tendency of the rate of profit to equalize".

In the first, competition presents all producers with a norm for the minimum necessary input of concrete labor time. This is a standard created by the social interaction of capitalist producers, "socially necessary labor time". This first clause of the law of value creates a norm for productive efficiency, which in practice need not result in enforcing equal productive efficiency among producers of the same commodity. As discussed in a later chapter, there are many reasons why productive efficiency might vary across an industry that would not be eliminated by competition. The interaction of producers establishes a norm which is the underlying basis of the market price of a commodity. Producers that achieve this norm realize their entire outlay of cost plus a profit when the commodity is sold. Producers that do not achieve the norm have part of their capital outlay rejected by the market when the product is sold, and the reverse for producers that are more efficient than the norm.

The operation of the second aspect of the law of value competition creates a tendency to a common rate of profit across industries, which is a process of distribution among capitalists generated by the movement of capital among the industries, a movement based on free wage labor. As we shall see, this implies that the law of value, the law of the exchange of equivalent quantities of social labor, is the law of surplus value, the law of the appropriation of unpaid labor and, thus, the law of the exploitation of labor.[15]

The "necessary illusion"

A valid social theory should explain reality, and through that explanation reveal why competing theories would explain the same reality differently. To this point, we have engaged only in the former task: to develop the concept of value and demonstrate the circumstances under which it becomes socially significant as a regulator of the interactions of producers. The analysis implied by the Marxian law of value should explain why competing explanations would view value in a completely different and opposed way. This is not an exercise in the history of economic thought, but a task that allows one to reveal the illusions, obfuscating forms, generated by the process of the circulation of capital. The labor theory of value is not only a theory of the social regulation of production. It is also a theory of how that production becomes fetishized: why it appears as something it is not.[16]

The analysis of exchange by Engels began with a society in which every producer had the right to her or his labor. While making no explicit statement about the social relations of production and ownership, Marx would appear implicitly to begin as Engels did. The temptation to interpret the early chapters of the first volume of *Capital* as a consideration of individual small producers, so-called petty commodity production, is almost irresistible. This interpretation makes the analysis in *Capital* much simpler and much less an intellectual and analytical challenge. But it is a very serious misinterpretation which trivializes the analysis as little more than an extension of Ricardo.

From their points of analytical departure Engels and Marx embark on two distinct approaches, the exoteric and the esoteric. In the former case, the presumption that individuals hold right to their labor is maintained until it becomes necessary to deal with the historical emergence of capitalism. In the latter case, the analysis reveals step by step that the assumption of individual private property is inconsistent with the actual operation of the law of value and must be discarded.[17] For Marx, the right to one's labor was *merely an assumption;* for Engels it characterized an actual society.

In capitalist society, wealth presents itself as commodities. If we abstract from class relations, commodity circulation appears as the exchange of equivalents. By beginning with a commodity once it has reached a market, what we observe is the commodity exchanged by the seller for money; then the seller uses the money to buy another commodity. Marx called this sequence "simple commodity circulation", with the notation C-M-C. Viewed in isolation, C-M-C implies no exploitation because the value of each of the three moments is the same. Equal exchange presupposes a measure of "equalness". Value is this measure. The magnitude of value presupposes that the means of production and labor power are commodities, which implies capitalist relations of production. In the absence of capitalist social relations, the equivalence is merely formal, because it is not based on norm established through the interaction of producers, a socially necessary norm in labor time. When purchase and sale are not ruled by capitalist relations, exchanges appear as equal; when circulation is ruled by capital the appearance of equal exchange is the manifestation in the interaction of circulation and production of a socially necessary labor time for each commodity.

Only under capitalist relations is it possible to compare the living labor objectified across commodities. The formal equivalence in exchange is the manifestation of the real equivalence resulting from the circulation of capital. One can begin the analysis by assuming individual property in commodities, but it is quickly revealed that the starting point, the simple circulation of commodities, implies the opposite, the circulation of capital. The simple cycle of selling one commodity in order to buy another, C→M→C (commodities sold for money, money used to purchase different commodities), implies M→C→M′ (money used to buy commodities, commodities sold for money), where M′ is greater than the initial M.[18]

Consideration of selling to buy (C→M→C) revealed that this process is subsumed within another, buying to sell (M→C→M′). For the first, all the terms are of equal exchange value: C→M→C implies and requires C=M=C. This cannot be true for buying to sell. The purpose of C→M→C is to sell one commodity in other to obtain a different one. The purpose of buying in order to sell is to have a larger amount of money at the end of the circuit than at the beginning, an increase of exchange value. This increase of value requires the introduction of an additional concept, which, following the terminology of Marx, we name surplus value. At this point, surplus value has a simple definition, M′ minus M (M′–M>0).[19]

Concepts now emerge quickly from the unfolding analysis. The circuit C→M→C implies M→C→M′, which implies (M′>M), a surplus value. The appearance of surplus value immediately presents the question, what is its source? The source is revealed by elaborating the insight that (C→M→C) is subsumed within (M→C→M′), shown in Table 2.1. What began as a superficially simple process in Chapter 1 of Volume I of *Capital*, buying and selling, with an apparently simple question of determining exchange value, is revealed by Marx's method to imply the full development of exchange and circulation within the social relations of capitalist society.[20] Again the analysis calls for a concept, the one word title of Marx's most famous book, "capital", and supplies its definition: capital is buying in order to sell with an increased exchange value, or, more simply, capital is self-expanding value.

In the process of its expansion, capital appears as money, exchanging for the ingredients of production (hiring labor and purchasing non-labor inputs),

Table 2.1 Circulation of commodities implies circulation of capital

M	*→C >>*	*[Production]*	*→C′→*	*M′*
Money capital	**Productive capital**	Workers produce commodities and surplus value created	**Commodity capital**	**Money capital**
	Capitalists hire labor		C_1 (bought by capitalists for production)	Surplus value realized
	Workers buy commodities	>>>>>>>>>>	C_2 (bought by workers)	

followed by the use of those ingredients in production to create a new set of commodities, which are sold. The terms used to describe this process are as straightforward as the process is esoteric: money capital becomes productive capital through exchange; through a labor process productive capital is transformed into commodity capital; and the conversion of commodity capital into money capital realizes a surplus value.

The circuit of capital reveals the source of the surplus value. The use of money to hire labor and buy materials has no quantitative impact on either the value of what is bought or the money spent. The same applies to the sale of the commodities after production, which again involves an amount of money exchanged for commodities of equal value. It follows that the increase in commodity value (C→C′), and the increase in money (M→M′), must result from the process of production. This is a conclusion reached by every serious theory of value and profit, Marxian, Ricardian and neoclassical,[21] and in itself is not a major revelation. The contribution of Marx's approach to the analysis of value is that the pursuit of the apparently simple and general question, what determines prices in general, reveals the inner nature of capitalist society in specific.

In the production process capital appropriates part of the product of labor for itself. Marx was not the first to recognize this appropriation, that part of what workers produced was appropriated as the property of capital. All contemporary writers recognized this, the dominant analytical explanation of profit until the second half of the nineteenth century. The term "exploitation" will be used for the appropriation of part of the output of producers by a non-producer. Exploitation is a relationship or phenomenon that occurs in production. It can be applied to any class society. One of Marx's great contributions was to explain the mechanism by which exploitation occurs in capitalist society, by distinguishing between the output a worker creates and the worker's capacity to work, which he called "labor power".

In capitalist societies, workers sell their capacity to work, their labor power, to capitalists. This sale implies that the capitalist purchases the right to the production of the workers he or she has hired. The worker receives the exchange value of labor power, then uses this to regenerate that labor power through the purchase and consumption of commodities. The capitalist obtains the power over the use value of labor power, and by doing so takes ownership of what workers manufacture, construct and cultivate. Separated from the means of producing, workers sell the capacity work and by doing so surrender the fruits of their labor.

The apparently simple concept of labor power reveals the source of profit and nature of capitalist exploitation. Unlike in feudal and slave systems in which appropriation (exploitation) is direct and obvious, in capitalist society it is hidden by the exchange of money for labor power, which, as shown in detail in the next chapter, is an equal exchange. The brilliance of Marx's insight cannot be exaggerated: by recognizing the existence of the commodity labor power, he demonstrated the mechanism of capitalist exploitation, and, at the same time, why the existence of that exploitation could be credibly denied by the defenders of capitalism.

A logical progression reveals the social reality beneath the exchange of equivalents. Commodity exchange is ruled by value when labor power itself is a commodity, which implies the historical process by which labor was separated from the means of production. As a result of this separation, workers must sell their labor power in order to obtain their means of subsistence, and capitalists must buy it in order to initiate production. The exchange of equivalents is an illusion based on the buying and selling of labor power, which involves the appropriation of unpaid labor (surplus value). This appropriation occurs in production, as the capitalist literally exploits the use value of labor power, and the worker labors beyond the time necessary to produce the commodity equivalent of the wage.

The illusion of equivalent exchange is not ruse. Capitalist competition enforces a tendency toward minimization of concrete labor and equalization of profit rates across industries. The equivalence is an equivalence among capitalists, whereby each tends to maximize the return for the capital he or she mobilizes.[22] For the worker, the equivalence is of a different sort, since he or she only has labor power to sell. For the working class, the sale of labor power is equality in form and exploitation in essence, because the worker surrenders the right to the product of his or her labor as a result of the exchange.[23]

The contradictory illusion, equal exchange concealing appropriation of unpaid labor, corresponds to the illusion of private property under capitalist relations of ownership. Commodity exchange is legally based upon private property. In law all members of a capitalist society are guaranteed the right to own, accumulate and exchange property. In practice, the operation of capitalist society negates this right. Capitalist accumulation is based upon the appropriation of unpaid labor through the buying and selling of labor power. For society as a whole, labor power becomes a commodity when the vast majority of the population is separated from its means of production. The productive property of the majority is expropriated by the process Marx called “primitive accumulation”.[24] Capitalist private property is not a system of individual rights to property. It is the monopolization of the means of production by the few, the “bourgeoisie”.[25] To state it simply, a few members of society accumulate wealth because the vast majority cannot.

The appropriation of unpaid labor, direct and obvious under slavery and serfdom, appears as the exchange of equivalents under capitalism. This façade of equality is built upon a façade of private property for all, and conceals that the only productive property of the worker is his or her capacity to labor. This “property” of the worker can only be sold to capitalists. The principle of exchange under capitalism is that capitalists exchange at value, appropriate surplus value and accumulate; workers exchange at value and surrender unpaid labor.[26]

That the law of value first becomes operative under capitalism and not before is an insight of considerable political importance. To argue that the law of value applied to exchanges long before capitalist society can be interpreted to imply that exchange can occur among independent, self-employed producers without exploitation. This suggests the possibility of a society of competing producers, exchanging their outputs (their labor), without any contradictions that would give rise to the concentration of economic power by capital. It follows from this logic that commodity exchange can be socially egalitarian, and is characterized by exploitation only when it comes under the domination of capital.

Within this view of exchange commodity production and competition are not sources of exploitation and economic crisis, but they become so under capitalism. The underlying, fundamental assertion is that the interaction between use value and exchange value is not antagonistic. It follows that commodity production need not be controlled and contained in order to end the crises, class antagonisms and environmental destruction associated with capitalism.

This benign view of exchange is found in the work of Proudhon, which Marx attacked vigorously (see Marx 1955). As demonstrated in this chapter, the production of commodities necessarily implies capitalism, and, therefore, capitalists and proletarians. The debate over whether commodity exchange implies capitalist exploitation has a long history among anti-capitalist writers. V.I. Lenin, first leader of the first country in which capitalism was overthrown, berated the Norodnik economists in Russia at the end of the nineteenth century over this issue. The Norodniks, spokesmen for the peasantry, argued that a society of independent, proprietor farmers and craftsmen could form the basis of an egalitarian commodity-producing society, and that capitalism distorted commodity production by creating exploitation. Lenin rejected their argument, maintaining that commodity production necessarily implies capitalism,

> [S]eparate producers, each producing commodities on his own for the market, enter into competition with one another: each strives to sell at the highest price and to buy at the lowest, a *necessary result of which is that the strong become stronger and the weak go under*, a minority are enriched and the masses are ruined. This leads to the conversion of independent producers into wage-workers and of numerous small enterprises into a few big ones. The enrichment of a few individuals and the impoverishment of the masses – such are the inevitable consequences of the law of competition.
>
> (Lenin 1972: 93, 95)

The logical progression in Lenin's argument is quite different from Marx's analysis. In this quotation and elsewhere, Lenin argues that a society of small-scale commodity producers inevitably results in capitalism through the attrition generated by competition among them. Marx's analysis was fundamentally different: no general system of commodity production existed or could exist prior to capitalism. To put the difference in its simplest form, in Lenin's analysis petty commodity production generates capitalism; in Marx's analysis, capitalism generates petty commodity production.

The fundamental difference in the analysis of Marx and the other writers we have considered (e.g., Engels, Prouhdon and Lenin), is that Marx fully recognized the dominance of social relations over relations of exchange. It may be true that competition results in the elimination of smaller producers, an issue pursued in the chapters on competition. The process of competition that would generate this outcome derives from capitalist relations of production and ownership rather than being the result of it.

The law of value summarized

Every society has a division of labor that generates the products that ensure the sustainability of that society. In precapitalist society, this division of labor was directly social, achieved through a conscious regulation prior to production and distribution, and mediated by exchange only at the margin of society. These societies were constructed on servile social relations, slavery and serfdom being the best known forms. With the separation of labor from the means of production, production appears socially isolated, with each capitalist arriving at his or her production decisions in a formally independent manner. In this sense capitalist production is anarchic.

This anarchy is both reflected in and rendered orderly through exchange. The exchange of the means of production and labor power presents each capitalist with a standardized monetary cost for a given quantity of these means of production and labor power. Capitalist competition requires that these quantities be consumed productively subject to a standardized selling price. As some capitals use the ingredients of production more efficiently, their profits increase. The less efficient capitals must emulate the more efficient or be eliminated from production. It is by this process that socially necessary labor time is established in each industry.

The labor consumed in production, both currently expended and that objectified in means of production, is rendered comparable in exchange and normalized through competition. In this manner, value comes to rule production. The socially determined normal labor time exists "behind the backs" of each capitalist, and regulates their production without entering the consciousness of capitalists. This is the operation of the law of the minimization of concrete labor in production.

In the accumulation process, qualitative changes in the organization and size of the workplace and through the combination and merger of ownership[27] result in a change in the composition of aggregate production. In this process the law of value becomes the law of the social division of labor. Shifts in supply and demand result in deviations of exchange value from value, which result in profitability varying systematically across industries. Profit differentials are reduced by the movement of capital among industries. Workers are shifted among industries, and concrete labor, rendered abstract through the exchange of the products of their labor, becomes abstract to the worker. The shift of labor between industries by capital separates the concrete labor carried out in the production from the worker himself or herself.

Increasingly there is no relationship between the particular knowledge or skill of most workers and the work he or she performs. With the mobility of the proletariat among labor processes, the worker's labor power is rendered an abstract force, alien to him (Marx 1970b: 402ff.). This abstraction of the concreteness of labor from the worker can result in the so-called deskilling of labor, though the process is more general. Capitalist production is the negation of the work of the artisan and the small farmer. Highly skilled, both the artisan and the farmer applied themselves to a range of tasks each involving specific knowledge and specific manual or mental techniques. In capitalist production the concentration of labor into workplaces is accompanied by the division of labor into small tasks. Whether the result increases or decreases the skill of the workers, it involves abstraction from the overall process of producing the commodity in question.

The social process of value formation is the law of labor allocation under capitalism (division of labor), the law of surplus value (exploitation) and the mechanism of alienation in society. When capitalism is immature and laborers carry to the workplace skills and knowledge necessary for production, this alienation is fundamentally the separation of the worker from his product; i.e., the appropriation by the capitalist of the product from the producer as a result of the wage bargain. As capitalism develops and the division of labor increases within the production process, the worker increasingly becomes alienated from the work process itself, reduced to a mere source of homogeneous, abstract human energy. The worker appears as, and in essence is, an extension of capital. The productive power of the masses of the population, achieved through cooperation, appears as the productive power of capital (ibid.: Chapter 12).

Appendix

Marx and Engels on the law of value

History and the law of value

There is an unfortunate tendency in the Marxist literature to rely upon quotations from authorities rather than analytical argument. In Chapter 2, I used quotations from Marx only when their clarity was so striking that they seemed to cry out for inclusion. This appendix will employ many quotations, because its explicit purpose is to compare the analysis of Marx and Engels, a comparison that demonstrates unambiguously that their views on basic issues differed fundamentally. The issues considered are: (1) history and the law of value, (2) perception and knowledge in the operation of that law and (3) the transition from precapitalist to the capitalist mode of production.

Engels begins his treatment of exchange by considering a society of independent producers, producing a surplus, in which this surplus is exchanged to satisfy needs that each producer cannot satisfy by his own production. This presupposes individual property in the product of labor, the existence of a surplus and a complex division of labor. Marx rejected each of these presuppositions explicitly. Writing of the precapitalist period, he says,

> [Merchant's capital] therefore merely promotes the exchange of commodities, yet this exchange *is not to be conceived* at the outset as a bare exchange of commodities *between direct producers.* Under slavery, feudalism, vassalage ... it is the *slave-owner, the feudal lord, the tribute collecting state, who are the owners, hence sellers, of the products.*
>
> (1971a: 326, emphasis added)

Further, the existence of a surplus product is not a natural phenomenon arising from physical productivity. Its existence must be explained in terms of the social relations that create it: "favorable natural conditions alone, give us *only the possibility*, never the reality, of surplus labor" (Marx 1971b: 460; and Marx 1970b: 482–3).[28] The discussion of the division of labor by Engels presupposed private property and a surplus product. Engels argued that the division of labor arose spontaneously and naturally because "[the peasant] lacked the raw material or because the purchased article was much better or very much cheaper" (Marx 1971a: 897). This formulation assumed what it sought to establish. It assumed that families "had to obtain" some items they required, which presupposed the need for things, and presupposed that specialization existed. This approach was also taken by Prouhdon, and Marx criticized him as follows:

> A very large number of products are not to be found in nature [Proudhon writes] ... If man's needs go beyond nature's spontaneous production, he is forced to have recourse to individual production.... A single individual, feeling the need for a very great number of things, "cannot set his hand to so many things". [However] so many needs to satisfy *presuppose so many to* produce – there are no products without production.... Now, *the moment you postulate more than one man's hand helping in production, you at once presuppose a whole production based on the division of labor.* Thus, need ... itself presupposes the whole division of labor. In presupposing the division of labor, you get exchange, and, consequently, exchange value. One might as well have presupposed exchange value from the very beginning.
>
> (Marx and Engels 1976: 111–12)

By postulating that some people can produce things cheaper and better, one presupposes the need for them in the first place and the division of labor that allows for someone to produce them cheaper and better. Implicit is the suggestion that exchange arises voluntarily and individualistically. Having assumed the division of labor, assumed many needs and assumed, in effect, exchange, Engels then considers the quantitative basis of exchange. For him, this derives from the answer to a rhetorical question, "What had [the producers] expended in making these products? Labor and labor alone.... [T]hey spent nothing but their own labor power" (Marx 1971a: 897).

By definition human beings expend their labor power on products, but this is of little analytical value until one specifies the social relations within which a person's work is carried out,

> Labor is *not the source* of all wealth. Nature is just as much the source of use value ... as labor ... Man's labor only becomes a source of use values, and hence also of wealth, if his relation to nature, the primary source of all instruments and objects of labor, is one of ownership from the start.
>
> (Marx 1974: 341)

The answer to Engels' question presupposes private ownership, which he assumes *ex machina.* He has ignored the social relations of production of peasant society and the exploitation that was the basis of that class society. Marx's treatment of exchange in precapitalist society recognizes that these societies were characterized by servile relations of production in which the direct producers, while united with the means of production, had no right of property. Because they did not and because the means of production they used were not monetized, value did not determine exchange; indeed, it did not exist, as Marx explicitly stated.[29] The law of value did not exist prior to capitalism because:

> [T]he product wholly assumes the form of a commodity only as a result of the fact that the entire product has to be transformed into exchange value and that also all the ingredients necessary for its production enter it as commodities – in other words it wholly becomes a commodity only with the development and on the basis of capitalist production.
>
> (Marx 1971b: 73)

Marx repeatedly argued that value rules *only* under capitalism, and the exchange of equivalents that Engels placed in precapitalist times occurs only under capitalism and, most importantly, the exchange of equivalence hides exploitation. In Chapter 2 there was a quotation from the *Grundrisse* to this effect, and almost the same passage appears in *Capital*, Volume I,

> [I]t is evident that the laws of appropriation or of private property, laws that are based on the production and circulation of commodities, become by their own inner and inexorable dialectic changed into their very opposite. The exchange of equivalents, *the original operation with which we started*, has now become turned round in such a way that there is *only an apparent exchange.*
>
> (Marx 1970b: 547)

This inversion does not occur historically; it is the relationship between surface appearance ("necessary illusion") and the underlying reality of that appearance,

> At first, the rights of property seemed to us to be based on a man's own labor. At least, some such *assumption* was necessary since only commodity-owners with equal rights confronted each other, and the sole means by which a man could become possessed of the commodities of others, was by alienating his own commodities ... Now, however, property turns out to be

> the right, on the part of the capitalist, to appropriate the unpaid labor of others or its product, and to be the impossibility, on the part of the laborer, of appropriating his own product. The separation of property from labor has become the necessary consequence of a law that *apparently* originated in their identity.
>
> (ibid.: 547, emphasis added)

Having made this line of argument, Marx refers sarcastically to a society of independent producers exchanging equivalents as the "paradise lost of the bourgeoisie, where people did not confront one another as capitalists, wage-earners, landowners, tenant farmers, usurers, and so on, but simply as persons who produced commodities and sold them" (1970a: 60). It is such a lost paradise of unexploited producers that Engels creates in order to analyze exchange.

Neither the importance of this insight nor the difficulty in fully appreciating it can be exaggerated. Commodities exchange, an amount of money for an amount of a commodity. The money is the equivalent of the commodity, and from this equivalence is generated a great ideology to justify capitalism as a social system. For example, from the commodity–money equivalence derives the belief that people are free to choose their work, that through diligence they can advance by the fruits of their labors and that this society of the economically free brings forth a society of the politically free. Marx demonstrated that the real basis for this exchange of equivalence is the monopoly of productive wealth by a few. In exchange commodity-producing society appears as "free markets, free people", and its basis is "free markets, exploitation".

Marx wrote, "[c]ompetition implements the law according to which the relative value of a product is determined by the labor time needed to produce it", and this implies that "the determination of value by labor time … is therefore merely the scientific expression *of the economic relations of present-day society*" (Marx and Engels 1976: 134, emphasis added.).

Perception of labor time

Engels and many other writers explained equivalent exchange on the basis of the knowledge of producers, the argument that by having knowledge of the production activities of others, the exchanging parties would be "stupid" to accept other than equivalent exchange. As shown in Chapter 2, this explanation confuses concrete and abstract labor, and there is no need to repeat that argument. In the analysis of Marx, the value was objective, independent of perception,

> The "circumstances" which determine the value of a commodity are by no means further elucidated by being described as circumstances which influence the "mind" of those engaging in exchange, as circumstances which, as such, likewise exist (or perhaps they do not, or perhaps they are incorrectly conceived) in the consciousness of those engaging in exchange.
>
> (Marx 1971b: 73)

Marx has a well-earned reputation for ridiculing his opponents, earned in part by his attacks on Prouhdon:

> Begin, he [Proudhon] says, by measuring the relative value of a product by the quantity of labor embodied in it, and supply and demand will infallibly balance one another … [T]he product's price will express exactly its true value. Instead of saying like everyone else: when the weather is fine, a lot of people are to be seen going out for a walk, M. Proudhon makes his people go out for a walk in order to be able to ensure them fine weather.
>
> (Marx and Engels 1976: 131)

"Supply and demand" refer to the process of the interaction of producers and consumers. It is this interaction that results in socially necessary labor time, which is the essence of value. The introduction of perception into the determination of prices reverses reality, positing a social outcome (value) to have a physical, non-social existence prior to its manifestation as price. As part of this reversal, the function of price in exchange is misunderstood. The principle function of price is not to be equal to value as Engels suggested, but to express or represent value. Marx's makes this point, albeit rather obscurely, "[A]lthough price … is the exponent of [a commodity's] exchange ratio with money, it does not follow that the exponent of this exchange value is necessarily the exponent of the magnitude of the commodity's value" (Marx 1970b: 104).

This rather awkward passage can be rephrased: "although price is the expression of value in money, it does not follow that price is necessarily the expression of value itself". By expressing value rather than precisely measuring it, the money price allows producers momentarily to realize profit above or below normal, so that the deviation of price from value signals commodity producers to vary their supply.

Transition to capitalism

Engels argued that the development of capitalism could be explained in "purely economic" terms, "without the necessity for recourse in a single instance" to any "political inference". In contrast, Marx devoted the final section of Volume I of *Capital* to the violent methods that accompanied the emergence of capitalism. Just the titles of two chapters in this volume indicate his view that violence played a major and necessary part in the emergence of the capitalist mode of production.[30]

One quotation demonstrates Marx's conclusions on the role of force:

> Direct force, outside of economic conditions, is of course still used, but only exceptionally [in nineteenth century Britain] … *It is otherwise during the historical genesis of capitalist production.* The bourgeoisie, at its rise, wants and uses the power of the state to "regulate" wages, i.e., to force them within the limits suitable for surplus value making, to lengthen the working

> day and to keep the laborer himself in the normal degree of dependence. *This is an essential element of the so-called primitive accumulation.*
>
> (ibid.: 689)

This is a specific case of Marx's general conclusion that "force is the midwife of every old society pregnant with a new one" (ibid.: 703). The other aspects of the transition to capitalism in the approach of Engels, that it was brought about by merchant's capital, that it involved artisans voluntarily choosing wage labor, were also criticized by Marx when he found these arguments in the work of others. On the latter question, Marx argued that the wage employment resulted because workers had been separated by force from their means to produce. As a result they had no choice about becoming proletarians. He viewed self-employment not as the original basis for capitalism, but as a barrier to its development, which had to be eliminated through the force of the state (Marx 1973: 515–518; 1970b: 681–5, 686, 694). Equally important is the treatment of merchant's capital by Engels. In Marx's analysis, merchant's capital was the form of capital (M→C→M′) without the essence of capital (control over production). As a consequence:

> [All] development of merchant's capital tends to give production more and more the character of production for exchange value and to turn products more and more into commodities. Yet *its development … is incapable by itself of promoting and explaining the transition from one mode of production to another.*
>
> (Marx 1970b: 327)

Marx did explicitly consider the case of the merchant extending his control over production and comes to a conclusion opposite to that of Engels:

> This system [merchant's capital] presents everywhere an obstacle to the real capitalist mode of production and goes under with its development … The transition from the feudal mode of production is twofold. The producer becomes merchant and capitalist … This is the really revolutionizing path. Or else, the merchant establishes direct sway over production. However much this serves historically as a stepping stone … it cannot by itself contribute to the overthrow of the old mode of production, but tends rather to preserve and retain it as its precondition.
>
> (1971a: 334)

Merchant's capital did not provide the path to capitalism, because it did not generate the separation of labor from the means of production ("primitive accumulation"). As a final note, it should be pointed out that Marx and Engels had quite different explanations of the origin of surplus value in the initial stages of capitalist development. Engels, as part of his view of the development of wage labor, argued that independent artisans willingly accepted lower wages in exchange for regular employment. The idea that capitalists (and capitalism) can deliver "regular employment" is a quite astounding idea. The capitalist mode of production is the first to generate idleness for a part of the laboring population as an endemic and *systematic* characteristic of its operation; capitalism creates its own specific form of poverty that did not previously exist, mass unemployment.

At the level of production units (individual capitals), a basic advantage of capitalist relations of production is that capitalists can hire and fire workers at will. Irregular employment is the *sine qua non* of capitalism. It is a necessary characteristic for a mode of production based on production for exchange value and constant technical change. Inherent in capitalist accumulation is what Marx called "that monstrosity, an industrial reserve army, kept in misery in order to be always at the disposal of capital", and the reserve army and the fluctuations of the market "dispels all fixity and security in the situation of the laborer" (1970b: 457). Engels reversed reality. It is the control of the means of production that gives the direct producer any security at all, and separation from the means of production eliminates that security. Only slightly less astonishing is the argument that producers would willingly accept a lower standard of living, even if such security of employment were magically guaranteed. Such an explanation for the production of surplus value comes very close to the arguments of a social contract type.[31]

Marx's explanation of surplus value was entirely different. First, the forced, violent process of the separation of labor from the means of production (particularly land) created a free, impoverished proletariat which had the "choice" between vagabondage or wage slavery. Given a large pool of free wage labor, impoverished and politically powerless, capitalists could force down the standard of living of their workers to a base minimum and ruthlessly extend the working day (ibid.: Chapters 11 and 10).

Why theories differ

It is possible at a general level to account the analytical differences in the works of Marx and Engels. In *The German Ideology*, written by Marx and Engels in the 1840s, the theoretical method places circulation and production on the same analytical level, co-determining the development of society. Engels maintained this analytical position, and clearly stated it in his 1877 polemical work attacking E.K. Dühring:

> Political economy, in the widest sense, is the science of the laws governing the production and exchange of the material means of subsistence in human society. [E]ach has what are also for a large part *its own special laws.* But on the other hand, they constantly determine and influence each other to such an extent that they might be termed the abscissa and ordinate of the economic curve.

By the time he wrote *A Contribution to the Critique of Political Economy* in 1844, Marx had broken with this position. In the *Grundrisse* he made this clear, stating, "the structure of distribution is completely determined by the structure of production" (1973: 95), which can be compared to a statement in *Anti-Duhring* by Engels, "[d]istribution, however, is not merely a passive result of production and exchange; it reacts just as much on both" (1976: 190). In both the *Grundrisse* and *A Contribution* Marx establishes the analytical position that would be the basis of the method of the three volumes of *Capital*:

> But (1) no exchange is possible without division of labor, whether this is naturally evolved or is already the result of a historical process; (2) private exchange presupposes private production; (3) the intensity of exchange, its extent and nature, are determined by the development and structure of production. Production is the decisive phase both with regard to the contradictory aspects of production and with regard to the other phases.
>
> (Marx 1973: 139; repeated in Marx 1967: 204)

The theoretical differences between Marx and Engels arise because Engels held to the view that production and distribution are equally determining moments in the circuit of capital. As a result, he like many others did not grasp what Marx called the "science of modern economy", which "only begins when the theoretical analysis passes from the process of circulation to the process of production" (1971a: 337).

3 Exploitation and surplus value

Social production and surplus value

The previous chapter explained that the payment of wages conceals the exploitation in capitalist society. One of Marx's greatest contributions to the science of capitalist societies was to demonstrate not only the form of exploitation, but also that wages, or to be more precise, the wage form of appropriation, socializes exploitation. While value originates in production, the concrete labor time expended in each work process does not measure the magnitude of value. This is because, first, the labor is concrete, not abstract; and, second, it may be above or below the normal labor time established by the interaction of capitals through competition. Value is socially necessary, abstract labor time, and the value created in each workplace is a part of total social labor. In each work process, concrete labor is expended, then rendered abstract in exchange. The interaction of all capitals generates a social norm that each capital must emulate, and the abstract labor created under the domination of each capital appears as part of society's total socialized labor.[1]

Abstract socially necessary labor time, value, exists separate from each particular production process, implying exploitation is a society-wide phenomenon in capitalist society. The exploitation of labor by capital occurs in production, through capitalist consumption of the use value of labor power. The total amount of surplus value and the rate of surplus value are determined in a process that involves abstraction from each specific labor process. The quantity and rate of surplus value are in the first instance social or society-wide, not the result of an aggregation of quantities and rates prevailing in each workplace.

This characteristic of exploitation, which reflects the socialized nature of production under capitalism, is clarified by considering exploitation in precapitalist society, particularly a peasant–landlord society. In what broadly can be called "feudal society", production occurred in isolated workplaces and farms, but was directly social within the social organization. It was isolated in that each manor, the area over which the landlord's authority extended, was largely self-contained. Inputs, the means of production, were not exchanged between production units to any great degree. To the extent that the domains of landlords were linked, this linkage was in the social relations between landlords and higher authorities.

The linkages reflected the social organization of society, not the links of an intermingled production matrix.

As a consequence, differences in the productivity of labor among production units, even among peasant holdings within these units, was specific to each. For example, differences depended upon fertility of the soil, the particularities of the landholding pattern and other characteristics internal to the manor. Similarly, the size of the surplus product appropriated depended upon these characteristics and the degree of oppression the exploiting class could bring to bear upon the direct producers. In any social system there is a tendency toward normalization of social practice, for reasons of custom if no other. But since land was not alienable nor peasants free to move to any significant degree, there was no mechanism, short of a local revolt of peasants, to bring about a normalization of productive efficiency and a system-wide level of exploitation. By contrast, under capitalism the movement of capital would tend to eliminate relatively unfertile land from production. In contrast, when land cannot be bought and sold, the landed exploiter has no choice but to use the land over which he or she had been granted rights.

In such a society, the distinction between necessary labor and surplus labor was direct and obvious. The work of the peasant was divided between the time worked for the support of the family and the time worked for the landlord. This division often took the form of the peasant laboring a certain number of days per year in the landlord's fields, in which case the actual working process itself was divided. Alternatively or in combination with this, the peasant delivered a portion of his production directly to the landlord. It is possible to distinguish objectively between necessary labor, the labor necessary to reproduce the peasant family and surplus labor, the labor performed for the exploiter of labor, since this division existed in reality (Marx 1970b: 227).

A rate of exploitation for feudal society as a whole in the sense of a quantitative measure did not exist as an objective phenomenon. This would require that the concrete labor of the direct producer be reducible to abstract labor in order to be aggregated. In the absence of exchange, no such reduction occurs in reality, and to make it conceptually is purely arbitrary. Because products are not rendered commensurate though a social process, it is arbitrary to impose this upon them. It is, however, heuristically useful to create a hypothetical feudal society in which a measurement of exploitation would be formally possible. To do so, assume the existence of a society of self-sufficient feudal manors in which only one product is produced, maize. Assume also that the same amount of corn is consumed by all agriculture workers, which will be named "necessary corn". Production in excess of necessary corn is appropriated by landlords.

In this hypothetical society, there is a "rate of exploitation" for the society as a whole, the ratio of surplus corn to necessary corn, but this aggregate rate has no social significance. It exists only as a numerical average of each individual rate of exploitation. Each isolated rate of exploitation in this case is the result of the particularities of the soil and social organization internal to the unit of social production. Since the means of production and labor power are not commodities, there is no tendency for individual rates of exploitation to move toward the societal average. In this hypothetical society, and in precapitalist society in general, labor was directly social, characterized by conscious organization directly among people, but production was not socialized, not integrated across society.

Capitalism involves an opposite process: labor expended in production is not directly social, and production necessarily becomes socialized. With the separation of the direct producer from the means of production and the division of labor that implies, the self-sufficient production that characterized feudalism came to an end. Through exchange each producer became dependent upon the activity of other producers. This creates the contradiction that there are no direct social links between producers, but these producers are enmeshed in an interdependent production system. The law of value resolves this contradiction by establishing norms in the use and allocation of concrete labor that are independent of each producer (each capital).

The rate of surplus value

It is now possible to consider the rate of surplus value at the appropriate level of abstraction. This is facilitated by considering the work of a non-Marxist strongly influenced by Marx's work, Michio Morishima (Morishima 1972). Morishima argued that under capitalism, the mobility of workers equalizes the length of the working day and equalizes wage rates. Workers, because they are not tied to capitalists by servile social relations, move from industries and enterprises where wages are below average and the working day above average length, and this process will continue until a normalization of remuneration and the working day is achieved. Because wages represent the value of labor power, their equalization standardizes the value of labor power throughout the economy. The equalization of the length of the working day equalizes the amount of surplus value each worker produces, and the result is an equalized rate of surplus value for the system as a whole.

It follows that the aggregate rate of surplus value is the weighted average of all the rates across each unit of social production, and competition among capitalists for workers tends to reduce the variation around the statistical mean which is derivative from the individual parts. Though logically consistent, this approach misunderstands the social nature of production under capitalist relations, and reduces necessary and surplus labor time to a problem of measurement. Absent is a theory of what determines the level to which wages normalize. When this element is included, the order of logic must be reversed, and the aggregate rate of surplus value is established *prior to* considering individual units of capitalist production (capitals).

Morishima's explanation of the equalization of the rate of exploitation requires the counterfactual assumption of full employment, or at least a relatively small reserve army. If the reserve army were large, capitalists have a pool of unutilized labor power, and the "mobility of labor" is the mobility from employment to unemployment if workers object to their working conditions and pay. While there are moments when the reserve army falls to a low level, this is the moment when the competition among capitals for labor power accentuates and systematically generates differences in wages rather than equalization (Weeks 1979). The reserve army is reduced in the accumulation process when the demand for labor by capital outweighs the growth of labor productivity, a relationship considered in detail in a subsequent chapter. When this occurs, capitalists bid against one another to obtain workers for expansion, and the necessary consequence of this is to increase the variance in wages, not to decrease it.[2]

The implicit assumption of full employment equilibrium reflects a formalistic and mechanistic treatment of wages in capitalist society.[3] The treatment is formalistic in that it is divorced from the process of accumulation, in which wages are capital advanced, not primarily income to the working class. Wages are treated as if they were merely one component of the net product, qualitatively no different from profits. A parallel argument could be made for the equalization of the profit rate, so the difference between profits and wages is purely formal, almost semantic, insofar as the equalization of each across industries is concerned.

Explaining the rate of surplus value requires a theory that explains the determination of the length of the working day and the wage level. One cannot consider the equalization of either profits or wages across capitals until one explains to what level equalization will gravitate. In capitalist society the working day becomes a period of time defined independently of the direct producer, which confronts her or him as predetermined by the employer. In precapitalist society, when the direct producer is united with means of production, the time of work is determined indirectly, by the need to reproduce the family and to satisfy the demands of the appropriating class for a surplus product. Under such circumstances, the division of the peasant's life between work and non-work has little objective meaning, because work does not present itself as something external to the producer out of her or his control.

The separation of labor from the means of production means that workers and tools are reunited by capital and under the domination of capital. The length of the working day becomes a subject of class struggle as capitals attempt to extract as much unpaid labor as possible. The existence of surplus value requires that the working day extend longer than necessary labor time. The duration of work is a source of conflict between the two great classes of capitalist society, and in every capitalist country it has been an epochal struggle that defined the political role of the two classes for decades.

The struggle over the duration of work has two aspects. Capitalist relations create the working day as something distinct from the rest of the worker's life. The working class fights to prevent capital alone from establishing the duration of the working day; i.e., that there be a working day of definite limits agreed by labor. This struggle takes the form of its second aspect, the limitation of the hours of work. What is at issue in the struggle is much more profound than a question of time; it is a struggle over the extent to which capital controls labor. The establishment of a limit to the working day reflects an assertion of the collective power of the working class.[4]

The successful struggle by the proletariat to limit the working day is historic in a second sense, in that it creates the period of capitalist accumulation when the raising of surplus value by working people harder and longer is no longer the dominant source of accumulation (Fine and Harris 1979). What before was a technological possibility, the reduction of necessary labor time by improvements in the means of production, which reduces the values of commodities, becomes an objective necessity if surplus value per worker is to be increased. In the new era of a limited working day, surplus value is increased by reducing the portion of the day required to produce what workers require for their subsistence. The historic change that facilitated raising surplus value through technical change did not, however, bring the practice of increasing exploitation by workplace oppression to an end in the advanced countries.[5]

One can understand and explain why the working day becomes a source of class conflict, but it is not possible to determine the length of the working day theoretically. It is determined in the concrete practice of class struggle, historically by legislation and the fight to ensure that that legislation be enforced. In Marx's famous phrase, "the working day is, therefore, determinable, but is, per se, indeterminate" (1970b: 223). The process by which the working day is equalized across branches of industry, be it by mobility of workers or class struggle, presupposes a process of class conflict at the level of society as a whole.[6]

The restriction on the length of the working day applies to a society as a whole, and differences across industries and workplaces are variations around that predetermined level. The same is true for the value of labor power, or necessary labor time. In all class societies, total production can be divided conceptually between necessary product and surplus product, where the former is the livelihood of direct producers and the latter appropriated by the ruling class. In capitalist society, necessary product or necessary labor is valorized. Workers exchange their labor power against money, and exchange money for the commodities they consume. Because of the intermediation of money, exploitation is veiled under capitalism. It appears that the wage covers the entire working day; i.e., the wage is formally exchanged for a contracted period of time. Surplus labor and necessary labor are not separated, as they are under feudalism. Their division in capitalist production is as real as in precapitalist society, and wages are one historical form in which the direct producer obtains his means of subsistence.

The form taken by labor's share of capitalist production, wages, reflects the value of labor power which has two components, the collection of use values consumed by workers and the unit values of these use values. Each component is socially determined, and the wages paid in each industry and workplace derive from a socially established norm. It is obvious that the standard of living is socially determined. The struggle of the working class as a whole, in the context of all the complex factors that tend to divide and unite it, in combination with the productivity of labor, set the standard of living.

However, it is not primarily the social nature of the standard of living of the working class that socializes the value of labor power. Given the standard of living, the labor time necessary to produce the use values that comprise the standard of living depends upon the overall development of the productive forces. This does not happen under precapitalist relations. When producers are self-sufficient, necessary labor is particular to each, a consequence of the fertility of the soil, size of the family and other influences. Under capitalism, necessary labor time is established independently of the efficiency or inefficiency of production in any specific industry or workplace. Given the standard of living, the value of labor power is determined by the productivity of labor in all branches of industry that produce commodities that workers consume, and in the branches that produce the means of production for these consumption commodities.

To establish a general rate of surplus value by beginning with the relationship between wages and profits in each industry, as Morishima did, ignores the socialized nature of capitalist production and its complex division of labor. In effect, it assumes that each worker produces his own means of subsistence in isolation. In reality, each worker labors and receives a claim on the total value produced in society. He then exchanges this claim in the form of money against a collection of use values that is the result of the combined, cooperative labor of all workers (including her/himself).[7] The rate of surplus value exists first for capital as a whole, because both the working day and necessary labor time are determined at this level of analysis. This does not ignore variations in wages, which reflect skill differences, historical particularities and divisions within the working class. But these differences do not affect the determination of the rate of surplus value, which arises from the class struggle and the development of the productive forces as a whole.

The foregoing analysis produces the abstraction that all workers produce equal amounts of surplus value per unit of time, and we make this abstraction without reference to industry and workplace. In summary, under capitalism exploitation is socialized, in contrast to precapitalist society, where exploitation was particular and one could speak of a rate of exploitation. Each capitalist exploits his workers to the extent and degree which capital as a whole exploits the working class as a whole, an aspect of what Marx called "the operating fraternity of capitalists". Thus, it is not political hyperbola but literally true that in a capitalist society two great classes, capital and labor, confront each other.

The rate of profit

The analysis of the rate of exploitation leads one directly to consider the rate of profit.[8] Capital appropriates unpaid labor through exploitation in the workplace. The profit is the form in which surplus value appears to capitalists, and the rate of profit reflects the "equitable" distribution of surplus value among capitalists. The rate of profit also functions secondarily as a disciplinary mechanism among capitalists. In neoclassical theory, the profit one observes arises at the level of the enterprise, and aggregates across all enterprises to total profit. This conclusion is based upon the illusion that the labor objectified in means of production ("dead labor") creates value.[9] By developing the rate of profit from the rate of exploitation, one can demonstrate the source of this illusion.

In order to initiate production by uniting workers with the means of production, capitalists advance money. The money capital they advance is divided between variable capital, which purchases labor power and creates value, and constant capital, exchanged for the means of production which does not create value. The aggregate rate of profit will be defined as the ratio of total surplus value to total capital advanced, constant and variable.[10] This aggregate rate of profit, like the rate of surplus value, exists for capital as a whole, behind the backs of capitalists, as the basis of the profit rate in each industry.[11] The conceptual movement from the rate of surplus value to the aggregate rate of profit is a simple algebraic exercise that reflects the social relations of capitalist society. Because both the means of production and labor power are temporarily tied up as capital, the profit calculation is on the sum of the two, though only living labor creates surplus value.

When the aggregate rate of profit is generalized to all sectors of industry, becoming the general rate of profit, an adjustment process across industries is required. The ratio of constant to variable capital varies among industries. Every worker in every industry creates the same amount of value per working day and, therefore, the same amount of surplus value is appropriated from each.[12] If commodities exchanged according to their values (abstract labor time), the rate of profit would vary inversely with the ratio of constant to variable capital, because only the latter creates surplus value. This apparent contradiction gives rise to a transformation process, which in academic literature is typically called the "transformation problem". The transformation is from the value of commodities into their exchange values, which are called "prices of production". A price of production is the exchange value of a commodity that conforms to the capitalist law of distribution that profit rates equalize across sectors of industry.

It is important to understand the sense in which there is a "problem". The problem is not conceptual, but practical, a problem of distribution among capitalists. The basis upon which surplus value is produced is inconsistent with the inherent mobility of capital, which calls forth a general or equalized rate of profit. While considering how this distribution of surplus value is affected by the requirement that the rate of profit be equalized, we must consider the question of efficiency. The efficiency of production in capitalist society is determined by the extent to which any particular capital conforms to the social norm established for the use of concrete labor in the production of its commodities. This norm is socially necessary abstract labor time (value), and it is established through the interaction of producers.

The norm includes both the productive consumption of the means of production and of labor power. Consider the case of two industries, in which all the producers (capitals) within each use the same technique of production, but in one industry the prevailing technique involves a higher ratio of constant to variable capital than in the other. If commodities sell at their values, the industries will display different rates of profit. This greater profitability of the sector with the low composition of capital implies that the distribution of surplus value does not conform to the distributional requirements of capitalist social relations. The difference in profit rates does not imply that one industry is more efficient in production than the other, nor does it indicate allocative inefficiency. Further, the equalization of the rate of profit has no impact upon the aggregate rate of profit, the rate of profit for society as a whole.[13]

On a purely formal level, profitability differences do not reflect efficiency in the use of the means of production and labor power because we have assumed that all producers within a sector use the same prevailing technique. In this respect, neoclassical theory would concur, because in that theory every producer is always both economically and technically efficient.[14] Neoclassical theory argues that differences in profit rates reflect allocative inefficiency, because their theory of profit implies that the "productivity of capital" must be lower in the sector with the lower profit rate. On the basis of the labor theory of value this is not relevant, for dead labor does not create value or surplus value,[15] and any distribution of gross output is consistent with an equalized rate of profit, given the technology of production.

The movement of capital to equalize the rate of profit has little to do with productive efficiency and is not a process of generating an efficient allocation of resources. Capitalist production is anarchic (unplanned), and variations in profit rates are the signaling mechanism to which capital responds. There is nothing efficient about this method of achieving the division of labor, except from the viewpoint of capital, by bringing about an "equitable" distribution of profit.

The movement of capital in response to differential profit rates does result in major qualitative changes in a capitalist society. These movements and their effects are the result of the differential or uneven development of technology within each industry. We have abstracted from changes in technology in order to clarify the process of the equalization of the *rate* of profit. Once we move to the level of many capitals and their differences in production techniques, we shall consider the centralization and concentration brought about by the movement of capital. These processes are treated in later chapters on competition and fixed capital.

Illusion of capital productivity

In summary, the law of the equalization of the rate of profit is part of the law of value, the part that brings about the distribution of surplus value among capitalists. This redistribution of surplus value according to the capitalist principle of equity resolves the contradiction that surplus value is produced by living labor, but cannot be distributed on this basis. This contradiction arises only under capitalism, and the law of the equalization of the rate of profit is relevant only within capitalist relations.

This distribution of surplus value among capitalists generates an illusion that is the basis of the ideological justification of capital's monopoly of the means of production and dispossession of the working class. This is the capitalist superstition that means of production, dead labor, create value. This superstition generates the further illusion that the movement of capital achieves allocative efficiency. The illusion is the capitalist interpretation of the process through which the rate of profit is equalized by an adjustment of values into prices of production.[16]

Living labor, workers toiling in offices, factories and fields, creates value. Dispossessed from the ability to organize their own production, they toil under the control of capital. The surplus value that capitalists appropriate must be distributed according to a socialism of the capitalist class, shared out on the basis of total capital advanced. The creation of value then appears as its opposite: the result of the power and creative genius of capital rather than of the collective power of labor. Perhaps there is no better example of the power of Marx's insight that the sphere of production is primary than the exposure of this illusion for the secular religious canon it is.

Marx's analysis leads us to discover that the apparently crucial regulator of capitalist society, the general rate of profit, is in essence a distributive algorithm for the "operating fraternity of capitalists". The redistribution of the unseen, esoteric surplus value among capitals as the observed, exoteric profit demonstrates historically specific and universal nature of capitalist production; historically specific in that it requires products to be commodities, and universal because of the social division of labor. It appears that production under capitalism occurs among many, isolated units of production, and becomes socially integrated through exchange and competition, through the circulation of products as commodities. Reality is quite different: a capitalist factory or call center is part of a huge integrated system of inputs and outputs, no individual element of which could or would exist without the others. In order for this socially integrated system of production to function as capital, the products generated by each element must exchange as commodities.

The great vertically and integrated factory of capitalist society appears as its opposite, a loose collection of isolated operations in constant rivalry. As a result of the development of the productive forces in a capitalist system, this real integration increases over time. Capitalism appears as production in competitive isolation; it is integrated production based on the collective of the workers it exploits. The great irony or contradiction of capitalist society is that its development progressively renders production social while it requires and perpetuates an ideological illusion of individualism.

4 Circuit of capital[1]

Clarifying concepts

Marx demonstrates that the nature of capitalism is hidden by the illusions created by commodity circulation. Chapters 2 and 3 revealed two of these illusions: (1) the productive power of the working population appears as the productive power of a few (capital organizes production because it has established a monopoly of the means of production not because of its productive role); and (2) the apparent reward for the productivity of capital is no more than the rule for distribution of income among the dominant class of society (capitalists appropriate part of the labor of workers and distribute it among themselves).

This chapter addresses another, closely related ideologically charged aspect of capitalism, the purpose of productive activity. The central tenet of the defense of capitalism is that its production must satisfy the demands of the masses of the population. This ideological defense is formulated by defining people to be consumers, and asserting that the production decisions of capitalists are by necessity guided by the desires of consumers. Some critics of capitalism maintain that this "sovereignty of the consumer" is propaganda, because capitalist enterprises through excessive and misleading advertising create the needs and desires which those enterprises claim to satisfy. This criticism can be restated to say, in a properly functioning market system consumers would be sovereign were it not for the distortions consciously created by capitalist misinformation. Marx's rejection of the ideology of consumer sovereignty was more profound than this.

In the mainstream analysis of commodity circulation in the aggregate, the key concepts are "aggregate demand" and "aggregate supply", and it can be summarized as follows. While the price of a product includes the cost of intermediate commodities (constant capital), for purposes of analysis of social production as a whole intermediate costs should be subtracted out. This subtraction leaves one with "value-added", the value created by living labor during the time period in question. If all income payments go to workers and capitalists, this net value or new value is wages plus profits, called "aggregate supply". These money incomes derive from the sale of commodities, the sum of consumption expenditures by workers and capitalists, plus investment expenditure by the latter, which is "aggregate demand". These are two ways to view the net product corresponding to what standard textbooks call the "income approach" and "expenditure approach" to national income accounting.[2]

With these two concepts, aggregate supply and aggregate demand, one proceeds to analyze social production. If aggregate supply exceeds aggregate demand, then commodities go unsold and the level of the net product falls. If aggregate demand exceeds aggregate supply, the level of net product rises. Taking the former case, net product falls because aggregate supply is both the value of net production and the income flow generated by that production. If aggregate demand, consumption plus investment in the simplest case, is less than the net product, then commodities go unsold and capitalists reduce their level of production. This, in turn, reduces the income generated, and because aggregate demand derives in part from income, aggregate demand falls by more, inducing capitalists to again reduce production, etc. This feedback is called the "multiplier process", well known to anyone who has taken introductory college economics.

The contraction or expansion process does not go on forever because of the particular theoretical formulation of the determinants of personal consumption and expenditure on investment. Personal consumption expenditure is explained in the simplest case by personal income flow. Analytically, personal consumption expenditure is determined simultaneously with the level of the net product, via a "consumption function", whose most important parameter is called the "marginal propensity to consume". Because personal consumption expenditure is derivative from the net product (and vice versa), the process of contraction or expansion would go on to zero or infinity without the inclusion of an element of aggregate demand that is independent of the level of the net product. If there is no government expenditure or exports, the autonomous element is investment in fixed means of production.[3] Investment functions come in many varieties, with neoclassicals preferring a simple relationship determined by the interest rate, and Keynesians one in which investment reflects profit expectations, in some cases with those expectations approximated by past profit levels and profit rates.

With these concepts clarified, one can summarize the process by which the net product is determined. The past history of profit performance provides the starting point or "initial conditions". This determines the level of investment. The level of investment, via the multiplier (whose value is implied by the consumption function), determines the level of the net product, and the latter determines the level of personal consumption expenditure. Expansion or contraction occurs until personal non-spending ("saving") equals the autonomously determined investment. Cycles and instability are the result of the volatility of investment.

This analysis, so familiar to students of undergraduate economics and, to an extent, the view of economics by the informed public, was challenged by Marx. He rejected the analysis of the circulation of commodities in terms of the net product, whether this net product be defined as aggregate demand, aggregate supply, value added, the product of living labor, the net national product or simply as income. More specifically, his theory of circulation has no consumption function and, therefore, no multiplier process.[4] Closely related to this, there is no investment function in his analysis, endogenous or exogenous.[5]

Net and gross production

The fundamental difference between Marx's theory of aggregate circulation and the prevailing mainstream analysis is that the mainstream treats the aggregate economy as the circulation of value and Marx treated it as the circulation of capital. The production of wealth in capitalist society takes the form of the production of commodities. These commodities are capital. They are produced as capital and circulate as capital. The circulation of commodities is part of the process of the reproduction of capital and should be analyzed as such. The reproduction of capital has two aspects, exchange value and use value: reproduction of capital in the abstract (reproduction of value), and the reproduction of capital in the concrete (material replacement). When one considers these two aspects and their interrelationship, the relevant *time period* of analysis is the turnover period of capital, not a year, quarter or some other arbitrary segment of time.

The central concept of a commodity-producing society is capital and it must be at the center of analysis. During the process of circulation, capital assumes various forms, means of production and labor power, commodities and money. It assumes all these forms during its function as the social relation in which money serves as a general claim on society's wealth.[6] Capital is the historically specific relationship based upon the monopoly of the means of production by the dominant class, predicated upon the prior dispossession of labor from those means of production. This separation of labor from the means of production, proletarianization, requires that labor and the means of production be reunited through the medium of money. The circuit of capital begins with the exchange of value in abstract form, money, for the use values by which the material process of production is possible. Marx called this step the advance of money capital, and when the exchange is made, capital has transformed itself into productive capital, from capital in the abstract to capital in the concrete, labor power and the means of production, the potential to produce use values.

Within the sphere of capitalist production, all of the ingredients of the labor process are capital, the buildings, land, machines, raw materials and the labor to work the machines. In this context Marx used the phrase "investment in wages",[7] a phrase which may seem quaint and old-fashioned if one has been trained to the neoclassical framework in which "labor" and "capital" are defined ahistorically and divorced from the social relations of production. Labor power in use or purchased in anticipation of use is as much capital as the machines that labor power is combined with. For this reason money exchanged against labor power is called "variable *capital*", and money exchanged against raw materials, intermediate commodities and machinery, "constant *capital*".[8] Production creates a new set of use values and these, too, are a form of capital, commodity capital. This commodity capital is the material form of the surplus value created in production. The exchange of commodity capital against money returns to its initial form of money capital, and the process begins again.[9]

Fundamental to the circuit of capital is the twofold nature of commodities, because capital must be reproduced both in money form and material form.

On the material side, labor power and means of production must be reunited in each successive circuit. On the value side, capital must achieve its metamorphosis into money in order that it be exchanged against use values and resume its productive role. Marx's analysis of circulation was the study of this opposition and interaction of the abstract (value) and the concrete (use value).[10] This approach is not obscure or theoretical, but quite practical: because value must have a material form (be objectified in a commodity), the circulation of value as capital requires that we consider both value and use value. If one considers only the circulation of value, as is done in the "circular flow" diagram found in economics textbooks, the process of production becomes a tautological process of generating value added. If only material circulation is treated, as the Sraffians do, the capitalist nature of circulation is lost (Sraffa 1960).

Using the net product to analyze circulation is partial, in that it does not include the process by which productive inputs are replaced,[11] and is fundamentally misleading. Because it treats the product of living labor as income to workers and capitalists on the "supply side", the nature of the material output of living labor as capital is lost. The net product also proves unsatisfactory on the "demand side", where it misrepresents the relationship between the production of use values and the production of value. In the simple Keynesian model, wages plus profits equal expenditure on personal consumption plus expenditure on fixed means of production. This implies that the value created by living labor must be equal to the value of consumption and investment commodities.[12]

This equality can hold only under simple reproduction, when the level of gross production (and, therefore, net production) does not change. In the case of no expansion, the sum of all variable capital and surplus value equals the total value of the articles of consumption, which is the sum of constant capital, variable capital and surplus value in that sector.[13] If there is expansion, then part of the surplus value has been transformed into additional capital. This additional capital has three parts: the increment in fixed constant capital (if existing fixed means of production cannot accommodate the expansion), the increment in circulating constant capital (since all commodities require raw materials or intermediate commodities) and the increment in variable capital. The material form of the increment in fixed constant capital is plant and machinery (investment). The increment in variable capital becomes additional wage income and has as its material form articles of consumption. This appears in the net product model as consumption induced by the payment of wages. The increment in circulating constant capital exchanges against raw materials and intermediate commodities. By definition these are excluded in the net product model, because constant capital has been subtracted from both sides.

There is an inconsistency in modeling and in the concrete: to produce commodities, material inputs as well as labor power are required. To produce *more* commodities than before, more inputs are required and the value equivalent of these is part of the net product. Except in the case of simple reproduction, when no expansion or contraction of material and value production occurs, the value of the net product cannot be equal to the value consumption and net fixed investment. Wages plus profits cannot equal “consumption” plus “investment” except in equilibrium.[14]

Appearance and essence in the circuit of capital

A capitalist society reproduces itself through the circuit of capital, and the circuit of capital provides the appropriate analysis for capitalist society. As we consider this circuit, the categories of the net product framework present themselves, but as distorted forms of the metamorphosis of capital. The circuit of capital takes the form of two moments of circulation around the moment of production:

$$M(CC+VC) \rightarrow C\mathrm{K}\ P\mathrm{K}\ C' \rightarrow M'$$

where M = money, C = commodities, CC = constant capital, VC = variable capital, P = production period and $M' > M$ and $C' > C$.

Production is the pivot around which the two moments of circulation turn and interact. It is the hub and the moments of circulation radiate as spokes. In the net product models, production is presupposed, viewed as a step in a sequential process, in which commodities are produced, and then must be sold. The sale appears as a separate and discrete process, but analytically separate from the advance of capital for the ingredients of production. To use net product terminology, M→C is an exchange in part for inputs and C′→M′ involves final demand.

Again Marx provides a great insight: the apparent end or “final” step, the sale of commodities for money, is part of the first step, exchange of money to initiate production. The perceived sovereignty of the consumer, the exchange of commodities for money, C′→M′, is subsumed under the sovereignty of capital. If this is not obvious, it can be demonstrated by inspection of the circuit of capital. Capital obtains the ingredients of production by the exchange of money capital, constant capital and variable capital, for productive capital, M(CC+VC)→C. This is followed by the consumption of labor power and the means of production in the production process, from which a new set of commodities results (C ... P ... C′). This new commodity capital is transformed into money capital (C′→M′). This transformation is nothing other than the initial step in the next circuit of capital. The net product framework treats circulation in the context of the post-production moment, C′→M′, which is a conversion of commodities into money derivative from the earlier circulation moment, M→C.

Marx enables us to transcend the confusion created by the circulation process. It appears that the three discrete and sequential steps occur: first, the elements of production are purchased, second, production occurs and, third, the final commodities are sold. It is the third step which the net product models treat as an independent process, analyzed in terms of their own specific concepts which are based in this step, consumption and investment and their functional forms derivative from incomes received by households and classes. The circuit of capital reveals there are only two steps or phases, circulation and production, for the first and the third (M→C and C′→M′) are the same, one the buying, the other the selling. The sale of commodities, step three (C′→M′), is the appearance of the first step (M→C) to the seller of commodities, while phase one is the same set of transactions to the seller in his necessary role as a buyer.

When capital first purchases the means of production (fixed and circulating) with the exchange M→C, this is simultaneously the final step, C′→M′, for the producers of the means of production. What serves as the first step of one circuit of capital is the last step for the previous circuit, so the end phases should not be treated separately. Similarly, the exchange of money for labor power uniquely determines the personal consumption expenditure of workers, so the part of C′→M′ that refers to consumption commodities is the direct extension of the advance of variable capital.

In a comment often quoted, Marx asserted that all relationships appear as their opposites in the circulation process. This is demonstrated clearly in the aggregate movement of social capital: it appears that the personal consumption of workers determines the realization of capitalist production, but it is the advance of capital that allows value to be produced and realized in money form. In the analysis of aggregate circulation, as in all other areas of capital's reproduction, Marx's fundamental insights, based on the distinction between value and use value, the abstract and the concrete, reveal the appearance of things to be an inversion of the actual operation of capitalist society.

In Volume II of *Capital*, Marx criticized Adam Smith for analyzing circulation in terms of the product of living labor, value added or the net product. Marx argued that one should analyze the circulation process using the *gross* product, what he called the "total annual product". He referred to the procedure of resolving the total product to the net product, subtracting out circulating constant capital, as "Adam Smith's first mistake", and at another point as an "absurd formula".[15] The reduction of the gross product to a net product should not be made, and cannot be made if theoretical consistency is maintained. Marx specifically took Smith to task on the supply side for trying to resolve production into wages plus surplus value.[16]

After ridiculing Adam Smith rather unkindly, Marx relents a bit and concedes that Smith's "first mistake" has a real basis, in the obfuscation of the concrete (use value) by the abstract (value).[17] After criticizing Adam Smith, Marx adds, as a final comment (somewhat disgustedly, no doubt):

> John Stuart Mill likewise reproduces ... the doctrine handed down by Smith to his followers. As a result, the Smithian confusion of thought persists to this hour and his dogma [of the net product] is one of the orthodox articles of faith of Political Economy.
>
> (1967: 373)

Over a century after Marx's death, the faith is stronger than ever.

Value and aggregate demand

The analysis of the circulation of the gross product of capital enables the understanding of why and how capitalism suffers from periodic crises, which is treated in Chapter 9. It also provides insight into confusion arising from application of the net product framework to crises. The publication of *The General Theory of Employment, Interest and Money* by Keynes in 1936 had a profound impact on progressive economists and Marxists were no exception. The common interpretation of Keynes was that mature capitalist economies suffered from an endemic instability of aggregate demand resulting from fluctuations in investment.

Many Marxists, strongly influenced by Keynes, developed crisis theories based on the instability of aggregate demand. This theory of capitalist crisis was much older than Keynes, appearing in the work of Thomas Malthus and Sismondi.[18] In the United States Paul Sweezy was particularly influential in making aggregate demand analysis the generally accepted Marxist theory of crises (Sweezy 1966). Notwithstanding considerable criticism,[19] crisis theories based on insufficiency of aggregate demand remain extremely influential among radicals and Marxists, with the "profit squeeze" hypothesis a rather distant second.[20]

Despite their influence, aggregate demand theories are inconsistent with the circulation of capital as explained in the previous section. More important, they contradict value theory. For this reason, advocates of aggregate demand theories, even when identifying themselves as Marxists, make little use of the labor theory of value in their analysis. This absence is not surprising, because if the capitalist system were endemically afflicted by the inability to sell all that is produced, then the Marxian concept of value *must* be rejected.

As shown in Chapter 2, the central concept in value theory is that of socially necessary abstract labor. Socially necessary abstract labor operates at two levels of abstraction: capital as a whole and among individual capitals. Marx developed abstract labor for capital as a whole, then moved to the more complex level of many capitals. This move required an explanation of the realization of value, because the conversion of commodity capital to money capital determines socially necessary abstract labor in the aggregate. A determination of value at the aggregate level is necessary before socially necessary abstract labor can be applied at the level of each commodity.

Marx did not assert that general overproduction does not occur in capitalist societies, which would be absurd. Rather, he argued that the analysis of general overproduction follows from first considering value at the level of capital in the aggregate. Again, Marx provides an insight whose esoteric nature makes it appear as self-contradictory: value is the basis of the circulation of commodities if there is no overproduction; overproduction is explained by value being the basis of the circulation of commodities. Within this apparent paradox lies the explanation of capitalist crises, including that which swept the globe in the late 2000s. Crises themselves are considered in Chapter 9. The basis for that discussion is the demonstration that capitalist societies do not suffer from endemic overproduction, which is done by revisiting the embodied labor explanation of value explained in Chapter 1.

In capitalist society social reproduction occurs through the circulation of capital. In its circuit capital undergoes the three transformations explained above. This circulation of capital is simultaneously circulation of use values and values. Table 4.1 provides a numerical example of the circuit of capital.[21] The basis upon which different use values can be aggregated is the key to the crisis theory of Marx, and is discussed in detail below. At this point we assume that the two commodities in Table 4.1 can be aggregated in units of labor time. In Table 4.1, output is made up of use values used in production, steel measured in tons, and use values consumed by people, wheat, measured in bushels. On the left side of Table 4.1 are values measured in labor days, and on the right side are the corresponding physical quantities.

In the example, capitalists in sector 1 initiate production by advancing an amount of money representing 210 labor days, with which they buy sixty tons of steel and hire 100 workers for a day each (shown on the right-hand side). In sector 2, where the composition of capital is lower (ratio of steel to workers is lower), capitalists advance money equal to 160 labor days, divided in the value-ratio 10:6. For the two sectors taken together, production involves 100 tons of steel and 200 workers. Part B presents the result of the production process, in which productive capital is transformed into commodity capital. The conditions of production result in 100 tons of steel being produced in the first sector and 100 bushels of wheat in the second sector.

Part C of Table 4.1 summarizes the conversion of commodity capital back into money capital (realization of commodity capital). The example is simple reproduction, in which each successive circuit of capital is at the same level of production as the previous. The 100 tons of steel are sold to each sector in the ratio 6:4, duplicating the distribution in part A of the table. Wheat is realized by sales to workers (sixty bushels) and to capitalists (forty bushels) for their consumption.

The purpose of Table 4.1 is to demonstrate the symmetry between the production and distribution of use values (right-hand side of the table) and "value" (left-hand side). In Part A of the table (M→C), the capital value advanced (210 in sector 1, 160 in sector 2) corresponds to an amount of steel and labor, use values. In Part B the production of value (250 and 200) also corresponds to amounts of steel and wheat. In the first sector 160 tons of steel represent output equivalent to the constant capital value advanced, twenty-four tons to the variable capital advanced, and sixteen tons to the surplus value produced, and similarly for the production of wheat. In the realization process, an amount of steel exchanges for the constant capital value advanced for the next period, and the wheat production corresponds to the expenditures of workers and capitalists.

The numbers on the right-hand side are the material characteristics of the use values; i.e., steel can be measured by its weight, workers by their number and wheat by its volume. As explained in Chapter 2, measurement cannot be the sum of the labor time carried out in the production processes. Steel and wheat cannot

Table 4.1 Numerical example of the circuit of capital

A. Conversion of money capital to productive capital (M→C)

Sector	*Values*		*Use values*	
	Constant capital	*Variable capital*	*Means of production*	*Labor power*
1. Production	150	60	60 tons	100 workers
2. Consumption	100	60	40 tons	100 workers
Total	250	120	100 tons	200 workers

B. Transformation of productive capital into commodity capital (C … P … C′)

Sector	*Values*				*Use values representing*			
	Constant capital	*Variable capital*	*Surplus value*	*Total value*	*Constant capital*	*Variable capital*	*Surplus value*	*Total value*
1. Production	150	60	40	250	60 tons	24 tons	16 tons	100 tons
2. Consumption	100	60	40	200	50 bushels	30 bushels	20 bushels	100 bushels
Total	250	120	80	450				

C. Realization of commodity capital as money capital (C′→M′)

Sector	*Values: spending by*			*Consumption of use values as*		
	Constant capital	*Workers*	*Capitalists*	*Means of production*	*Workers' subsistence*	*Capitalist "luxuries"*
1. Production	150	60	40	60 tons	30 bushels	20 bushels
2. Consumption	100	60	40	40 tons	30 bushels	20 bushels
Total	250	120	80			

be added. As shown in Chapter 2, the problem of adding steel and wheat is not a problem of units of measure. It would be legitimate to measure wheat in tons, but this would not make meaningful the addition of wheat to steel. The aggregation problem arises from the physical properties of the two use values, and a common unit of measure does not itself allow aggregation to make sense.

The production of steel and the production of wheat involve qualitatively different laboring activities, concrete labor. Aggregating these concrete labors in units of time no more solves the problem of aggregation than using tons to add steel and wheat. Aggregation of the two commodities requires the conversion of concrete labor into abstract labor, which also applies to the aggregation across production units of the same commodity. Assume that all the workers in a sector perform the same activity in every production unit, which eliminates aggregation problems due to skill and other differences in workers and the work process. In all industries there is a distribution of production units around some average level of efficiency. This implies that not all labor time, even when identical, creates value. In Table 4.1, the standard or normal labor time is given in each department on the left-hand side, and this presupposes a process by which a norm is brought about. The establishment of abstract labor (value) is not primarily a problem of the aggregation of labors of different skills.[22] The fundamental transformation in value formation is from concrete to abstract labor not from skilled to unskilled.

The abstraction from concrete labors and differences in efficiency among producers is demanded by the social relations of capitalism. Because value cannot be directly observed, theory is required to reveal and understand it. The abstraction of concrete labor appears as a creation of the mind, which it is in the sense that theorizing is a mental process, but the abstract labor is as real as the concrete labor. Value, hidden by price, is a real abstraction[23] generated by capitalist relations, that exists independently of people perceiving its role in commodity production.[24]

Were price determined by the labor one can observe, it would also be hidden, because commodities do not come to market marked with hours, minutes, seconds, but by pounds, dollars, yens, etc. But abstract labor is hidden in a different sense. Value is established by the interaction of capitals in competition, the subject of a subsequent chapter. This interaction presupposes specific social relations, labor power and the means of production circulating as commodities. Once these *social relations* exist, organizers of production (capitalists) must by necessity interact, as they compete to convert money capital into productive capital. This conversion is simultaneously the conversion of commodity capital into money capital, realization of commodity capital for some capitalists, since the purchase of the means of production (CC→MP) is also the process of the realization of the means of production (see previous part of the chapter). The advance of money capital cannot be separated from the realization of capital-value, as Table 4.1 demonstrates numerically.

This abstract labor is the hidden regulator of price, and, as a result, the mechanism by which formally isolated production is rendered social. The law of value is the law of the social division of labor in capitalist society, one of whose corollaries is the law of price determination. With this clearly in mind, we return to the hypothesis that capitalism is characterized by an endemic tendency for aggregate demand to be insufficient. A simple statement of the hypothesis is as follows: if workers spend all of their wages, insufficient aggregate demand results if the sum of capitalist personal consumption and capitalist investment is less than capitalist income. The problem of inadequate demand arises from the instability of investment.[25]

We assume this hypothesis to be correct and pursue its implications for value theory by reference to Table 4.1. All commodities would not be converted into money capital if investment plus capitalist consumption is less than capitalist income (part C). The consequence of incomplete realization for the value side of Table 4.1 depends on the theory of value. If one has the labor-embodied view, incomplete realization does not affect the value calculations. If use values could be aggregated directly by the expenditure of concrete labor, then value is determined independently of the interaction of capitals, one aspect of which is realization. In other words, the circulation of commodities has no impact on their value.

However, if there is systematically incomplete realization of commodity capital the determining role of value disappears. Consider one commodity, produced under differing conditions of efficiency by various capitals. Assume that competition results in the commodity being realized such that the median capital receives a rate of profit equal to the aggregate rate, which is determined by the rate of surplus value and the composition of capital as a whole. Capitals in this industry that produce below median efficiency will receive a lower rate of profit. Part of the labor time expended in production under the domination of these capitals cannot be realized and is *socially unnecessary.* This redundant labor time does not circulate as commodity capital. It is not validated by competition as socially useful labor. The competitive nature of capitalist production relations implies that not all working time is transformed into value, even when performed under capitalist social relations. However, there is still a definitive relationship between labor time expended in production and the quantitative relationship between commodities, determined by the industry norm of efficiency.

In Table 4.1 a capital value of 370 is advanced, which results in a production of a commodity value of 450. The quantity of value objectified in the produced commodities is determined by labor time expended if money exchanged against these commodities is equal to a value of 450. If the money exchanged for commodities is less than this, *in the aggregate* a portion of value goes unrealized. There are now two senses in which abstract labor time is not validated in exchange. One arises from the differences in efficiency within a sector of production (it is not *necessary*). When all value is realized at the aggregate level, the structure of efficiency and competition in each sector determine the value produced in each sector.

If the realization of the value of commodities in the aggregate is less than 450 units of abstract necessary labor time, the relationship between the expenditure of labor time and labor time realized as money becomes indeterminate. Any proportion of what under full realization was total value can emerge as socially necessary labor time. Production and competition set the upper limit of abstract labor time (value), but nothing more. If under-realization is endemic, and the upper limit is rarely reached, "total value" becomes "maximum value", a construction of the mind.[26] The expenditures of workers and capitalists determine value, not relations and conditions of production. Production still plays a role, but a limited one. The differences in efficiency among capitals determine which survive and which do not, and the realized labor time in any sector of industry depends upon how the shortfall in aggregate demand is distributed through the economy.

Stated in a more formal way, part A of Table 4.1 begins with certain parameters: the composition of capital, the rate of surplus value and the degree and intensity of competition. On the presumption of full realization, these imply a total value for production. If full realization is not presumed, these parameters become irrelevant for the determination of value. They give no indication of how much value or how many commodities will be produced and circulated in the subsequent period. The *ex ante* rate of surplus value no longer determines the profit realized by capital. Because labor time expended in production no longer determines either realized abstract labor time or the profit of capitalists, the relevance of the analysis of production becomes primarily sociological.[27]

The value of commodities has no meaning in an analysis of the circulation of commodities that is continuously constrained by incomplete realization. This is why in *Capital* Marx considered the process of realization prior to elaborating his theory of crisis. He treats aggregate realization at the end of Volume II, where he abstracts from changes in the values of commodities.[28] His purpose is twofold: (1) to demonstrate the analytical possibility of realization, and (2) to show that incomplete realization is the consequence of what he has omitted, changes in values. In this process he justifies his previous use of the labor theory of value, which can be methodologically sound only if complete realization is presumed within the context of a determinate set of values.

Instability and crisis in capitalist economies are not caused by problems of the realization of value. They result from problems inherent in the accumulation process. The analytical tools and concepts developed to this point are adequate to understand the circulation of capital, but not the accumulation of capital. Understanding accumulation requires the analysis of money, the manifestation of money as credit, the nature of capitalist competition and technical change. These are the subjects of the chapters that provide the basis for our analysis of crises.

Appendix

Marxian and mainstream economic categories[29]

Aggregate production

The purpose of this appendix is to demonstrate in detail the relationship between the measurement categories of mainstream economics and Marxian analysis. This is done for two purposes: (1) to demonstrate formally conceptual concordance and (2) to show the analytical advantage of the approach used by Marx. To do this, we begin with the definition of the price of a commodity, non-labor cost, plus labor cost, plus non-labor incomes. For simplicity, we assume that all machinery and plant is consumed during the current production period and all non-labor income goes to capitalists as profit.

The fundamental conceptual divergence between Marxian and mainstream categories is price itself. As strange as it may seem to the uninitiated, the mainstream school of economics defines price as wages plus profits, as shown in Figure 4.a.1, while the Marxian category is the common sense one, though its components are conceptually complex. The difference reflects method. Marx began his analysis with the empirical categories use value and exchange value, and with his theory revealed what lay beneath those categories. The mainstream economics treatment of price as wages plus profits reflects its underlying production theory in which workers and machinery ("labor" and "capital") combine to produce exchange values, not use values.[30]

The aggregation from one price to the value of output for the economy as a whole, from Figure 4.a.1 to Figure 4.a.2, appears as repetition, but is not. In mainstream economics the aggregates refer to a flow of output over a discrete time period, for example one year. During that time period, workers generate a quantity of output by transforming an amount of intermediate products, and from the sale of this output wages are paid to labor and profits retained by capitalists. Mainstream "output", neoclassical and Keynesian,[31] is the sum of all the wages and profits, which is called "value added".

	Inputs of materials	**Inputs of labor**	**Income to ownership**	
Marxian terms	Constant capital +	Variable capital +	Surplus value	= Price
		Net product or living labor		
Neoclassical terms	Intermediate cost	Labor cost/wages +	Profit	= Price
		Value added		

Figure 4.a.1

	Inputs of materials		Inputs of labor		Income to ownership		
Marxian terms	Constant capital	+	Variable capital	+	Surplus value	=	Gross product
			Net or living or living labor				
Neoclassical terms	Intermediate cost		Labor cost/wages	+	Profit	=	National product
			Value added				

Figure 4.a.2

At the aggregate level, value added equals what the mainstream analysis calls "final goods and services". While the theoretical specification of this concept can be clearly stated, its empirical application is quite arbitrary. Theory requires that "final goods and services" be the value of commodities which is equal to the sum of incomes (wages plus profits in the simple case). This can be seen in the lower part of Figure 4.a.2. Wages plus profits, value added, corresponds to an equivalent money value of some collection of commodities. If the wages plus profits are not entirely spent by workers and capitalists, part of aggregate production will not be sold, and capitalists would produce less in the next time period because of lack of sufficient demand. The theoretical definition of "final goods and services" is circular: incomes equal value added, which corresponds to an equal quantity of commodities, and these commodities are called final goods and services whether their use is in consumption, investment or as inputs into production.

As one might expect, this circularity in theoretical definition results in empirical definitions which are arbitrary. In every capitalist society, labor income is almost entirely spent on consumption commodities. However, only part of profit goes to capitalist consumption, with the remainder advanced for new plant and equipment. If steel sheets used to produce an automobile are an intermediate good (commodity), it would seem logical to define the machine that forms the steel sheets into the desired shape also to be intermediate. With respect to the output, the difference in function between the steel sheets and the machine would seem to be no more than longevity. If this argument is accepted, the concept of "final goods and services" breaks down.

The issue of "final goods and services" does not arise in the Marxian formulation. While mainstream price and aggregate output are specified as a flow for some period of time, the Marxian analysis occurs in one moment of time, in which an amount of the means of production (the inputs) produced in a previous time period has been combined with a quantity of productive labor, that processes those means of production into a different set of commodities (the outputs). The difference in the value of the inputs and the outputs is the money value of the quantity of labor expended (wages plus profits). If the economy is exactly reproducing itself, what Marx called "the simple reproduction of capital", the output (gross production) must include the same inputs that laborers used to produce it.

It is now possible to identify the fundamental problem arising in the mainstream analysis of aggregate output. Assume the simple case of a capitalist economy with no government, no international trade and all income payments go to workers or capitalists. The quantitative level of production over a specified time period in this capitalist economy will be stable if everything produced is sold, if the following equality holds:

	(*Gross product*)	
Money spent by workers plus money spent by captalists	Equals	Total money value of commodities
Minus *Inputs of materials*	(*Net product*)	Minus *Inputs of materials*
Value added	Equals	'Final goods and services'

The first equality states the obvious, when everything produced is sold the money value of expenditures on commodities equals the money value of the commodities sold. If the money value of all the non-labor inputs is subtracted from the expenditure on commodities, one obtains value added on the left, and on the right an equal money value which the mainstream calls "final goods and services", without clarifying its material form (use value). "Final goods and services" is nothing more than another name for value added.

Value added under the name of final goods and services plays a key role in mainstream macroeconomics. It is the money output which under still another name, "final demand", is used to determine the equilibrium level of output. This equilibrium requires that all value added become expenditure on commodities. Table 4.a.1 is an aid to understanding this equilibrium. The expenditure of wages

Table 4.a.1 Simple reproduction of capital measured (outputs in equilibrium)

Sectors/categories	*Constant capital*	*Variable capital*	*Profit* (π)	*Output*	*Profit rate*
1 Intermediates/means of production	$CC_1=155$	$VC_1=51$	$\pi_1=51$	$\lambda_1=257$	25.0
2 Final goods/means of consumption	$CC_2=102$	$VC_1=51$	$\pi_2=40$	$\lambda_2=193$	25.0
Totals	$CC=257$	$VC=102$	$\pi=91$	$\lambda=450$	25.0

Notes
Where $CC_1+CC_2=CC$, and $VC_1+VC_2=VC$, $\pi_1+\pi_2=\pi$ and $\lambda_1+\lambda_2=\lambda$.

is for the output of the consumption commodities sector in Table 4.a.1 (sector 2), which creates no analytical difficulties. However, the expenditure of profit is in part for fixed means of production (means of production that last more than one time period), which the mainstream analysis labels "investment". If the means of production purchased with profits come from the first sector in Table 4.a.1, a logical contraction results: equilibrium requires that final demand (value added) be equal to final goods and services, but part of value added (profit) is spent on the commodities of the sector defined as producing intermediate goods.

To resolve the inconsistency, either the two sectors must be redefined or the equilibrium rule abandoned. The equilibrium rule can be formally maintained by removing plant, machinery and equipment from means of production (the first sector in Table 4.a.1) and reassigning them under the term "investment" to the category of "final goods and services" (second sector in Table 4.a.1). This would seem to solve the equilibrium problem, with the condition becoming,

(Wages + profit) = (value added) = (consumption + investment) = (final goods)

Two serious matters cast doubt on the meaning of this equilibrium condition. First, investment must exclude the physical depreciation of fixed means of production. In mainstream categories, the equilibrium includes net investment (additions to the stock of fixed capital), and excludes replacement (depreciation). No general theoretical method exists for distinguishing between the two.[32] This implies that part of the definition of final goods remains circular: net investment is that portion of investment that equals the difference between value added and consumption expenditure.

Second, and more serious, even if one could define net investment independently of the money used to purchase it, its inclusion as a final good is inconsistent with equilibrium, because by definition it increases the stock of fixed capital. Neither in theory nor practice can an economy with an expanding stock of fixed capital be in equilibrium at a constant level of output. If initially aggregate output were in equilibrium, the expanding fixed capital stock would create unused capacity, investment would fall and output would decline in the next period.[33]

Mainstream analysis avoids this contradiction by the counter-factual assumption that the investment that is part of final demand creates no new capital stock. By doing so the mainstream accepts, perhaps without being aware of it, that Marx's specification of the simple circulation of capital, formulated in a gross production framework, is analytically superior for the analysis of macroeconomic equilibrium.

An expanding economy

This purpose of this tedious presentation has been to demonstrate the logical and practical inconsistency in the mainstream specification of the conditions under which a capitalist economy will reproduce itself at the same level. This specification is made more difficult, not simpler, by the introduction of the concept of "final goods and services", which proves to be logically flawed. The flaw is considerably more serious than a bicker over how to define inputs that last more than one time period (plant and machinery), and more serious than how to specify equilibrium.

Table 4.a.1 provided a numerical example of a capitalist economy with two sectors, with one producing intermediate inputs (means of production), and one producing means of consumption ("final goods"). We assumed that inputs are entirely used in one production period, and that in each sector the same amount of labor is employed.[34] All value added goes to labor or capital, and the economy is in equilibrium, producing at the same level period after period. The process of capitalist distribution has allocated surplus value and adjusted the two commodity prices to enforce an equalized rate of profit, the capitalist principle of distribution.[35]

The conditions for simple reproduction or equilibrium can be verified by the numbers in Table 4.a.1. The outputs of means of production (intermediates) and means of consumption (final goods) require 257 money units of the input (155 plus 102, the "constant capital" column),[36] which is equal to the output of that sector. The output of means of consumption ("final goods") is equal to wages plus profits. The capitals in both sectors enjoy a rate of profit on capital advanced of 25 percent.[37]

The expansion of an economy, in this example and in practice, requires that the current production of inputs exceed their current use, as shown by the numbers in Table 4.a.2. This is an obvious necessity of the real world: the inputs that can be used at any moment must have been produced previously. In symbols, the requirement is:

Means of production used	Less than	Means of production produced
$(CC_1 + CC_2)$	$<$	$(CC_1 + VC_1 + \pi_1)$
$(162 + 103)$	$<$	$(162 + 54 + 54)$

This obvious requirement of an expanding economy implies that the value added arising in production must be less than the production of what the

Table 4.a.2 An expanding economy (output of means of production exceed their use)

Sectors/categories	*Constant capital*	*Variable capital*	*Profit* (π)	*Output*	*Profit rate*
1 Intermediates/means of production	162	54	54	270	25.0
2 Final goods/means of consumption	103	51	40	194	25.0
Totals	265	105	94	464	25.0

mainstream analysis calls "final goods and services" (VC+π less than λ_2). This creates a serious problem for the mainstream, because it implies that its analysis of equilibrium at a constant level of output is inconsistent with the analysis of an expanding economy. This problem is avoided rather than resolved by creating two distinct areas of inquiry, the analysis of static macro equilibrium and the analysis of economic growth, which can be found as separate sections in all macroeconomics textbooks.

The price of a commodity consists of all of the components of its production, including the materials required in production. Similarly, the aggregate of all commodities at any moment in time consists of inputs and value added, gross output. Including materials (means of production) in the aggregation of all commodities does not involve "double counting" as the mainstream argues. Marx's treatment of the aggregate economy involves viewing it at a moment in time, as if it occurred in one great factory. At a moment in time in this aggregate factory current means of production wait for processing, new fixed means of production await to be installed and consumer commodities rest on the shelves of the shop where workers do their shopping. There is no double counting when all of these commodities are added together.

The aggregates of the mainstream represent flows through time, which is the source of the double counting. Divorced from the means of production, these flows appear as exchange values, quantities of money. Attempts to relate these flows of money to flows of commodities results in logical contradictions except in the case of simple reproduction, what the mainstream calls static equilibrium. It is for this reason that Marx analyzed capitalism as it is, "an immense accumulation of commodities", not as a homogeneous flow of value added.

5 Commodity money

Introduction

Capitalist society is the first mode of production in which the class structure and society itself require the circulation of products as commodities. Production is for exchange and commodities must be converted into a general form that can be used in all exchanges. This general form is "money". This chapter follows Marx in unveiling the mystery of the money form.

Despite the central role of money in capitalist society, and even though almost the entire work of Marx analyzed capitalism, his theory of money was largely ignored in the English-speaking world until the final decades of the twentieth century.[1] Even the best treatments of Marxian theory refer to money in passing, leaving the reader to conclude either that Marx had no theory of money, that he had one but it is not relevant to contemporary capitalism or that it does not differ significantly from the theory of money in mainstream economics, and therefore does not require separate exposition. The purpose of this and the following chapter is to develop Marx's theory of money and credit, to show how it provides the basis for a critique of the mainstream monetary theory as it reveals the contradictions inherent in commodity circulation.

Marx's treatment of money is frequently dismissed on the grounds that it assumed a money commodity (gold), or "convertible" money. This argument concludes that because legal convertibility no longer plays an important role in capitalist economies, the analysis is an anachronism.[2] I show below that the convertibility of money is not an assumption in Marx's theory of money. It is derived as a theoretical conclusion with general validity for capitalism in all periods. This conclusion represented and continues to be a radical break with all other treatments of money. The development of non-Marxist theories of money, from David Hume in the eighteenth century, is a history of an analysis that, step by step, seeks to treat money almost exclusively as a valueless facilitator of exchange (see appendix to this chapter for a critique of the neoclassical theory of money).

When analytically separated from commodity production and circulation, money can be treated as having no value; i.e., not a commodity. In the mainstream treatment of money, derivative from the neoclassical quantity theory of money, it is analytical necessity that money has no value itself. Analogously, commodity money is an essential feature of Marx's theory of value, and it provides the basis for a general theory that explains why money appears to be a medium of exchange with no value in itself.

Because products exchanged long before capitalism developed, many theorists have sought an explanation of money applicable to all its historical manifestations. A general theory cannot be formulated, because it would by necessity ignore the relations of production that determine exchange and, therefore, determine the nature of money.[3] Seeking a general theory of money applicable across different historical periods results in abstracting from the circulation of commodities as capital (M→C→M′). This reduces exchange to simple commodity circulation (C→M→C). Treating simple commodity circulation as the general case analytically subsumes the circuit of capital within simple commodity. As has been shown, the opposite is the case: simple commodity circulation derives from the circuit of capital.

Seeking a general theory of money applicable to all modes of production is a mistake because such a theory would by definition abstract from social relations of production as they change through history. As a consequence, a general theory could not relate money to the production of commodities. A general theory would focus on the aspect of money common to all epochs, exchange, rather than on the social relations that create the possibility for exchange. Therefore, the theory of money elaborated below is not general in the sense of applying to various modes of production. It is general that it incorporates and explains the various forms of money in capitalist society, commodity money, fiat money and credit, and how these perform the functions of money.

Commodities and money

Marx begins *Capital* with general commodity circulation and production without specifying the nature of society. He proceeds to reveal, step by step, that he had necessarily been considering capitalist society from the outset. He develops his argument in this way to demonstrate that commodity circulation requires private property, which implies a social system in which capitalist property is dominant. This implies that competition is specifically capitalist competition that brings about the concentration and centralization of capital.

Because Marx presented the commodity, value, and money before capital and exploitation, it appears that these concepts were developed independently of capitalist relations of production. This appearance prompted Engels to believe that Marx's method was "logical-historical"; i.e., that the logic of Marx's presentation followed the order in which they present themselves in history. Marx explicitly denied having done this and criticized it as an invalid method (Engels in Marx 1970a: 225ff.).[4] Marx's treatment of value in the first chapter of *Capital* presupposes capitalist relations of production, which he soon makes explicit. Similarly, his discussion of money is specific to capitalist relations.

I begin with the simplest manifestation of exchange; barter. The barter of one commodity for another establishes equivalence: commodities exchange, they are equivalent. This is what Marx called the "equivalent form of value", in which the value of one commodity is represented by an amount of another. Both commodities were produced and have value, but neither can express its own value. The value of each commodity appears as a certain quantity of the other.[5] While this may seem obvious to the point of trivial, that when one commodity exchanges for another its value is revealed through the other commodity, pursuing its implications will lead to the inner (esoteric) nature of money.

The use value of a commodity is unaffected when it serves the role of measuring the value of another commodity. For example, if the commodities are wheat and iron, and they exchange on the basis of one ton of wheat for 100 pounds of iron, the value of a ton of wheat is 100 pounds of iron, and the value of iron is unexpressed. The use value form of the equivalent commodity (iron in this case) becomes the value form of the other commodity (wheat).[6]

The foregoing was not a game of words. It expressed that one commodity becomes the value representation or the value *form* of the other. When more commodities enter circulation and they all exchange against the same commodity (iron in the example above), the value of each is expressed as a certain quantity of a specific commodity (iron in this example), and that commodity becomes a general equivalent. By serving as the general equivalent, the value of iron is not affected, nor is its use for other purposes affected, such as making steel.

The development of a general equivalent allows for the abstract labor in each commodity to be quantitatively expressed as a weight or volume of the equivalent commodity. The units in which the equivalent commodity is measured are the calibration of the price of other commodities. As it becomes more common for a commodity to be used as the general equivalent, that commodity takes on an entirely new form of existence. While other commodities are desired by some people but not others because of their specific use, everyone wants the money commodity, and its specific use is spectacularly general: it is a claim on all other commodities, what it can purchase now or in the future. In a fundamental sense, the money commodity becomes all other commodities.

As a result of its attribute of transformability into all others, and the closely related attribute of being held idle without loss of function, there will be a tendency to select as the money commodity a product which has few alternative practical uses. The ideal arrangement for the general equivalent would be that it has no use value, in which case there would be no tension between its allocation into use as money and its direct use in production (the example of iron) or consumption. However, and this is the point of Marx's "equivalent form of value", a commodity with no other use but to be money could not be money because it would have no value. No one would exchange anything of value for a commodity which itself had no value; it could not serve as an "equivalent form".

As its use as the general equivalent is established, the money commodity undergoes a profound change. Its primary function, therefore, its primary use value, becomes its representation of abstract labor in general. The money commodity has intrinsic use value, gold, for example,[7] but this becomes obscured so it appears that its primary use is to represent the value of all other commodities.

While the use of other commodities reveals their intrinsic nature, the nature of the general equivalent is hidden by its use, and its price is subsumed within itself. The general equivalent cannot express its own value, just as a ruler a meter long cannot itself verify its own accuracy; nor can it express its intrinsic nature which its function as money denies. By becoming the general equivalent, a commodity separates itself from other commodities, and separates itself from its self, standing alone as the apparently valueless representation of all things of value.

To summarize, the process of exchange results in the complete abstraction from the intrinsic properties of the money commodity, such that it appears that it has no purpose but exchange. This appearance creates the illusion that the money commodity was selected arbitrarily, and that its value was irrelevant to its role as money. This illusion is validated in the eyes of commodity producers when the state issues representations of the money commodity to circulate in its place. When this happens, its use value in practice is its use to represent exchange value, though it remains the product of human labor and a commodity, not a valueless convention.

Representations of money hide the reality that commodities exchange against commodities, and in this process one commodity establishes itself as a general equivalent. This is not a process that occurred in some remote time when exchange was less complex and society more simple, and now has no relevance. It is a process of capitalism that occurs continuously, alongside the determination of exchange value by value. A legal link formalizes the money commodity, but its role is no less real in the absence of such a link.[8]

Money appears as a valueless medium of exchange, and this appearance hides its true nature, a produced commodity whose intrinsic use value has been lost in exchange. Capitalist circulation spreads the perception that money itself has no value and need have no value. This is an illusion created by capitalist circulation. The statement, money itself has no value, is analytically equivalent to the statement, commodities have no value.

Circulation and money

Because of the almost universal rejection by Marxists and non-Marxists of money as commodity, I should be explicit and unambiguous. The rest of this chapter and the next are devoted to convincing the reader of the following arguments: (1) in capitalist society money achieves its fullest and most complex forms, (2) a commodity is the basis of money and all its forms and (3) the observed prices in markets are determined by the abstract necessary labor time (value) of each commodity and the money commodity.

The first step in the argument is to demonstrate that treating money as valueless implies that exchange of commodities is analytically equivalent to barter. That is, in an analysis based on valueless money, money has no role. I start with the apparently simple case in which gold circulates as money and is used to purchase wheat. Because both gold and wheat are the products of human labor, in isolation their exchange is the barter a quantity of one for a quantity of the other.

Assume a slightly more complicated case, in which representations of gold circulate (tokens or coins). A producer sells wheat for tokens, and uses these tokens to buy a book. If the representation of money has no value itself, the second case reduces to the first, gold for wheat or wheat for a book. Because a representation of gold facilitated exchange, this token is equally a representation of wheat, a book and gold itself, a mere "veil" as the classical economists called money, which hides the barter nature of the exchange.[9]

Few writers other than the most orthodox neoclassical economists, and certainly few laypersons, would agree with this analysis that money is a mere veil over market exchanges which in practice are barter. However, the belief that money has no intrinsic value implies precisely this assertion. It implies that an exchange involves the following thought process: (1) the five dollar/pound note I hold has no value itself,[10] (2) its exchange for five liters of gasoline is purely formal because (3) the real exchange is between my working time and the gasoline, in which the five pound note is no more than a convenient intermediary.

The key characteristic of this treatment of exchange is its isolation from the general circulation of commodities. Treating the money commodity like all others implies its negation, its non-existence. If the money commodity is like all others, then it plays no distinctive role, there is no money commodity, and money is a convention agreed upon by commodity producers.[11] Placing each exchange into an interrelated process of commodity circulation reveals the fallacy in this treatment of money.

Commodity circulation is the mechanism by which capitalist producers are formally integrated into a system of social production. Price, the denomination of value in units of the money commodity, is the form in which value manifests itself, but price need not equal value, except momentarily. Each capitalist producer marshals the means of production and labor power by advancing money. The price each capitalist receives for her/his commodity is the signal of the extent to which her/his productive capital was used according to the norm for that industry's efficiency. If industry demand conditions result in capitals enjoying a rate of profit greater than that in other industries, capital flows into the sector. In such a case, price was greater than value, the abstract labor realized in exchange in the form of the money commodity exceeds the abstract labor objectified in the commodity in production.[12]

The deviation of exchange price from value is necessary during the interaction of capitalist production and circulation in order that labor and the means of production be redistributed in response to shifts in demand and changes in technology. Value must appear in a form that allows for a quantitative divergence of value from exchange value. Labor time itself cannot be the calibration of value, because this would not allow for the necessary divergence.[13] In capitalist society the market price reflects the necessary contradiction between value and exchange value. If value determines exchange value, then the two must diverge, otherwise it is not a relationship in which one determines the other, but an identity.

The denomination of all commodities in the general equivalent commodity is the vehicle for this divergence. The two important causes of divergence are (1) the systematic divergence required to enforce the capitalist distribution rule of a tendency for profit rates to equalize across sectors of production; and (2) the unsystematic divergences due to momentary shifts in market demand and supply conditions. I consider only the first, which at this point is theoretically more important.

The role money plays in this divergence can be demonstrated by use of algebra. Commodities fall into three analytical categories, those that are produced to be inputs (designed as 1), those produced for consumption (designed as 2) and the commodity that serves as money, which I note as commodity "e", for general equivalent. The value, abstract socially necessary labor time, of each commodity is given by the following equations:

commodity value = (value of materials) + (value of labor power) + (surplus value)

$$\Lambda_1 = (a_1\Lambda_1 + w_1n_1\Lambda_2) + \pi_1$$

$$\Lambda_2 = (a_2\Lambda_1 + w_2n_2\Lambda_2) + \pi_2$$

$$\Lambda_e = (a_e\Lambda_1 + w_en_e\Lambda_2 + \pi_e$$

where Λ_i = abstract socially necessary labor, measured in units of time, a_i = amount of the input required in production, measured in physical units, w_i = amount of the consumption commodity paid to a worker during the time period, measured in physical units (the "real wage"), n_i = amount of abstract labor time required to produce the output and π_i = surplus value arising in the production of each commodity.

To further simplify, I assume that the consumption of workers is the same for each commodity, and I define a unit of each commodity as the amount produced by one worker in one day.[14] This implies that the production of each commodity differs only by the amount of the input (means of production) required, the a_i terms.

$$\Lambda_1 = (a_1\Lambda_1) + (w\Lambda_2) + \pi$$

$$\Lambda_2 = (a_2\Lambda_1) + (w\Lambda_2) + \pi$$

$$\Lambda_e = (a_e\Lambda_1) + (w\Lambda_2) + \pi_e$$

If all three commodities have the same labor input and, therefore, the same surplus value, but different amounts of the material input, the rate of profit will be different for each. This inequality results in a process by which surplus value is distributed through the realization of commodities, the so-called transformation problem which is discussed in a subsequent chapter.[15] Marx named the unit values that result when each commodity yields the capitalist the same profit rate "prices of production". I designate these as λ_i and the common rate of profit as r, and rewrite the commodity equations as:

$$\lambda_1 = (a_1\lambda_1 + w\lambda_2)(1 + r)$$

$$\lambda_2 = (a_2\lambda_1 + w\lambda_2)(1 + r)$$

$$\lambda_e = (a_e\lambda_1 + w\lambda_2)(1 + r)$$

I can now define the price of means of production and consumption items in terms of the money commodity as the ratio of their values to the value of the general equivalent:

$$p_1 = \lambda_1/\lambda_e$$

$$p_2 = \lambda_2/\lambda_e$$

In both cases the commodity price is expressed as an amount of the general equivalent commodity; e.g., ounces of gold. The value of total production, measured in labor time, is the sum of the price of production weighted by their quantities. The price of this output in units of the money commodity for n number of commodities, which could be called the commodity money value of total output is:

$$\Sigma(p_i x_i) = \Sigma(x_i\lambda_i)/\lambda_e \text{ for } i = 1, 2 \ldots n$$

The algebra of prices is completed by specifying the ratio of fiat money to units of the money commodity. Let α be the number of currency units (dollars, pounds, euros) per unit of the money commodity. The prices of the commodities in fiat money are:

$$P_1 = \alpha p_1 = \alpha\lambda_1/\lambda_e$$

$$P_2 = \alpha p_1 = \alpha\lambda_2/\lambda_e$$

The central theoretical and practical question is whether the value of α must be tied to a commodity, or, to put the question crudely, can it be any number? In other words, could we have omitted algebraic and analytical reference to a money commodity? To pursue this question, we note that the calibration of price can be arbitrary even with a money commodity. In the case of gold, it can be measured in various physical units and these units can be assigned different names (dollars, pounds, euros and so on). This is trivial. The theoretical issue is, whatever may be the units of measurement of price and a currency, what determines the value of α, which is the same question as what determines the level of prices and changes in the price level?

The answer to the question is the most important element in any theory of money. A money commodity provides a theory of the absolute price level with relative values given, and a theory that rejects the necessity of a money commodity must provide an alternative explanation of the price level. In 250 years, only one alternative to commodity money has been proposed: that α and therefore the general level of prices is determined by the quantity of money in circulation.[16]

The two theoretical explanations of the general level of prices contradict each other. If money is a commodity, the general level of prices is determined by the cost of producing the money commodity. If the general level of prices is determined by the quantity of money, then money can have no value. They are also contradictory with respect to their implications for the supply of money. If money is a commodity, its supply is basically determined by the tendency of profit rates to equalize across sectors. If money has no value, its supply must be determined in a manner exogenous to the circulation of commodities.

We shall refer to these two theories as commodity-based and quantity-based monetary theory. Essential to the second is that all that is defined as money must circulate, or if some is held idle, this is done as part of a systematic and stable process. In the discussion that follows, I assume the simple case in which all such money circulates, and this is an accurate representation of quantity-based theory, capturing the essence of the analysis.[17] In the theory money has four functions, but the primary function is means of circulation. The other functions are either trivial or become subsumed as part of means of circulation.[18]

The quantity-based theory of money assigns very little importance to the role of money as a store of value, which is the form in which claims on social labor can be hoarded in a capitalist society. By definition, hoarded money does not appear in circulation.[19] It is ignored by neoclassical quantity-based monetary theory because with few exceptions the mainstream analysis is carried out within a framework of general equilibrium that excludes the possibility of financial instability. Critique of the monetary analysis based on money in the context of financial instability is pursued in the next chapter. This chapter focuses on the implications of commodity money.

In the circuit of capital, capitalists advance money for commodities that will be used in production (including labor power), and workers use the materials to produce a new set of commodities, which through sale are realized in money form. This circuit of capital can be summarized in symbols as before.[20]

$$M \rightarrow C \ldots [\text{Production}] \ldots C' \rightarrow M'$$

where $C > C'$ and $M > M'$.

The exchange on the left, $M \rightarrow C$, leaves the capitalist with a collection of commodities to employ in production. The other exchange, $C' \rightarrow M'$, realizes the newly produced commodities, the conversion of commodity value into money value. As shown in the previous chapter, the two exchanges occur sequentially for individual capitals and concurrently for capital as a whole. With the one exception considered below, commodities are not an adequate form in which to hold capital. This is obvious for productive capital, which if sold rather than used for production would at best yield the capitalist no gain and could result in a loss. In practice the commodity capital could be hoarded by delaying its sale. This hoarding requires that the commodity has a durable value, and the necessity to covert it to money capital remains.

It is obvious that money, the general equivalent, is the most appropriate form for a capitalist to hold wealth. What differentiates money from commodities in general is that it need not be realized, because it is abstract labor in general. In a society that produces for exchange, money *is* all other commodities. The important question is not, in what form would capitalists hold value? This has the obvious answer, money. The important question is, what form of money serves as an adequate hoard of value?

Functions of money

If money has no value, then it is not a commodity, and its worth is potentially indeterminate. This makes valueless money unsatisfactory as a store of wealth if inflation occurs or is anticipated. In such a period, when the purchasing power of valueless money falls, hoarding must occur in the form of specific commodities, not a general equivalent.

Our analysis appears to reach an impasse: holding wealth in the form of commodities is problematical because it may prove impossible to sell the commodities at the value when purchased. Holding wealth in the form of money makes their holder vulnerable to the ravages of inflation. This apparent dilemma, wealth as commodities is uncertain, wealth as money may be more uncertain, is resolved in practice and in theory by commodity money.

Marx observed that money is always convertible, in practice if not in law (1970a, Part I). He meant that the circuit of capital necessarily requires capitalists to hold wealth, and that valueless money is inadequate for this function precisely because it is valueless. However, periods of inflation would appear to provide clear evidence that money is valueless and ruled by its supply. The analysis of Marx reveals the opposite: inflation, the depreciation of paper money demonstrates the principle that money must be a commodity. If the value of the money commodity is constant, inflation reflects the quantitative inconsistency between the expansion of representations of money and the performance of social labor (production of value).

The fundamental difference between Marx's theory of money and almost all others is captured in a further function of money that is closely related to store of value: means of payment. This function of money hardly appears in neoclassical theory.[21] In capitalist society, most transactions are by capitalists using credit, which is another word for debt, a promise to pay in the future. Credit involves a separation in time between purchase and payment.[22] In neoclassical monetary economics this separation is trivial. It exists but has no analytical implication.

In Marx's theory, the separation of purchase and payment is central to commodity circulation, because the form of money adequate for purchase is not in general satisfactory for payment. If the separation of purchase and payment occurs during a period when the purchasing power of money changes, the conditions under which payment is made will differ from the conditions when purchase occurred. The use of money implies the use of credit, which in turn implies purchase that requires a subsequent payment.

The several roles served by money, medium of exchange, measure of value, store of value and means of payment are more than different functions of the same thing. Money is not a general purpose tool such as a hammer that can be easily shifted among different uses. The different functions imply different roles that require different things. As a medium of circulation, money can be a symbol, even an informal agreement to pay at some future date. As store of value and means of payment, money must assume a form adequate to these tasks, in which its relationship to socialized labor is firm and fixed. The form of money that serves to circulate commodities cannot in general satisfy the other functions required of money.

Understanding the complexity of money and its forms provide the key in a subsequent chapter that unlocks the nature of the financial disasters that swept the world at the end of the 2000s. With the purpose of clarifying this complexity of forms, the analysis of money to this point can be summarized as follows:

1 in the general exchange of commodities one commodity comes to serve as a general equivalent, which is money, and the use of this commodity as money makes it appear that this is its only function and would exist for no other important purpose;
2 the simple function of means of exchange can be served by representations of money which can take many forms;
3 capitalist exchange is defined by the advance of capital in anticipation of the production of commodities which implies that credit serves as the principle means of exchange;
4 credit implies deferred payment, in which money as means of payment serves to cancel debts;
5 the deferment of payment implies the further function of money as store of value;
6 the separation of exchange and payment creates the possibility of changes in the value of commodities in the course of commodity circulation; therefore,
7 while anything may serve as means of circulation, means of payment and store of value require a direct link to a money commodity.

To state the essence of Marx's theory of money in a sentence, in exchange anything may and does serve as money; in the circuit of capital the need for commodity money asserts itself. This apparent contradiction is pursued in the next chapter.

6 Capital and money

The nature of money

Money is a commodity whose use value and value become obscured by its function as means of exchange. The mainstream treatment of money as valueless endorses this obfuscation as if it were fact, and Marxian writers should not follow them by doing so. As with all obfuscations created in the circulation of capital, the misperception of money as valueless has a material basis: anything can serve as means of exchange, and this leads to the syllogism, anything can serve as money, so money can be anything.

The mainstream or neoclassical treatment of money, which is explained in the Appendix to Chapter 4, extends the syllogism: exchange is the most important function of money; anything accepted by buyers and sellers will facilitate exchange; therefore, money can be anything that has the agreement of buyers and sellers. This train of deductive logic is based upon an analysis that presumes capitalist economies to have an automatic tendency to a stable equilibrium characterized by the full employment of labor. This full employment results from the absence of uncertainty, which implies that the plans of capitalists are always and completely realized as outcomes. If it were the case that capitalism was characterized by certainty and intentions were always realized, the functions of money would collapse into the single role as means of exchange. Money could be without value and prices determined by its supply.[1]

The practical requirement for a money commodity does not preclude moments when representations of money appear to function autonomously. These moments do not invalidate the general conclusion, just as price deviating from value does not invalidate that value is the basis of price. They are understood by first considering money in its commodity form, gold, for example. Marx develops his theory of money by abstracting from all the complicated developments of the money form, fiat money, credit and others, which I treat later. He did not assume that gold was money in the simple sense of a counterfactual simplification. Rather, by beginning at this with a money commodity, the development of the more complex forms could be explained, and the laws governing those forms revealed. This is the method I shall use, in which the abstract concept reveals the complexity for the concrete (Marx 1973: 105–8).

I begin with the abstraction that gold serves as the medium of exchange.[2] The parameter α, introduced in the previous chapter, is the inverse of the value of gold.[3] Given the values of all other commodities, the price level rises and falls with increases and decreases in the productivity of gold production. Since the value of gold determines general price level,[4] what is the role of the supply of gold? To phrase the question more specifically, would an increase in the production of gold affect the general level of gold-denominated prices?[5]

One possible interpretation would be that an increase in the supply of gold generates a scenario similar to that predicted by quantity-based theory: with the increased availability of gold there is more gold to exchange against all other commodities. This excess supply of gold would drive the price of gold down and prices of other commodities up, until all gold was sold. This analysis suggests that an increased availability of gold has the same consequence as an excess supply of other commodities, and implies that the quantity-based analysis holds for commodity money. Ricardo used this logic in developing the monetary adjustment mechanism for his theory of comparative advantage (Shaikh 1979).

This interpretation of commodity money has a complication that Ricardo recognized.[6] An increase in the availability of gold that depresses its price in terms of other commodities would not be sustainable. A sustainable price for any commodity requires that the rate of profit in that sector be the same as the average rate of profit. If the rate of profit were the same for all commodities before the increase in the supply of gold, the subsequently higher gold price for all commodities would imply that the rate of profit for gold had fallen. As a result, producers of gold would move some of their capital out of gold production, reducing the supply until the original absolute gold price was re-established.

This interpretation of commodity money concludes that if the value of the money commodity is constant, a unique absolute price level is implied, from which the actual price level can temporarily deviate. The same conclusion would apply to all commodities, which implies that the only special property of the money commodity is its role as general equivalent. This in turn would imply that money could be valueless except during occasional moments when factors independent of money itself render valueless money unable to perform all the functions required of it. This interpretation of commodity money produces such modest insights that it does not justify designation as a theory of money.

In the monetary analysis of Marx, an increased supply of the money commodity, gold, would not in general lead to a rise in commodity prices even as a transitory phenomenon. How Marx reached this apparently absurd conclusion, the supply of money does not affect the level of prices, reveals the uniqueness of his monetary analysis. Though money must be a commodity, that does not mean that the money commodity is like all other commodities.[7]

All other commodities must be converted into money or the circuit of capital cannot be renewed. If an excess supply of one of these commodities occurs, either the price falls or a portion of the output is not sold. In both cases a part of the value produced is not realized. The use value remains, but it is useless to the capitalist for whom its use is its potential to be realized as money capital. The money commodity need not be realized; it is realized value.

As the general equivalent, the money commodity represents all commodities, and does so *because* it is a specific commodity. In the money commodity the opposition of use value and exchange value, the concrete and the abstract, is resolved. The use value of the money commodity is the abstraction to all other commodities. The money commodity is a commodity of its own type. It is itself the abstraction of all use values to value.

To continue with the simple case in which all exchanges are in gold, money is drawn into circulation or lies idle depending upon the aggregate value of commodities to be realized. If for some reason the production of commodities declines, some money falls out of circulation, accumulates in hoards, as a preserve of value and wealth. In the simple case of gold as money, such moments occur when commodity prices fall, and the value of money rises. When all other commodities fall in price because of excess supply, hoarding of commodity money is in its most attractive moment for capitalists. When accumulation accelerates, these hoards are reduced, as more money is required as means of circulation. While the money commodity must have specific physical properties to be hoarded (gold is hoarded not apples), hoarding and money itself are social relations.

A basic misconception of the quantity-based theory is to assume that all money must circulate.[8] This assumption derives from one of two mistakes, mentioned before. If the money commodity is treated like all others, then like all others it must be realized and cannot be dormant in hoards. If money is assumed to be valueless, there is no motivation to hoard, because money cannot adequately preserve value. Both misconceptions result from considering commodity circulation in isolation in exchange, in which money functions simply, as a medium of circulation. When exchange and money are placed within the circulation of capital, the preservation of value becomes a necessary function of money. The movement of commodities determines the movement of money, not the reverse. Marx summarized as follows:

> [F]or a given interval of time during the process of circulation, we have the following relation: the quantity of money functioning as the circulating medium is equal to the sum of the prices of the commodities divided by the number of moves made by coins of the same denomination. This law holds generally.[9]

His meaning is clear: the determination of money in circulation in the simple case of commodity money applies in general. As in all aspects of the functioning of capitalism, the important issue is not what Marx wrote about it, but understanding his analysis.

The circulation of money is determined by the quantity of commodities to be realized and their values.[10] Additional money is drawn into the circuit of capital as a result of an increase in the number and value of commodities to be realized.

At a later point in this book during treatment of interruptions in the circuit of capital, I show that the availability of a specific form of money becomes of paramount importance. This will not amend the general relationship in which the circulation of money derives from the circulation of commodities. In the process of production a certain mass of commodities is produced.

The social interaction of producers establishes abstract necessary labor time, which is the total value to be realized. These commodities must be realized as money. The total amount of money drawn into circulation is determined by this total value and the frequency with which money turns over in a given period of time (the velocity of money). Money not in circulation serves as a store of value. The value of the money commodity, not its supply, determines absolute prices.

In this simple case of commodity money only, circumstances might arise in which the growth of production was so rapid that all money enters circulation. At this point the availability of money would limit expansion. More commodities could be circulated only if the exchange value of money fell, in which case absolute prices would no longer be determined by the value of money, or if the velocity of money rose. We treat this issue in the following chapter.

Symbols of money

During the circulation of capital, money has four functions: a medium of circulation, standard of value, store of value and means of payment. Commodity money asserts itself in the last three functions and is obscured in the first. As a medium of circulation, money facilitates exchange by providing a general form that abstract labor can assume between exchanges. In exchange, money is a symbol, a representation of the value of commodities in general form. As a store of value, it is not only a symbol of abstract labor, but value itself in its most liquid form.

When money facilitates exchange, its role can be served with a symbol that can calibrate price (Marx 1973: 143–4). The substitution of representations for the money commodity endorses the symbolic role money plays in exchange. The replacement of the money commodity by symbolic representations does not imply that money need not be a commodity. The absence of the money commodity from transactions follows from a functional division: for a means of circulation a symbol will suffice, while a store value requires commodity money, "money as such", to protect against loss of value.

The use of symbols of money is a convenience in exchange, in part because commodity money is bulky and loses weight in use. A symbol of money becomes generally accepted through a social process, almost without exception the result of action by the state. The state creates an official substitute for money and, equally important, guarantees the property rights and enforcement of contracts that make the generalization of exchange possible. Without state regulation, commodity money would rule exchanges. The issuance of coins, tokens and paper money requires the state as the guarantor of the worth of these symbols. This guarantee is maintained by a legal promise of some form of convertibility. In its most rigid form this convertibility is achieved by limiting the issuance of symbols of money to the amount of the money commodity available for conversion.[11] In this case, the circulation of symbols of money can be considered analytically identical to the circulation of gold itself.

The necessary role of the state in creating valueless symbols of the money commodity is dramatically demonstrated when the states break down. When governments collapse, as during the civil wars Liberia, Sierra Leone and Somalia in the 1990s, what economic activity survived was carried out in commodity money such as diamonds and gold, or in international currencies, with the US dollar being the most common. While in the abstract world of free markets the control of symbols of money can be privatized, this has not occurred in practice in a major country since the nineteenth century.[12]

Issuing currency represents an integration of the economic and political spheres, and convertibility can be a weapon in the struggle among national capitalist classes. The development of symbols of money creates a separation between domestic and international exchange. What can serve as a satisfactory medium of circulation within a country may be unacceptable among capitalists of different countries. The tension among currencies reflects the underlying need for a money commodity. Symbols of money can circulate internationally only if national capitalists join to create supranational institutions to assure the worth of the international medium of exchange, the best known being the International Monetary Fund and the Bank for International Settlements.

Defenses of valueless money

Objections to assigning an analytical role to commodity money are typically based on apparently empirical arguments that transactions in modern capitalist societies do not involve gold or any other commodity as a means of exchange or means of payment. And while capitalists may hold gold as a store of wealth or value, gold is but one among many commodities that is held for speculative purposes. Almost all writers on the left, including Marxists, reject commodity money as practically and analytically irrelevant, pointing out that exchanges among capitalists are typically based on "promises to pay" (Foley 1982, 1983), with no reference to other forms of money.

As with value itself, the circulation of commodities hides the role of commodity money. The great contribution of Marx was insight that every aspect of capitalist reproduction reflects the specific social relations of capital and the historical process that generated those social relations. The medium of exchange in any transaction does not arise spontaneously in exchange itself. It is not the result of the choice and convenience of the parties to the exchange, though this will appear to be the case.

To be specific, promises to pay among commodity producers, which is short term indebtedness, presuppose money as a unit of account. While a group of producers might spontaneously create indebtedness for their trade, a common nomenclature of prices must be presented to them by some external agency.

To understand how promises to pay arise, one needs an explanation of the source of the units in which the promises are calibrated. Presupposed is a standard of value; i.e., the prior existence, both historically and analytically, of a money commodity that is the basis of monetary calculation.

Capitalists in developed and underdeveloped countries do carry out exchanges on the basis of debt promises; however, this method of facilitating exchange cannot be divorced from the historical and social bases that make such promises valid. The development of the credit system within capitalist relations of production makes possible the apparently spontaneous intra-capitalist debt that finances exchanges. The sophisticated forms of finance arising from credit and debt among capitalists requires prior understanding of simpler mediums of exchange.

Closely related to the argument that buyers and sellers can create their own valueless forms of finance is the role of the state in the capitalist financial system. With its monopoly over the issuance of fiat money, the state would appear to render commodity money unnecessary. To accept this appearance as causal fails to distinguish between the monopoly itself and the function of convertibility. A monopoly over the issuance of the means of circulation centralizes in the state the convertibility function, but does not eliminate the occasional need of capitalists to convert symbols of valueless money into commodity money.

Convertibility raises the issue of variations in the supply of fiat currency, the analysis of which requires review of the circuit of capital with commodity money. Capitalists advance money for labor power and the means of production. This exchange realizes previously produced means of production and the consumption commodities intended for workers.[13] Production occurs, which establishes the quantity of commodities to be realized at the end of the production period. If total value produced increases compared to the previous production period, additional money is drawn into circulation for the requirements of realization (hoards are reduced). The amount of the money commodity serving as a means of circulation expands and contracts, depending on the tempo of accumulation.[14]

For those reluctant to accept that commodity money plays an important and continuous role in modern capitalist society, the ebb and flow of money from and into hoards may seem nothing but a convenient assertion. What may appear as an assertion is the practical consequence of the unique characteristic of commodity money: it is the embodiment of realized value. Every holder of commodities must at some point sell, with the exception of the holder of the money commodity, who can hold it or sell it as opportunity requires. A specific objection to this key role for hoards is that capitalists would not hold money idle in any form except very briefly because doing so implies a zero return on capital. This is a valid but separate issue discussed in the next chapter. As in so many aspects of capitalism, Marx reverses the arguments of neoclassical economics. Where the latter explain hoards by the financial incentive offered by interest and dividends, Marx explained interest and dividends as the consequence of hoards.

Dispelling the illusions of money

The circulation of commodities is the reason for the circulation of money. This obvious statement implies that an increase in the availability of the money commodity with no change in its value results in increased hoarding. In a society of commodity producers, commodities must be transformed into money, commodity capital into money capital. If for some reason all commodities are not transformed into money, this appears as an excess of commodities compared to the money commodity. The money commodity appears to be in shortage. It is a short step to the conclusion that commodities failed to be realized because of a shortage of the money commodity.[15] This conclusion presupposes what it seeks to establish, namely that all money circulates, that there are no hoards of money and no motivation to increase them.

The general use of paper money endorses this illusion, because paper money serves primarily as a means of circulation. This and other representations of commodity money are a claim on commodities (social labor), but this claim is limited by the amount of value that can be realized, not by the volume of currency itself. If the quantity of fiat money exceeds the value of commodities including the money commodity itself, capitalists may attempt to convert this currency into commodities. The consequence can be a rise in prices denominated in units of the valueless currency; i.e., inflation. This process can continue until all of the valueless currency is absorbed in circulation.[16]

It appears that the introduction of valueless currency, even if convertible in law, has saved the quantity theory of money, since the quantity of currency affects the nominal price level in a more or less proportionate way. It would appear that one could argue as follows: if the money commodity itself circulated in exchange, prices would be determined by its value. However, paper money and other representations of the money commodity circulate, and prices are determined by the quantity of those representations.

This defense of valueless money, which is a defense of the neoclassical theory of money, is an extremely limited one. The interesting aspect of the relationship between fiat money and inflation is not its generality, but its specificity: when, how and under what circumstances it might occur. The quantity theory of money and its neoclassical elaborations claim much more than being an explanation of the price level. It is a theory in which all aspects of an economy are explained by the quantity of money, most importantly, the level of output and employment.

Because symbols of commodity money are representations of something else, the purchasing power they represent has the potential to decline as their quantity in circulation increases. Their symbolic nature asserts itself; the contradiction inherent in them, that they represent money but are not themselves money, is manifested in their depreciation. The depreciation of currency due to the increase of its quantity is not a theory of the price level. It represents recognition of the distinction between the real and the symbolic. No theoretical insight is required to predict a rise in nominal prices when the symbolic comes into contradiction with the real. The theoretical insight begins when one moves to analyze the consequence of this contradiction on the material process of the production and circulation of value.

Because the real basis of circulation is commodity money, the excess supply of representations of money results in a change in the calibration of price (Marx 1970: 122).[17] Variations in the supply of fiat money do not affect that a specific amount of gold (the money commodity) exchanges against a specific amount of iron. The change is in the symbolic representation of iron in terms of gold. The production of commodities determines total value and, therefore, the productive utilization of labor power and the means of production. More or less paper money in and of itself has no direct impact upon employment, production or the mass of commodities that circulate. Indirect consequences may occur, and these are considered in the next chapter.

In the neoclassical theory of money an increase in fiat money flows into circulation. If there is less than full employment, the price level increases more than the money wage, stimulating output,[18] and output increases until full employment is reached. If the supply of paper money continues to increase, all prices and wages rise proportionally to the increase in the supply of paper money. Increases in the availability of valueless money stimulate the real variables in the economy. The neoclassical theory of valueless money is not primarily a theory of the price level, but a theory of how the symbolic determines the material.

The neoclassical theory of money is weak even as a theory of the price level, because its view that all money circulates trivializes the relationship between commodities and money. Casual observation shows that large increases in currency almost always result in large increases in prices, excessive printing of money results in excessive price increases. It does not follow from this obvious relationship that any increase in currency results in an increase in prices or output. As with all aspects of instability, the analysis of inflation takes one beyond the circulation of capital to the process of accumulation, which is considered in subsequent chapters.

Money reveals and obfuscates the nature of capital in the cycle of the production and realization. Representing value in the abstract, money reveals the nature of capital as self-expanding value. The appearance of capital as monetized abstract labor obfuscates the basis of that expansion, expansion of value through exploitation of labor. As value alienated from its material basis, the money form of capital contains within it the potential for instability on crises.

Marx's single most important insight into capitalism was and remains that the appearances of capitalism are not only misleading, they are frequently the direct contradiction of the underlying relationships.[19] There is no better example than money, which appears to be valueless, but is a commodity. It is a mystery why this powerful insight has been rejected by almost all Marxists. As shown in Chapter 3, the distribution of surplus value as profit on the basis of total capital advanced creates the illusion that capital itself is a source of value along with labor. No Marxist is misled by this appearance. Certainly no Marxist has ever argued that the exploitation of labor was a phenomenon of Marx's time that no longer applies to capitalism.

Yet, this is what is argued for Marx's treatment of money. Marx's theory of exploitation is directly derivative from his theory of value, and that theory of value explains the process by which one commodity is differentiated from all the others as the general equivalent. This differentiation is not a historical event, but a continuous social process which is constantly repeated, just as the process and relations of exploitation are repeated. Conan Doyle has his famous detective, Sherlock Holmes, say, "after eliminating the impossible, whatever remains, no matter how improbable, is the truth".[20] Quantity-based monetary analysis is the impossible, and commodity money is what remains, though it is improbable only if one discards or fails to understand Marx's labor theory of value.

Appendix

The neoclassical quantity theory

The hypothesis that prices respond to the quantity of money available for circulation is hundreds of years old. The analytical and practical issue is not whether the hypothesis is valid, but to what extent, under what social and institutional circumstances ("the monetary regime") and for what definition of money. In various manifestations this hypothesis is consistent with Marx's monetary theory.[21]

Neoclassical economics has a version of the quantity theory that the nineteenth century economists would neither have recognized nor accepted. Indeed, the neoclassicals have given quantity-based monetary arguments such a bad name that the term "quantity theory" is used with a disdain bordering on contempt by Marxists and other radical economists. This appendix focuses exclusively on the neoclassical version because it has pretensions to be a comprehensive explanation of the level of output and employment as well as prices and interest rates. As a result it is inconsistent with monetary analysis based on commodity money.

The analysis of prices and money within the neoclassical framework presents two difficulties from the outset. The first and simpler is whether the term "price level" refers to a system with one or more than one commodity. The second more complicated ambiguity arises because no theorizing is possible without abstraction, and the analyst must specify the simplifications. The simplifications required in neoclassical money analysis prove so severely restrictive that even pretence to generality is lost. These will present themselves as the discussion of neoclassical monetary theory proceeds.

I begin as capitalist exchange presents itself. In a given time period, the sum of all sales is equal to the sum of all purchases. The sum of sales equals the quantity sold of each commodity times the price at which it was sold, and the sum of all purchases is the aggregation of the means of payment used for those purchases. Money is the means of payment, no matter what form it takes.

[sum of all purchases] = [sum of all payments] (6.1)

$$\Sigma(P_iQ_i) \equiv \Sigma M_i$$

where P_i = sale price of commodity i, and i = 1, 2, etc., Q_i = quantity sold of commodity i, and i = 1, 2, etc. and M_i = the means used to make the purchases.

All the M_is can be measured in the same units, so I can simplify and by division obtain the following, $v \equiv \Sigma P_iQ_i/M$. The letter v is the turnover rate of means of payment or turnover rate of money.[22] Moving from this to the behavioral relationship among money, prices and quantities requires a clarification of $\Sigma(P_iQ_i)$ and ΣM_i. The $\Sigma(P_iQ_i)$ we observe is the sum of all transactions, exchanges of means of production as well as of consumption commodities. This was the measure used in theoretical specifications of the two greatest post-Classical economists, Leon Walras and John Maynard Keynes.[23]

The standard approach in the neoclassical quantity-based monetary framework is to assume that the hypothetical economy has only one product, and that the quantity of the means of payment is determined *ex machina* by an entity usually identified as the "monetary authority". The symbol v is assumed a constant, designated the "velocity of money". While the assumption of a single, composite commodity may seem absurd (which it is for most purposes),[24] it is essential in the neoclassical monetary theory. The price–quantity–money relationship is reduced to a simple behavioral equation, in which v is constant and the single commodity is designated as Y.[25]

$$PY = vM^* \qquad (6.2)$$

and the price *level* is

$$P = vM^*/Y$$

When $(\Sigma M_i = M)$ is fixed at M* by the monetary authority and v is constant, causality runs from money to price and quantity. If output is not at full potential, an increase in the quantity of money will increase price and the quantity of the output in some unspecified combination, determined by one's theory of macroeconomic adjustment. Therefore, if Y is not at full potential, the level of price is in part determined by the level of output. In what might be called the pure neoclassical quantity theory of money, Y is fixed at full potential. The price level is unique with respect to the quantity of money, and changes in the quantity of money result in an equal proportional change in the price.[26] In principle price can be anything because it has no nominal anchor. It has a unique value because the quantity of money is fixed by a monetary authority.

The neoclassical "price level" in Equation 6.2 has no empirical counterpart. It is a purely theoretical construction that cannot be measured. Ignoring for the moment the difficulty of defining M*, the simple form in Equation 6.2 requires a physical measure of output which exists only in the case of an economy with one product. In the full version of Equation 6.1 the price level cannot be defined because the prices of commodities cannot be separated from their quantity weights.

Because it may seem to the non-specialist that it required a great deal of space and unnecessarily tedious discussion to present the obvious, I summarize why the analytical validity of the basic quantity equations, PY = vM and P = vM/Y, is not obvious, though neoclassicals wish us to believe so.

> *Complication 1.* The observed sum of transactions involves many commodities and many prices, and some of these commodities are inputs into other commodities. Over any discrete time period a commodity is likely to reappear subsumed within the price of another. This complication is eliminated by assuming there to be only one commodity.

> *Complication 2.* Some money may be held idle, and this idle amount may vary over time.[27] Thus, the quantity of money circulating in exchange may not equal the quantity created by the monetary authority. This complication is eliminated by calling v the velocity of money and assuming it constant.

> *Complication 3.* The equation PY = vM is valid only if Y is constant. This complication is eliminated by assuming that the system is always at full potential.[28]

> *Complication 4.* Not even in theory can there exist a monetary authority that determines the quantity of money. This is the focus of the rest of this appendix.

Quantity-based monetary theory might survive by eliminating the first three complications through assumptions, but it cannot assume that the quantity of money is fixed. That the quantity of money is determinate and independent of the prices it is alleged to determined is the *raison d'être* of the neoclassical quantity theory. In order that the theory not assume what it seeks to establish, it must provide a logically consistent explanation of what determines the quantity of valueless money. Further, it must link this theoretical explanation to a process in actual economies.

No neoclassical economist believes that even in theory, much less in practice, there exists a money supply determined by a monetary authority. Their theoretical and practical argument is that this simplistic assumption produces a monetary analysis whose conclusions are not fundamentally altered by the complexities of reality.[29] The critique that follows accepts the simplistic assertion of a monetary authority that can regulate a form of money. A concrete example would be a central bank granted the monopoly to print paper currency and strike coins. I name this the "monetary base".

The problem for neoclassical monetary theory to proceed further lies with its definition of money, of which the monetary base is a part. Following in the tradition of the American monetary economist Irving Fisher, neoclassical theory defines money in terms of exchanges: money is anything generally accepted as medium of exchange. Using this definition, a leading monetary theorist wrote that money is anything acceptable "as such", and "as such" refers to the property of general exchangeability (Johnson 1972: Chapter 7). The difficulty with this apparently sensible definition is it implies that money literally can be *anything*. If money can be anything, then its amount is indeterminate. In the absence of a money commodity as the anchor for nominal prices, and in the absence of a determinate quantity of money, the theory is left with nothing.

As serious as it is, this definitional indeterminacy reflects an even more serious problem in neoclassical monetary theory, which is accounting for the very existence of money. The theoretical problem is implied from the outset, because something which can be anything has no separate existence from all other things. The existence problem derives from the methodological core of neoclassical economics, the combination of the assumptions of individual utility maximization and full knowledge of the information generated by markets. If people have full knowledge of all markets, they will know the money price at which each commodity would be bought and sold. If they know this, they can exchange commodities directly without passing through the intermediary of money.[30]

As mad as this argument is, it is the necessary collateral damage arising from the equilibration process in competitive markets which is further elaborated in Chapter 8. If people do not have full knowledge, then ignorance can result in a commodity exchanging at different prices during a market period and commodities going unsold. If this happens, then markets do not generate economically and socially optimum outcomes, and there is a prima facie case for public intervention to correct their failings (see Chapter 8).[31]

Neoclassical writers have for the most part resolved the problem, in principle money can be anything, but for rigorous theory it must be something quite specific, by reference to practice. In practice, anything does not serve as money. By some process commodity-producing societies sort out a limited number of things to serve as money. Neoclassical textbook writers are content to leave the issue as settled: anything can be money, but in practice only a few things are. Custom and time have resolved the indeterminacy. On this basis theory proceeds with a supply of money that is exogenous with respect to the level of economic activity.

Without recognizing it, neoclassicals have refuted their definition of money. One is first offered a definition: anything can serve as money. This theoretical generalization proves to be absolutely central to the theory, for it is the basic defense of the argument that money has no value. However, this generalization creates a potential analytical problem of major importance: how are limits to be set on the definition of money so that its quantity can be treated as exogenous with respect to the transactions it finances? Second, one discovers that the theoretical prediction, "anything can be money", is refuted in practice because very few things serve as money. Third, the empirical rejection of the definition is taken as the vehicle to solve the major analytical problem created by the definition; empirical rejection of the definition is used to reconcile its own contradictory nature.

People in the street, and even most students of economics, go about their affairs largely unaware that the mainstream economists who set the public debate over inflation cannot resolve something as basic as why there is money and what it is. The hypothesis that there exists a supply of money which can be effectively adjusted by a monetary authority is not only unproved, it cannot be rigorously formulated. The essence of the neoclassical monetary problem can be simply stated: the theory provides no nominal anchor for prices. Without a nominal anchor, the need to define and restrict what can serve as money is absolute. With a nominal anchor, the quantity of money and the quantity of representations or substitutes for money remains important, but need not be subject to such analytical limitations. Marx demonstrated why and how a produced commodity can function as the necessary nominal anchor, and how it relates to its representations, fiat money and credit money.

7 Credit, crises and capital

The capital relation

In capitalist society, commodity money is hidden by fiat money (paper notes and token coins), and also by credit, which I define broadly, as contracted indebtedness. Credit allows for circulation without formal representations of money. The exchange of commodities coincides with the accumulation of indebtedness. When the debts fall due or cannot be rescheduled or renegotiated, money functions as a means of payment.

With the development of credit transactions, even fiat money falls out of use as a means of circulation and becomes the medium for canceling debts, which is the payment for transactions that have already occurred. As means of payment money does not circulate, but lies idle alongside indebtedness as "the independent form of existence of exchange value".[1] In this chapter I show that the functioning of credit involves the interaction between commodity circulation without money, and the emergence of commodity money when debts must be paid.[2] Credit brings forth the contradiction between the functions of money, which results in financial crises.[3]

The value of a commodity is its abstraction from its concrete form, and credit is the further abstraction of value from any material form that wealth takes. The great variety of commodities becomes represented for capital as one, the money commodity; state-created symbols circulate abstracting from the material form of money (the money commodity); and debt replaces and abstracts from those symbols as means of exchange. In these successive steps of abstraction, each more distant from concrete wealth, lies the potential for crises in capitalist society. An analysis of the instability and crises generated by capital by necessity comes to focus on money and credit.

Money in capitalist society is the medium by which labor power and the means of production are set into motion. This role of money does not occur spontaneously; it is the consequence of specific social relations. Money is not a claim upon the productive forces of society unless labor has been separated from the means of production with which commodities are made. The function of money as capital presupposes the "capital relation", which is the potential to purchase dispossessed and alienated labor; dispossessed from the means of producing and as a result dispossessed from the products of labor. The historical process by which people were liberated from servile social relations left them free to be exploited by capital. This liberation of people from servile relations was simultaneously created capital and gave it license to exploit labor. Capital is a relationship between classes in which money commands labor power.[4] The conversion of money into capital, the marshaling of the productive forces through exchange, represents the class relations that produce and reproduce capital.

In capitalist society reproduction of the class relations requires the circulation of commodities and alongside them money. Because capitalist society is the first in which the circulation of commodities and money is general, it appears that circulation is dominant over production. This appearance provides the basis of theories that seek to explain the operation of capitalism in terms of circulation of commodities and money, buying and selling. Neoclassical economic theory, the most sophisticated and arcane version, analyzes the circulation of commodities on the assumption that the conditions of production are given. When circulation rather than relations of production is treated as primary, it is a small step to attribute an active role to money. This is ahistorical, for money existed in varying degrees of development in many societies without giving rise to capitalist accumulation.

With the development of capitalist social relations, the accumulation of capital appears as the accumulation of money. The circuit of capital, M→C … P … C′→M′, begins and ends with money. Its apparent points of departure and culmination imply that its purpose is an expansion of money. It appears that the expansion of capital is not material, but the generation of money from money. From the point of view of capitalists, this irrational aspect of accumulation-money-more-money assumes a real existence. For part of the capitalist class, financial capital,[5] it is possible to convert money into more money without going through the process of production.

Financial capital is the faction of capital that is the vendor of money. When money is lent by a capitalist, the "price" is the interest rate that is charged. With the intention of avoiding confusion, the commodity that serves as money will be called commodity money. The credit that finance capitalists lend to other capitalists will be called "money as a commodity". The analysis of credit, money as a commodity, is the investigation of the development of money capital into a claim on surplus value that is independent of industrial or productive capital. Inherent in money as a commodity is the potential for financial capital to assert dominance over industrial capital, the realization of which is discussed below.

Hoarding and capital

The previous chapter explained that capitalist society generates hoarding of money due to the nature of money. Because the money commodity need not be realized (no one has to sell it), it comes to rest in hoards when not required for circulation. Hoarded money is unproductive, but remains capital,[6] and as capital maintains a claim on surplus value. The form of these hoards is fictitious capital, symbols of ownership and indebtedness, of which stocks and bonds are the most commonly known.

This form of capital is fictitious in the sense that it is a claim on surplus value, but not the direct claim of ownership of any material object. In capitalist society, means of production are capital, and the property of the owner is productive capital. The person who buys a stock in a company cannot go into a factory or office and claim ownership of a machine or desk; the ownership claim is fictitious, referring to a claim on profit not on real property. As a consequence, the link between the market value of these paper claims and the market value of the assets they nominally represent can be quite loose. The possible disjuncture between fictitious and real capital is key to the financial crisis of the late 2000s and of capitalist crises in general.

This fictitious capital, "financial assets", takes take two forms, claims of ownership to which profit accrues, and claims on debt to which interest is paid.[7] The markets for financial assets in a capitalist society provide the mechanism by which idle money can assert itself as potential capital. Mainstream economics is obsessed with these markets, treating them as mobilizing and allocating resources, as well as determining the return on investments. While financial transactions affect the distribution of money capital among capitalists, it is not this function that explains their existence. In mainstream economic theory, people hold money in financial assets for the income they generate, and buying and selling them allocates capital. As for so many aspects of capitalism, individual behavior and motivation do not explain an aggregate phenomenon.[8] Commodity production implies a money commodity, which falls out of circulation into hoards. Someone must hold these hoards, and in capitalist society this necessitates a payment. People hold fictitious forms of wealth because the system as a whole generates hoards of idle money.

Prior to the rise of capitalism, wealth accumulated in hoards, frequently in the form of money. Except for those specifically involved in money lending,[9] accumulated wealth did not command a return, because money was not a general claim on society's resources. If neither labor power nor the means of production are commodities, money is not a potential claim upon the surplus labor of society. In medieval Western Europe money entered the process by which resources were allocated to a very limited degree, because production was organized within non-monetized social relations, serfdom, guild system and other institutions.[10] Because money in such societies played a restricted role in wealth expansion, it claimed no return, it was not capital.[11] Precapitalist interest-bearing money existed to facilitate luxury consumption, state expenditure and trade among countries.

Once money has command over resources, access to money becomes access to surplus value. Access to money takes the form of credit provided by financial capitalists. There, we reach the point at which the analysis of credit in capitalist society requires the introduction of interest-bearing forms of money into the circuit of capital.

$$M^* \rightarrow M \rightarrow C \ldots P \ldots C' \rightarrow M'$$

Financial capitalists lend money to productive capitalists (M*→M). The first M is assigned a star to indicate that while M*=M, the financial capitalists make a profit in their operations. Before considering how this profit is determined, it is necessary to explain why M*→M occurs. Its function is not obvious, since no value is created by it. It is also true that no value is created in the two other moments of circulation, M→C and C′→M′. However, these have a clear function, to change the form of capital. The first, M→C, changes money capital to productive capital, and C′→M′ realizes surplus value as profit by the conversion of commodities into money. These changes provide for the reinitiation of the circuit of capital in its cycle of production, realization and recapitalization of value. The purely financial transaction M*→M seems redundant, since it involves no change in amount, nor a change in form. It does not seem a transaction in any meaningful sense, only a transfer of money.

The step M*→M is not necessary in order to finance the expansion of production. The level of production for capital as a whole in any turnover period is set by the material production of the previous period (see appendix to Chapter 4). The surplus product of one period sets the limit to production in the next, since only what has been produced can subsequently be employed as means of production and means of consumption for the working class. If the realization of value (step C′→M′) occurs smoothly, capital as a whole can convert money capital into productive capital.[12] Money capital is unproductive, what Marx called “a dead weight of capitalist production”.[13]

Irrelevant for capital as a whole, the transaction between financial and productive capital, M*→M, arises from the interaction of many capitals. In the aggregate, accumulation results from the capitalizing of realized surplus value. If this were the case for individual capitals, it would imply that each could increase by no more than the amount of its profits. A major aspect of the dynamism of capitalism is the expansion of some sectors and the producers in them and the contraction of others. This dynamism of capitalism requires the redistribution of profit among producers and sectors.[14] This redistribution allows the more efficient to expand at the expense of the less efficient, either in the same sector of industry or by invading another. This redistribution would be extremely slow if capitalists were limited in their accumulation to the profit realized in the moment C′→M′. Redistribution of capital requires, in Marx’s phrase, that money capital be “wholly detached from the parent stock”.[15] The development financial capital personified in bankers and other financiers allows for this detachment.

Credit and debt facilitate two distinct and related types of distribution of capital: (1) the reallocation of capital across sectors in response to changes in demand, and (2) redistribution of capital within a sector as part of the competitive process that I discuss in the next two chapters. Both involve qualitative as well as quantitative changes. Reallocation within a sector qualitatively changes that sector through mergers, takeovers and collapse of enterprises. Redistribution across sectors appears quantitative, more capital in some and less in others, and it is also qualitative because new entrants to a sector bring changes in technology.

In summary, for capital as a whole, the system of credit and fictitious capital exists as a consequence of hoarding. At the level of many capitals, it provides the mechanism by which capital can be redistributed in order to bring about changes in the structure of production and application of technology. Redistributed are claims on the surplus product of society, surplus value. In order that some capitals expand beyond the limit set by the surplus value they realize as profit, surplus value must become detached from its source. This detachment mechanism involves the development of what Marx called social capital (Marx 1971a: Chapter 27).[16]

Credit, interest and social capital

In order that surplus value be redistributed from some capitals to others, it is necessary that ownership can be detached from units of production. The initial development of capitalism requires the abolition of individual private property in favor of capitalist private property (see Chapter 2). The maturing of capitalism requires the abolition of individualized private property among capitalists in favor of the socialization of ownership to capital as a whole. Increasingly capitalists do not own factories or hold any direct claim upon the material means of production. Through ownership of fictitious capital they hold a claim on a portion of total surplus value wherever and in whatever form it is produced. In Marx's words,

> The capital … is here directly endowed with the form of *social capital* … as distinct from private capital, and its undertakings assume the form of social undertakings as distinct from private undertakings. It is the abolition of capital as private property within the framework of capitalist production itself.
>
> (Marx 1971a: 436)[17]

Ownership passes to the financial capitalist, thereby "transforming the actual functioning capitalist into a mere manager" (ibid.: 436).[18] The industrial capitalist as a property owner, personifying the capital relation in the youth of bourgeois society, later became an obstacle to capitalist development by limiting the mobility of capital. The change in the mode of ownership from individual to collective capital resulted from the processes of concentration and centralization, facilitated by the development of credit. This socialization of capital implied the formal ascendancy of financial over industrial capital.

The ascendancy of financial capital derives from the development of capital itself rather than on specific institutions.[19] In the last two decades of the twentieth century and into the twenty-first century, the immediate impulse to the ascendancy of financial capital was the reduction in state regulation of the freedom of capital, which is elaborated in the final chapter. Whatever institutional form social capital assumes, finance capital reigns dominant in the sense that the claim on surplus value becomes detached from the level of the production unit. This dominance may appear to be the result of conflict between two portions of the capitalist class. However, that conflict is the manifestation of a process generated by the continuous reorganization of capital as it expands.

In summary, with the development of credit, the ownership of capital becomes the ownership of surplus-value-production in the abstract, not the ownership of specific use-value-producing means of production. The concept of capital as a whole moves from the realm of analysis to an actual social category, as capitalists become those who own wealth in its most abstract form, fictitious capital. These contractual documents represent claims on social labor, which is the source of expanded value in the material process of production.[20] That contraction, ownership of the abstract by the few and material production by the many, is the extension of the fundamental opposition of use value and exchange value. With this contradiction lies the source of capitalist crisis, not least the great financial collapse of the 2000s.

Capitalist credit is the commodity form of capital, money as a commodity. It is the existence form of the commodity "capital". The potential confusion shown by this manipulation of words gives evidence to the elusiveness of the concept, an elusiveness that increases with each new abstraction created by financial capital. Money as a commodity is capital in the transaction, M*→M, as a result of which there is no expansion (production) of value, nor any change in the form of capital. The recipient of the finance gives up no commodity or money when the transaction occurs, promising to pay a larger amount at a future date.

Without exception, every commodity has a use value and an exchange value. The use value of money as a commodity is to function as capital, exchangeable for commodities whose use in production creates surplus value. This use value arises from the nature of the capital-relation, which allows money or finance in credit form to be a claim upon surplus value.[21] For credit, the concept of use value applies in a unique way. In the case of all other commodities, use value is the result of natural, material properties. For those commodities used in the labor process, their use value is consumed either at once or over time, depending upon whether they are circulating or fixed capital.[22] How they are consumed will differ in each labor process, and they are all cases materially consumed, transformed or discarded when their usefulness is over, "their substance disappears".[23]

In contrast the use value of money as finance lies not in its material form. It is not consumed, transformed or discarded after use. It is a claim on the resources of society, a social relationship, capital. Capital takes the form of money, commodities and the means of production, and each of these can and does exist without being capital. Money spent by the working class is not capital. Commodities are not capital if they are not produced under capitalist relations, for example peasant production in underdeveloped countries. Machinery and tools existed long before capital. Capital is a relationship among classes in which money, commodities and means of production each serves momentarily as the form this class relationship takes in its life cycle.

It follows that the use value of capital as a commodity is purely social, completely dependent upon the prior existence of the general production of commodities, capitalism. The recognition that the nature of capital is purely social reveals that capital has no intrinsic material form, though it must assume material form in its life cycle. As money capital, it could be in the form of gold (a money commodity); as productive capital it exists as a claim on human effort and purchased means of production; and as commodity capital it is newly produced commodities awaiting realization to money capital again.

None of these material forms represents the use value of capital. Their use values are material characteristics of the objects that momentarily function as capital. As capital, their consumption occurs in a specific context, for a specific purpose, the production of surplus value. A tree may yield fruit that can be eaten. If the tree grows in an orchard of a capitalist farm, it is not capital that yields fruit; the tree remains the generator of fruit whether or not it is capital. Ignoring the distinction between the production and the social relations under which production is organized gives rise to the neoclassical concept of capital as a factor of production which is analytically parallel with a labor input. Treating the social relationship of capital as an object is the essence of commodity fetishism. The contradictions that arise have been demonstrated in detail in the neo-Keynesian critique of neoclassical production theory (Harcourt 1973: *passim*; Weeks 1989: Chapter 10).

Capital itself is not consumed but moves through the process of commodity production and circulation intact, as the socialized, abstract representation of commodities. As a commodity, loan capital or credit must have a price. This definitional and practical necessity presents a paradox, since loan capital is itself an amount of money. For all other commodities, price is the money form of the commodity. In the case of credit, the commodity exists as money, implying the apparently absurd contradiction that capital has a price, prior to functioning as a commodity. In the circulation of capital as a commodity, a price form is needed for what already is in price form.

The "price of capital" is treated in the next part of the chapter. Prior to this, I pursue the implications of the social nature of capital. As a social relation capital has a definite role in society but no fixed form. In the form of finance its manifestation can vary with the imaginations of capitalists, to the extent that the development of the financial system can accommodate the creations of those imaginations. Toward the end of the twentieth century and into the twenty-first, the collective imaginations of the capitalist world produced a range of manifestations of capital under the general term "collateralized debt obligations" (CDO).[24]

These strange and often bizarre forms of capital may have come from the feverish imaginations of financial houses, but the possibility of their existence lies in the essentially social and non-material nature of capital. The collapse in value of these debt forms was the inevitable consequence of the contradiction between the purely social, non-material nature of the capital relation and the requirement that at some point in its life cycle that social relation must pass through the material process of production. This contradiction between the social and the material is the basis of all capitalist crises.

Interest on capital

Interest is the price of loan capital or credit, which Marx characterized as irrational in the logical sense that a price cannot itself have a price.[25] This faux price serves as a redistribution mechanism within the capitalist class. The capital commodity cannot exchange at its value. If it did the price would be zero. Loan capital is a claim on a specific amount of social labor (value), and the price of this capital is the mechanism to deduct a share for finance from surplus value.

When one begins with the simple exchange of commodities, the analysis by necessity moves on to consider money, and money implies the division of surplus value between two analytically distinct elements of the capitalist class, financial capital to which interest accrues and productive capital that receives profit. For all commodities but capital itself, the fluctuations in supply and demand occur around the value of the commodity, which is its center of gravity (socially necessary abstract labor time). In a process of intra-capitalist redistribution, competition tends to enforce a common rate of profit in all sectors.

The capital commodity represents value, but has no value. Therefore, it has no center of gravity around which the market interest rate would fluctuate. In the ideology of capitalism it is extremely important that the rate of interest has a clear, material determination. If it cannot be demonstrated that the rate of interest has a center of gravity, then financial capital does not justify its existence by making market economies more efficient. Despite this necessity, neoclassical economics has been unable to produce an explanation for interest which is not tautological.[26] The essentially irrational and indeterminate nature of the rate of interest is demonstrated by it being the only price in an economy that has no upper or lower boundary; most bizarre, it is the only price that can be and sometimes is zero or negative.[27]

Declaring interest as irrational by Marx did not represent an ideological objection to money lending, nor was it a moral judgment based on the unproductive role of financial capital. His treatment of interest followed from his analysis of commodities, which implied that value arises in production. If by some magical stroke the class of money capitalists were swept away, there would be no interest category.[28] This would be impossible. Mainstream analysis is correct in arguing that the financial sector is essential for a capitalist economy, albeit correct for the wrong reason. In the absence of financial capital the necessary redivision of surplus value that brings about shifts in the division of labor among sectors could not occur.

The division of surplus value between interest and industrial profit ("profit of enterprise" Marx called it) is essentially different from the division of new value into surplus value and the value of labor power. In purely quantitative terms, the value created by living labor appears in three categories, wages, profit and interest,[29] reflecting the claims of three groups; proletarians, industrial capitalists and financial capitalists. Prior to these three categories is the fundamental class division between surplus value and the value of labor power. The proletariat, separated from the means of production, surrenders its control over the labor process and, in doing so, cedes to capital the entire product. The proportion of new value that reaches the proletariat as wages is determined by the value of labor power. Without this qualitative differentiation between workers and capitalists, no surplus value is possible. A class division, derived from the relations of production, generates a quantitative division of value. This quantitative division is determinate, since it is based upon a commodity with a determinate value, labor power.

The division between interest and profit of enterprise is secondary. It requires the prior division of value into surplus value and the value of labor power. The division of interest and profit of enterprise is purely quantitative. It is not based on a class division, but on a division within a class. The two parts of the capitalist class are partners in the process of capitalist exploitation, having established a division of labor between themselves in order to facilitate that exploitation. The division of surplus value between them is the result of their intra-class competition and takes the form of fluctuations in the price of a valueless commodity, loan capital.[30] This competition generates a contradiction that manifested itself in virulent form toward the end of the twentieth century. As discussed at a later point, the unproductive part of capital (finance) increased its claim on surplus value, undermining the productive role of capital, in a growing ascendancy of the redistribution of surplus value over the production of surplus value.

The division between the value of labor power and surplus value is determined in production, while the division between profit of enterprise and interest is determined in circulation. In the former case, exchange between capital and labor reflects a division prior to that exchange, while in the latter case it is the exchange itself that creates the division. The exchange between capital and labor is part of the value creating process in which production and circulation interact. The material process of production is the basis for the value of the commodities that workers consume, and these commodities and their values establish the value of labor power. Total net value is determined in part at the point of production by the class struggle over the intensity and duration of work. The exchange between capital and labor is a manifestation of a process of material production and class struggle.

The exchange between industrial capitalists and money capitalists is a determining factor itself, because the commodity exchanged, capital, has not been produced. The interest form and the moment when it appears in the circuit of capital create the illusion that the rate of interest determines the rate of profit, though the reverse is true. Chapter 3 developed the concept of the aggregate rate of profit, the ratio of surplus value to capital advanced for capital as a whole. This aggregate rate of profit is the basis for the rate of profit received in each industry.[31] Because surplus value undergoes the quantitative division between profit of enterprise and interest, the aggregate rate of profit cannot be observed directly. Like value itself, it has no empirical form.[32] What one observes is a rate of interest and a rate of industrial or commercial profit. Further, the interest form appears as the reward for owning capital, thus the return to capital itself.

The money capitalist, by lending to the industrial capitalist, can obtain the formal ownership of the capital employed in the production process. Financial capitalists then represent capital as ownership, while the industrial capitalists represent the functioning of capital.[33] To the industrial capitalist, it appears that profit is a residual, derivative from the interest rate. A higher interest rate implies a lower profit of enterprise, and the rate of interest confronts the industrial capitalist as a contractual obligation prior to production. The profit received by the industrial capitalist seems not to be the result of owning capital (since this may shift formally to the financial capitalist), but from her or his own skill and enterprise in organizing production.[34]

The twofold division of surplus value makes it possible to argue that the distribution of new value reflects a difference in productive contributions: the worker supplies labor power and receives a wage, the entrepreneur supplies organizing ability and receives profit, and the money capitalist provides capital and receives interest. This is the view of neoclassical theory, in which each of these, labor, entrepreneurial ability and capital, is treated equally as material inputs to production.

The basis of this illusion is the quantitative division of surplus value, rendered necessary by the accumulation process, which requires the continuous redistribution of surplus value among capitals. The twofold division of surplus value rises from no productive division of labor or productive functions. The division reflects the separation of the financing of capital from the functioning of capital, the separation of surplus value from its origin for the purpose of converting it into capital for expanded production.

Credit crises

The division of surplus value derives from the development of credit, and the development of credit generates financial crises. Pursuing the analysis of credit in capitalist accumulation requires a brief review of the function of money as a means of payment. Credit allows exchange without payment. A credit transaction is an exchange in which the borrower receives commodities with a promise to make payment in the future. This may be direct, as when one industrial capitalist provides another with short term credit in a particular sale. Such credits in Marx's time were called "bills of exchange", though I shall use the general term "supplier credit".

Alternatively, one industrial capitalist may borrow from a financial institution to purchase commodities from a second industrial capitalist. While the two types of credit transactions can have different implications in the financial system, they both create a debt. As a result commodities circulate as a consequence of growing indebtedness, not as a result of the parallel circulation of money. In these exchanges, money is not a medium of circulation, but a means of payment for previous transactions. If credit is defined as money, such a distinction cannot be made, and the function of money as a means of payment becomes identical with the function as means of circulation. A central insight of Marx's theory of money in capitalist society is that the distinction between money and credit implies the distinction between money as means of payment and means of circulation. These distinctions provide an understanding of why, when the circuit of capital is interrupted, "the whole crisis seems to be merely a credit and money crisis" (Marx 1971a: 490).

To consider how the contradictions in the relationship between credit and money arise, I assume that the expansion of capital is proceeding normally, the aggregate rate of profit is stable, commodity capital is fully realized as money capital, then converted into productive capital. Expansion results from the successive advance of more capital, and the demand for the means of production, a demand among capitalists, expands. Because some capitals expand by more than their realized profit, the aggregate growth of capital requires that some of the intra-capitalist exchanges occur with credit. As the expansion continues, exchange becomes increasingly independent of money and credit indebtedness grows. In this expansionary process, the predominant form of credit may be among industrial capitalists, and there need be no limit to the expansion of such credit, except the production process, which sets the material limit to the means of production that can circulate.[35]

In this expansionary period, industrial capitalists require a means to purchase the ingredients of production. This limited role can be satisfied by a symbol of future payment, either through borrowing from financial capitalists or by mutual agreement between producers. Industrial capital may have independence of money capital, for if money capitalists decline to supply sufficient credit, industrial capitalists can meet their need for means of purchase by credit among themselves. However, when conditions are prosperous there is no reason financial capital should decline to provide credit. What Marx called "the regularity of returns" on industrial capital insures the interest owed on debt.

The key characteristic of a period of prosperity is that the dominant monetary function is means of circulation, so that the demand for money as such declines with the accumulation of indebtedness. Under these circumstances the demand for money is the demand for means of circulation, and this can be satisfied by any acceptable representation of money, even a representation of future payment. Therefore, it appears that anything can serve as money. The period of prosperity endorses the illusion that money need have no value, because as a medium of circulation it need not. Because industrial capitalists are eager to expand production, convert surplus value into productive capital, the primary function of money is to circulate commodities. Therefore, all capitalists require is a monetary form to bridge the gap between commodity capital and productive capital. However, as accumulation continues, it creates the potential that indebtedness (credit) will exceed the amount of commodity money. The credit system has facilitated the expansion of production to its material limit,[36] unrestrained by any dependence on money as such; i.e., commodity money and fiat money.

When the expansion comes to an end, the dominant function for money changes to means of payment. In a subsequent chapter I consider why expansion should be arrested. Here I assume that the "regularity of returns" comes to an end for unspecified reasons and less money capital is advanced in each successive circuit. When this happens effective demand among capitalists declines, the volume of exchanges declines and previously contracted purchases fall due for payment. Now, industrial capitalists require a form of money adequate for means of payment. Money asserts itself as money capital, capital as ownership.[37] During a general slowdown in accumulation the shift in the demand, from money as means of purchase to money as means of payment, occurs across many sectors of industrial capital at the same time. The credit accumulated during prosperity was based upon a presumption of continued expansion. When that expansion ends, the accumulated credit transforms into a demand for payment.

In the prosperity period, capital as function is dominant, capital as self-expanding value. The social relations of production facilitate the production of surplus value, and the forces of production stretch to their limit. When expansion ends and the production–exchange–production cycle is interrupted, capital as ownership asserts itself. This contradiction between the material process of production and the social relations that make that production viable under capitalism manifests itself in a conflict between industrial and money capital that threatens to cause a credit collapse. What during prosperity appear as innovative mechanisms of wealth creation (e.g., derivatives) prove in time of crisis, such as the late 2000s, to be "financial weapons of mass destruction".[38]

Production in capitalist society is socially integrated, not isolated. The purpose from the standpoint of capital is the production of surplus value. Production of surplus value through exploitation of labor is not sufficient for the reproduction of the capital relation. Surplus value must also be distributed in a manner that allows for that reproduction. The circuit of capital involves both of these processes, production and distribution. The production process represents capital as function, the domination of labor to facilitate exploitation. The distribution of surplus value involves ownership, the institutional claims upon surplus value once it is produced. The credit system is the formal separation of the two, personified in the industrial capitalist and the financial capitalist.[39]

As long as the production of surplus value proceeds smoothly, the industrial capitalist achieves a certain independence from finance. Once the production of surplus value is no longer adequate, capital as a whole enters a period when losses must be distributed as well as gains. In this period the rivalry among capitalists asserts itself, and a struggle begins to determine who within the class will carry the losses. This struggle manifests itself as industrial capitalists are forced to liquidate their debts. Financial capitalists become the arbitrators of the struggle for survival. The availability of credit declines and part of industrial capital lies idle. At the same time, the sudden demand for money as means of payment threatens the value of fictitious capital, capital that represents ownership.

During prosperity, a volume of credit developed that bore no fixed relation to the money available to cancel those debts. Unless there is some drastic adjustment mechanism, a part of the accumulated debt cannot be paid and some assets will be valueless.[40] This drastic mechanism is the devaluation of commodities,[41] the process of price deflation. As the expansion of capital ends, commodities go unsold, and their market prices fall, which implies a rise in the value of money.

This rise in the value of money protects the market value of fictitious capital and its claims on indebtedness. The money necessary to redeem the accumulated debts inflates in exchange value.

What protects creditors, the decline in the prices of commodities, is a manifestation of the tension between use value and exchange value. A credit crisis causes the concrete, use values, to be sacrificed for the abstract, credit. Commodity production declines, employment falls and the ownership of capital is protected at the expense of its material function. In an extraordinarily prescient passage in *Capital*, Marx referred to the danger that "a depreciation of credit-money … would unsettle all existing relations",[42] which states succinctly the financial disaster of 2007–2009. A credit crisis occurs because the form of money adequate for facilitating exchange is not satisfactory for canceling debts. What was an adequate form of equivalency among capitalists during the expansionary period proves unsatisfactory when debts must be canceled.

The process that generates credit crises in capitalist society can be summarized as follows. The expansion of capital requires changes in the division of labor that are brought about by the movement of capital within and across sectors of the economy. Were individual capitalist enterprises constrained to expand on the basis of the surplus value each realizes as profit, the ability of the system as a whole to alter the division of labor would be severely limited. The credit system allows the redistribution of surplus value among capitalist enterprises for expansion. The credit system implies a differentiation between the control of the production process and the claim upon surplus value (capital as function and capital as ownership). As expansion proceeds, debt grows at a rate which is not limited by the growth of commodity money. When expansion comes to an end, the accumulated debt must be paid in all or large part. At that moment the demand for money is a demand for means of payment. Financial capitalists seek to redeem debts in a form protected from changes in value, and industrial capitalists seek to do the same with the commodities that have in stock.

The sudden rush for money as means of payment pushes up the rate of interest, which further reduces profit of enterprise. Commodities go unsold, some debts cannot be paid or only paid in part, and the market value of fictitious capital is depreciated. The intervention of the state during 2008 and 2009 in all the developed countries represented an attempt to prevent the full unfolding of this process. Direct state intervention in the financial to ameliorate the problems arising from the contradictions in the circuit of capital further demonstrates the essentially social nature of capitalist production. Despite their rhetoric of individualism, in times of stringency capitalists embrace comrades in exploitation by seeking the aid of the instrument of their collective interests, the state.[43]

Credit crises do not arise from financial processes themselves. They are the manifestation of problems in the production of surplus value, presupposed in the analysis, and explained in Chapters 9–11. The comprehension of those problems requires further analytical development of the fundamental contradiction in the commodity of the unity of the concrete and the abstract. The analysis of the first seven chapters followed the method of Marx, in which each new concept emerges from the previous, as the more complex issues arise. As in some mathematical inquiries, method, not the analyst, dictates the emergence of concepts and the unfolding of the analysis. At a number of points in this chapter the analysis required reference to the interaction of capitalist enterprises, competition, which is the subject treated next.

8 Competition among capitals

Introduction

Previous chapters stressed that capitalist society is historically unique in that its reproduction requires the circulation of the products of labor in the form of commodities. The circulation of commodities, along with the parallel circulation of money, is the mechanism by which formally isolated producers are integrated into a system of social reproduction. Competition, a concept to which I have repeatedly alluded, is the interaction of these formally independent producers. Competition is of central importance to the understanding of capitalist society. The development of Marx's concept of capital prepared the ground for an analysis of competition, and it remains to develop the analysis.

Marx's intellectual and political break with the political economy of his time represented a methodological revolution. This revolution came from the insight that capitalism is an historically unique mode of social reproduction. Most Marxian writers have recognized the methodological break, but elements of mainstream analysis continue to appear in Marxian writings, particularly in the treatment of competition. It is a common view among Marxists and non-Marxists alike that Marx broke new ground in other areas but not in his treatment of competition.

Derivative from this view was the suggestion that the analysis in *Capital* is historically specific to "competitive capitalism", and must be amended for "monopoly capitalism" (Baran and Sweezy 1968). This interpretation of Marx dominated the writings of Marxists after World War II. The concepts "competitive" and "monopoly" capitalism played a centrally important place in the analysis of post-war imperialism. Toward the end of the twentieth century the view that capitalist countries were dominated by a few large monopolies was complicated by the argument that capitalism was undergoing a process of "globalization".[1] The significance of the Marxian and also the radical treatments of competition and monopoly have been, and remain, their analytical and descriptive similarity to neoclassical economics.

Neoclassical economics provides the analysis to support the favorable role of competition, whose origins can be found in Adam Smith.[2] It is necessary to explain and critique neoclassical theory before turning to Marx because of the near universal acceptance that competition is a positive force. Little progress can be made toward understanding capitalist crises until the fallacies of competition are identified and the analysis rejected in its entirety.[3] Once the fallacies are recognized and the analysis rejected, it becomes possible to explain crises as arising not from the failures and weaknesses of capitalism, but from its strengths and dynamism. In the next part of the chapter I present the ahistorical neoclassical theory of competition and dissect it critically in anticipation of understanding capitalist competition.

False virtues of competition

Competition is the key element in the entire neoclassical theoretical system. On the level of vulgar analysis, competition ensures that "consumers" receive "value for money", forces producers to lower costs and generates the ultimate benefit of the market system, "choice". In the absence of competition benefits fade and markets whither. At the level of high theory, competition is more than just a good thing, is the Philosopher's Stone of neoclassical economics. Touch it to a market and efficiency prevails. When competition holds sway in the neoclassical sense, the working of the economy approaches the sublime; when competition is imperfect all necessary steps must be taken to purify it. In the economics profession and in the press, the truth of these arguments was taken as self-evident until briefly drawn into question during the financial crisis of the late 2000s. Rare is the progressive writer who does not argue that the evils of markets derive from monopoly power and would be eliminated or at least reduced by increased competition.

It is part of the folklore of mainstream economics and business journalism that perfect competition is best, but if that cannot be achieved, more competition is better than less. Fifty years ago the falseness of this argument was demonstrated by mainstream economists (Lipsey and Lancaster 1956–57). As surprising as it may seem to the non-specialist, neoclassical theory provides no rule for systematically analyzing whether more competition is better than less. Perfection is perfect and no conclusion can be reached about degrees of imperfection.[4] Suggestions that introducing "more" competition into a market will bring benefits have no analytical basis.

The agnostic conclusion about degrees of competition reflects the lack of an analysis of competition as process in mainstream economics. The standard economics textbook states that perfect competition is the result of a large number of small buyers and sellers, each acting on the belief that he or she cannot affect market prices.[5] This common statement is a logical muddle: the number and size of enterprises are characteristics; that the firms may or may not be able to "impact on market price" is an outcome. The two must be linked by a process. It may seem "common sense" that many buyers and sellers would believe themselves unable to affect price, but theoretical insights do not derive from laboring the obvious.

If perfect competition is defined as a situation in which no producer can have an impact on prices, producers in perfectly competitive markets are excluded by definition from price wars and the struggle for market shares.[6] They are also explicitly prohibited from product differentiation. The characteristics of a market that provide for competition in its most perfect neoclassical manifestation exclude the forms which competition might take.[7] The exclusion of the manifestations of competition from its definition explains why the concept of perfect competition offers no insight into circumstances in which price and product characteristics are instruments of rivalry. Perfect competition reveals itself to be a creation of the mind with no claim to existence in the material world.[8]

The standard definitions of competition from textbooks, many buyers and sellers, homogeneous product, etc., are low and vulgar theory. The high-theory neoclassical treatment of competition is found in what is called Walrasian general equilibrium analysis. The superficially simple idea that many buyers and sellers interact to create competitive prices has no analytical or real world meaning outside a general equilibrium framework.

Before entering into this arcane realm of general equilibrium, I should explain why it is necessary to do so in a presentation of Marx's theory of capitalist competition; indeed, why it is necessary at all. The purpose is to assess the theoretical basis for the argument that there is a process named "competition" which brings benefits and stability in market systems. If this argument was true, it would imply that competition is a source of stability: the solution to the potential volatility of capitalism. In its role as a solution, competition is alleged to foster efficiency, and this increased efficiency brings welfare gains to the population. Efficiency is achieved by the interaction of buyers and sellers generating prices which feed back upon those buyers and sellers, which results in an allocation of resources which is optimally efficient. Therefore, prices are the key: competition is good because it produces prices which determine "socially efficient" decisions by producers and consumers. The purpose is to discover if this characterization of competition has any place in the analysis of the production and circulation of commodities. To put the matter subjectively, should progressives favor greater competition in markets?

Under the circumstances described above, buyers and sellers view market prices as unaffected by their individual actions. To use the technical term, their decisions are *price constrained*, based on the prices they observe in the market. If it is the case that buyers and sellers make their decisions on the basis of market prices, then prices are beyond their control. Were this not the case, buyers and sellers ("agents" they are named by the neoclassicals) would not be constrained by prices. They would be making decisions *about* prices, not on the basis of prices. It follows that these agents are not constrained by their incomes or revenue. Buyers choose their incomes just as they choose how much beer, shoes, etc. to buy; companies consider all levels of output, no matter how large or small, and select the one that gives them their greatest profit.[9]

It may seem strange that firms would not worry about how much they can sell and people would not worry about obtaining the amount of paid work they desire. Yet, these propositions are inseparable from the argument that competition produces efficient and desirable outcomes; that competition is "good".

Keynes argued that these analytical outcomes represent a special case. For example, consider an economy with 10 per cent unemployment of the labor force and idle industrial capacity. In such a circumstance idle capacity exists because firms discover that they cannot profitably sell more output; the unemployed have looked for work and found none available. In this case, prices reflect that the economy is *demand* or *quantity constrained.* Were demand to increase, outputs would rise and prices would change. Some prices would rise and others would fall, generating a different allocation of resources. Only when all resources are active will prices assume the autonomous, allocative role that they play in the neoclassical parable of competition.

The benefits of competition cannot be justified on a market-by-market basis,[10] "partial equilibrium" in the jargon. Competition delivers its benefits only on the grander scale of aggregate full employment of resources, "full employment general equilibrium". In the absence of full employment of resources, it cannot be demonstrated theoretically that any specific competition-fostering measure will lead to increased efficiency (improved allocation of resources) and welfare gains to the population. An aggregate competitive full employment is the necessary condition for the efficient operation of each specific market. Achievement of general equilibrium is logically prior to establishing competitive outcomes in partial equilibrium. An example of this is international trade theory, which assumes full employment as the basis for initiating the analysis of the gains from trade.

The theory of general equilibrium, which is the *sine qua non* of neoclassical competition, was created by Leon Walras at the end of the nineteenth century (Walras 1926). In a Walrasian world, people come to "the market" with a fixed amount of commodities to sell, and the purpose of making exchanges to acquire a different set of commodities that will increase their subjective welfare. There is no production, and the buyers and sellers enter into the simple circulation of commodities, C→M→C. Market traders compare the prices of what each has to sell with the prices of what is to be bought and choose the most advantageous combination of buying and selling.

At first glance, this approach appears not very promising for the purpose of establishing competitive full employment, because no production is involved. Commodities come to the market already produced, with the only important action to determine a set of prices that will ensure that there are no surpluses or shortages (designated "excess demands" and "excess supplies"). The process of price formation in this simple system of fixed supplies is not very satisfactory. If traders are left to their own devices, the probable result will be a set of prices that leaves some commodities unsold. This would occur, for example, if on the basis of an initial set of prices the seller of beer received a price so low that that he or she was unable to make the required contribution to the total expenditure that would allow all apples to be sold. One way out of this problem would be to allow for commodities to be sold at different prices during the market period. This happens in real markets: leftover apples would be dumped at a below-cost price as the market closes. This cannot be allowed if the trading process is to produce an efficient outcome. If any commodity sells at more than one price during the market period, this is *prima facie* evidence that trading was demand constrained; i.e., sales were not determined by relative prices, but relative prices were established by the need to sell.

The Walrasian process is designed to avoid this outcome through the *ex machina* intervention of an "auctioneer". The auctioneer stands at the center of all traders and listens to the alternative offers by buyers and sellers. He or she is given with the draconian power to prohibit any trades at prices that leave excess demands and excess supplies, which are called disequilibrium prices. No trading at disequilibrium prices is permitted. The auctioneer is granted perfect foresight in which he or she knows in advance the trading outcome of every set of prices, even though they cannot be observed.

Actual markets do not have auctioneers except in very special cases, and real auctioneers do not care about the general equilibrium purity of the prices they gavel down. Markets, with or without auctioneers, do not clear simultaneously, but sequentially. There is no going back if the "wrong" price is established for a commodity. Nothing remotely resembling a Walrasian market exists in any exchange economy, yet Walrasian markets are the basis of neoclassical competitive theory. It is an interesting sociological phenomenon that such a patently absurd view of market operation should be incorporated into a social science. More interesting still, this theater of the absurd is treated as the norm and what actually occurs as a deviation from that non-existent norm that must be justified.[11]

After much tedious deconstruction of neoclassical logic, the meaning of "perfect competition" reveals itself. Many buyers and sellers will be unable to affect prices when they trade in a market with an omniscient auctioneer and no "false trading" is allowed. In other words, they will be unable to affect prices when a higher authority forbids it. The neoclassical version of "competition" is a considerably more problematical concept than the person on the street or most students of economics are led to believe.

The problematical nature of neoclassical competition becomes all the worse when one attempts to include within the Walrasian framework the most important traded commodity, labor power, or labor services as preferred term of the neoclassicals. It is the clearing of the labor market, above all others, that determines full utilization of resources in a capitalist economy. To include it as one of the many traded items in the Walrasian market requires the introduction of production into the system. Production creates many theoretical difficulties for neoclassical economics, the analysis of which lies beyond the scope of this book (Weeks 1989: Chapter 10).

The market for labor power cannot be treated like the markets for produced commodities and services without flights of fantasy that make the mythical auctioneer seem a credible construction. In a Walrasian world workers arrive on the market day with their labor power to sell, and a price is struck that satisfies every seller of labor power in terms of the amount of time contracted for work, and every employer is content with the contracted labor time. On this basis, workers determine their incomes by choosing the optimal amount of work in light of wage rate offers and their preferences between income and leisure. Under these circumstances, workers, too, are price constrained, treating employment opportunities as unlimited at the prevailing wage.

Even in the abstract problems arise with this approach to the labor market. It would be somewhat credible to argue that at the outset of a market day no potatoes have been sold, that the market for potatoes takes the form of a great collection of unsold potatoes.[12] This is not the case for the labor market. An excess supply of labor occurs when the vast majority of workers is employed. While it is reasonable to assume that the excess supply of any commodity other than labor would imply disappointment on the part of the vast majority of sellers, an excess supply of labor power is consistent with contentment for the vast majority of sellers. Further, the neoclassical equilibrating adjustment which would eliminate the excess supply, a lower real wage, would leave the vast majority of sellers (the employed) worse off (paid less per unit of effort). This contrasts with the situation of the seller of a non-labor commodity, who, if demand is price elastic, loses from the fall in price, but gains from the rise in quantity sold with no change in effort expended. At any moment the vast majority of workers is not on the market. If wages fall or rise for the newly employed, this is false trading, not evidence of allocative efficiency.

In summary, neoclassical theory has no adequate explanation for marketing clearing that has a remote resemblance to the operation of labor markets. The theory provides no analytical basis for concluding that exchange economies tend automatically to full employment. The theory provides no justification for treating economies as price constrained. Therefore, it cannot be established in the abstract that prices generate an allocation of resources that is economically efficient. There is no theoretical support for the view that competition brings welfare and efficiency benefits, except in the Walrasian fairy tale.

The assertion that competition is desirable and its absence lamentable, that restriction of competition has a negative impact on people's welfare, is an ideological defense of capitalism. It should be rejected by progressives seeking the end of the abuses of capitalism for the self-serving capitalist propaganda that it is. While neoclassical theory has no theoretical or empirical insight into competition, buyers and sellers do compete. Understanding competition and its consequences requires a methodological break which abandons the *ex machina* invoking of competition as a magic wand that turns the anarchy of the market into harmonious optimality. Karl Marx is the only writer who clearly and decisively made that break and developed a coherent alternative,[13] based on the governing principle that competition is part of the movement of capital.

Competition after Marx

As noted at the outset of this chapter, most Marxist and other radical writers have assumed Marx's treatment of competition was similar in most aspects to that of the neoclassicals.[14] For all but a few writers, competition is a self-evident, exoteric phenomenon of the number and relative size of competitors which has analytical implications, but itself is so obvious that it requires no analysis.

Almost everyone defines competition as individual buyers and sellers in pursuit of their interests, then lists the conditions necessary for competition to prevail: many buyers and sellers, free entry and exit from the market, etc. It would seem obvious that competition is a question of numbers and the size of competitors, a directly observable calculation of number and size of sellers and buyers in a specific market, what might be called the quantity theory of competition. If this is not competition, what is?

Because of this near consensus on this, the quantity theory of competition and its benefits, it comes as a surprise to discover from Marx a much more profound view, that competition does *not* result from many buyers and sellers; it is in the nature of capital and inseparable from it. The competition of both high neoclassical theory and the person in the street is a relationship purely in exchange, isolated from its historical origin and artificially separated from its class nature. The acceptance of this view of competition as a benign game of the numbers of players demonstrates the power of the ideology of capitalism to infect and mold the minds of even its critics.

The quantity theory of competition is ahistorical because it is applied to all modes of production when there is monetary exchange. The word "applied" is meant in its dictionary sense: any society can be inspected for whether it exhibits some of the requirements for "competitive markets", whatever might be the basis on which the social relations of the society rest. Divorced from the context of capitalism, this analysis is confined to the act of exchange, a social relation characteristic of modes of production other than capitalism (see Chapters 1 and 2).

The central revelation that unveils the mysteries of competition is the specification that what we seek to understand is not "competition", but capitalist competition. The phenomenon to which the neoclassical theory of competition addresses itself, the struggle among capitals for market shares, is a real process recognized by Marxists and non-Marxists alike. Certainly Marx argued that exchange has a central place in the analysis of competition. Incorrect is the treatment of exchange divorced from the class relations that are unique to capitalism. Marx's treatment of competition is not an alternative to the neoclassical approach; it begins in a different manner and encompasses the manifestation of competition in the exchange of commodities as a part of a general theory of competition.

In mainstream theory competition among capitals is introduced as an external force. In the absence of this external force production and consumption are no longer efficient, income distribution is indeterminate and the principles of supply and demand cannot be applied in the short run or long run. Especially in neoclassical analysis, competition serves not only as the vehicle by which economic relations manifest themselves, but also as the origin and cause of these relationships.

In value theory, accumulation is the key process that gives rise to all the important generalizations regarding capitalist reproduction. Although accumulation and competition are closely related, accumulation can be conceptualized and understood prior to the analysis of competition. Accumulation is the progressive expansion and internal transformation of capital. Accumulation is first analyzed for capital as a whole, without reference to the interaction of many capitals. Again we encounter one of Marx's apparent absurdities, that the analysis will explain competition among capitals by inspecting capital as a whole for which there are apparently no competitors. What initially strikes the reader as absurd becomes an insightful revelation: competition arises from the nature of capital and takes the form of the struggle among its parts.

Capital exists because of the separation of people from the means by which they can produce, and competition derives from that separation. The circuit of capital is the self-expansion of value, achieved through the production of surplus value. The production of surplus value requires the prior advance of constant and variable capital, and the subsequent application of labor to the means of production imply the extraction of absolute and relative surplus value. Absolute and relative surplus value correspond to concrete processes, the intensification and the lengthening of the working day (absolute surplus value) and the application of machinery to the labor process, which increases the division of labor (relative surplus value).

As capitalism develops, the production of relative surplus value becomes the primary way of increasing the extraction of unpaid labor and gives rise to what Marx called the general law of capitalist accumulation. This "general law" is the endogenous generation of surplus labor power in the form of a "reserve army" of the unemployed. This analytical sequence, from commodities to capital to accumulation, brings one through Volume I of *Capital*, during which no consideration of competition among capitals is necessary. Consideration of competition would obscure the analysis by introducing a complex concept, competition among capitals, prior to an explanation of the simpler concepts upon which it is predicated. The interaction of capitals in the accumulation process requires prior explanation of accumulation, itself is understood by the concept of capital as a whole.

It is possible to advance in the analysis of capitalism while abstracting from competition among capitals because accumulation is essentially a production process carried out under specific relations of production, and these specific relations of production require analysis of the exchange between capital and labor, but not the exchange between capitals. Every important aspect of capitalism derives from capital as a whole. Capital and capitalism are the separation of labor from the means of production. This separation results in a competition between capital and labor, a class struggle. Both analytically and in practice competition among capitals derives from the conflict between capital and labor. It is not subsequently developed through an independent analytical process.

The analysis of the competition among capitalist enterprises is the process that distributes surplus value among those enterprises, and the intra-capitalist allocation of surplus value as profit of enterprise, rent and interest. Previous chapters considered one aspect of this competition, between money and industrial capital. This was necessary to account for the process by which qualitative changes occur during the accumulation process. Prior to considering this particular aspect of competition it was not necessary to make an assumption of its existence or non-existence, because the division does not appear at the level of capital as a whole.

Neoclassical theory initiates its analysis of capitalism by postulating competition or non-competition among capitals and cannot advance logical steps without doing so. In contrast, value theory develops the theory of accumulation without reference to the interaction of capitals. Competition among capitals could be considered when establishing the basis of accumulation, in that the analytical elements of the concept are present in the concept of capital itself, but to do so would complicate the analysis without advancing it. For this reason Marx summarized the role of the competition among capitals as follows:

> Competition merely *expresses* as real, posits as an external necessity, that which lies within the nature of capital; competition is nothing more than the way in which the many capitals force the inherent determinants of capital upon one another and upon themselves. Hence, not a single category of bourgeois economy, not even the most basic, e.g., the determination of value, becomes real through free competition alone.
>
> (Marx 1973: 651)

Competition is the mechanism by which the underlying laws of accumulation manifest themselves. Competition does not generate or even make possible the operation of the law of value. The basis of value is free wage labor and the circulation of means of production as commodities. Competition allows for the expression of the law. The fundamental concept is the relations of production (free wage labor), and these relations create the possibility of both the law of value and the competition among capitals.

At points in his writings Marx states that competition is the mechanism by which the essence of capitalist social relations is transformed into their distorted appearance. Two examples can clarify this transformation. First, while the basis of capitalist accumulation is the appropriation of unpaid labor, the wage form masks this exploitation in the guise of an equal exchange. In the process of this exploitation workers compete among themselves over wages and capitalists compete with workers to extract unpaid labor. Second, the competition among capitals tends to equalize profit rates across sectors that causes a deviation of price from value, which gives the illusion that dead labor creates value. These examples can be multiplied, which led Marx to observe that in competition every relationship is reversed.[15]

This distorting character of competition makes it an analytical mistake to begin one's theory with it. Rather, one should begin at the level of social relations and ask why there should be competition.

The inner nature of capital

Marx places competition in the context of capital as a whole: "conceptually, *competition* is nothing other than the inner nature of capital, its essential character, appearing in and realized as the reciprocal interaction of many capitals" (Marx 1973: 414). The buying and selling of labor power reveals itself as the basis of the competition among capitals. The neoclassical theory of competition, ahistorical in method of analysis, is an idealized description of the particular historical character of capitalist production, the breakdown of feudal monopolies, guilds and agricultural estates.[16]

Prior to the development of capitalism, economic life was regulated within historically specific modes of production. In Western Europe these relations involved guild membership, state control of long distance trade through monopolies and many other mercantile institutions. With the emergence of capitalism as the dominant mode of production, economic life was also regulated, by capital. The intellectual spokesmen of the rising bourgeoisie, most famously Adam Smith, described the latter regulations as "free competition", giving an ideological justification to the new order. Strict regulation characterized capitalism and its predecessors, one by monopoly of the landlord class, the other the monopoly of the capitalist class. What Smith did not do, and his successors down to the present day have not done, was to analyze the conflict among capitals.[17] Marx took on this task. To suggest that competition is the existence of many competitors, the absence of monopolized and centralized production, is to employ ideology as theory. For example, there were a large number of manors in feudal society, but no competition. Numbers are not the key, nor is the size of competitors; the key is the social relations that determine and regulate the interaction of producers.[18]

Discussion of competition without first explaining why there are competitors is the same analytical mistake as initiating an analysis of value without asking why there are commodities. In both cases the general production of commodities is presupposed. Neoclassical theory initiates the discussion of competition at a relatively low level of abstraction. As a result, it treats competition in extremely complex manifestations that require the analysis at the outset to explain price competition, product differentiation, capital movements, the barriers to those movements and the growth and reduction in number of competitors. As a consequence, the analysis proceeds eclectically. The forms taken by the competitive struggle under capitalism do not derive from the concept of capital, but appear as exceptions to it, called "market failures". To avoid this eclecticism Marx defined competition as the "inner nature of capital", and with this simple concept one can move to more complex concepts such as competition among capitals and, more complex still, price competition.

Competition is the inner nature of capital in the sense that it arises from the contradiction between the process of production and the process of circulation, which are synthesized in industrial capital, "capital as such", Marx called it. While capital unites production and circulation, it does so in a contradictory way, through the medium of free wage labor. Because labor power is a commodity, the product of capitalist production must be exchanged. The reproduction of capitalist society necessitates that the use values arising from production be realized as money. It is first under capitalist society that the surplus labor of direct producers cannot be appropriated in material or natural form, but must be converted into money. The first and most basic form of competition is the competition between capital and labor, not for the distribution of the value, but over the organization of production. This competition is a class struggle over one of the most fundamental aspects of any society, the control of production. And the subsumption of labor to capital is the basis for the competition among capitals.[19]

Capital exists because of free wage labor, on the one hand, and the monopolization of the means of production by a class, on the other. The existence of free wage labor allows for the exploitation of labor in a specific form, in the service of capital and deployed at the will of capital; i.e., where it will bring forth the largest profit. The feudal ruling class exploited labor, but because labor was united with the means of production, this exploitation was of an essentially immobile labor force. Free wage labor liberated the exploiting class to extract unpaid labor under changing circumstances and conditions: "it is not individuals who are set free by free competition; it is, rather, capital which is set free" (Marx 1973: 650).

The full implications of the term "free wage labor" now become clear. Prior to capitalist society, labor was not free in that its mobility was narrowly limited within servile social relations, New World slavery perhaps the most extreme type of un-freedom. When such social relations were destroyed in favor of free wage labor, workers become free in the narrow sense of not being tied to particular exploiters. Capital, not labor, obtained the potential for unconditional freedom and liberation as a result of the demise of servile relations.

The inner nature of capital is the capital–labor relation. This social relation, involving the exchange of capital against labor power, brings the production process under the direct control of capital. Based on free wage labor, the capital relation begins with an exchange prior to production and prior to the circulation and realization of commodities. The purchase of labor power by capital creates the conditions for competition. The necessary conditions for capitalist production, free wage labor and a market for the means of production, allow the marshaling of the forces of production for an invasion of branches of industry where the rate of profit is higher.

Competition under capitalism is not determined by conditions in market for commodities; a market for labor power creates it. While a capitalist enterprise can momentarily monopolize the sale of a particular commodity, it cannot monopolize the market for labor power. In part this is because of the reserve army that is continuously generated by capital. The existence of the reserve army itself is the consequence of labor power being a commodity, the basis of competition among capitals.

Free wage labor involves the permanent separation of labor from the means of production, and necessitates the repeated uniting of labor with those means of production. This inter-class reunion occurs through each circuit of capital by the buying and selling of labor power. Since the combination of labor and the means of production is a moment in the circulation of capital and always incomplete for labor (the existence of the reserve army), each capital's control over labor power is momentarily and quantitatively incomplete.

The unification is fundamentally incomplete because capitalists do not buy workers; they buy their capacity for work for a discrete length of time. Once the workers' contracted period ends the link between that particular group of workers and the capitalist that employed them is broken. Capital as a whole asserts its monopoly over labor through the tendency of capital to eliminate all sources of livelihood except wage labor. This monopoly takes the form of the competition among capitals, none of which itself holds a monopoly over labor. It is in this sense that "free competition is the relation of capital to itself as another capital".[20] Capital's monopoly over the means of production prevents the sustained monopolization of production in any specific branch of industry because the form of capital's exploitation of labor continuously creates the conditions for competition, free wage labor and the reserve army.

At this level of abstraction, competition is an inherent tendency in the capital relation. The form of this competition depends in part on the stages of capitalist development, which is treated in the following part of the chapter. Competition as it appears is determined by the sophistication of the credit system, the role of the state and the development of the productive forces (Clifton 1977). The basis of competition can be analyzed, as we have done through abstracting from the complexities of reality, but competition as it manifests itself incorporates concrete complexities that cannot be generalized.

It is important to break with the commonplace view that competition is the struggle over sales of particular commodities. This is an aspect of competition, but an aspect that presupposes the buying and selling of labor power. The exchange of commodities pre-dated the development of capitalism. It was a characteristic of merchant's capital, which Marx called the form of capital (M→C→M′) without the essence (Marx 1971a: 326). Control over the market for a single commodity or a number of commodities by one or several capitals temporarily suppresses the manifestation of competition in a particular market, but does not eliminate and may not reduce competition among capitals. Control over a market does not touch the source of competition, which is the existence of free wage labor. To eliminate competition, it would be necessary to eliminate labor power as a commodity, as under feudalism.

Since a market for labor power is the necessary condition for capital, to "assume" market competition is to assume capitalism: the existence of capitalism implies competition. Capitalism involves the movement of capital; competition is this movement.[21] We can now understand why mainstream economists assume competition at the outset of their analysis though for the wrong reasons with the wrong analysis. Competition is the "inner nature" of capital, its force manifested in all the complex appearances that capital's movement assumes, and none of these appearances can be considered independently of competition.

The reduction in the number of competitors in a market, what Marx termed the centralization of capital, does not reduce competition; causality runs the other way from competition to the interaction of competitors. In rare cases, competition in a market generates monopolies, but monopolies are not the antithesis of competition, they are not the negation of competition.[22] In a rare explicit use of thesis–antithesis–synthesis, Marx made his analysis of competition quite clear:

> We all know that competition was engendered by feudal monopoly. Thus competition was originally the opposite of monopoly and *not monopoly the opposite of competition.* So that *modern* monopoly is not a simple antithesis, it is on the contrary *the true synthesis.*
> Thesis: Feudal monopoly, before competition.
> Antithesis: Competition.
> Synthesis: Modern monopoly, which is the negation of feudal monopoly as it implies the system of competition and the negation of competition insofar as it is monopoly.
>
> (Marx and Engels 1976: 194)

The contradictions inherent in the social relation capital generate centralization, but this does not result in the elimination of the competitive contradiction. Competition is the negation of feudalism and not a function of the number of competitors. Competition arose as a consequence of the elimination of the material basis for feudal monopolies. That material basis was the immobility of laborers, the appropriation of surplus product in material form and the union of labor with the means of labor. Capitalism arose through the separation of labor from the land and the means of labor in general, which created the conditions for the appropriation of surplus product in the form of surplus value. Modern, capitalist monopolies emerge as the synthesis of the competitive contradiction and the process of centralization. Capitalist monopoly is a "unity of opposites".

The buying and selling of labor power is not sufficient to establish the forms that competition takes or its intensity. The concrete aspects of competition require an analysis of credit and accumulation. As argued in the previous chapter, credit is the mechanism that realizes competition. Competition among capitals in essence is the attempt to redistribute or centralize capital, and the credit mechanism is the lever for the redistribution. Since the credit system develops and becomes more sophisticated as capitalism develops, competition among capitals is facilitated as capitalism matures. The process of accumulation sets the context of the competitive struggle, whether it occurs within a contracting or expanding circuit of reproduction of social capital.

Generalization of competition

Capital itself creates the possibility of competition prior to any consideration of many capitals. The existence of many capitals is the consequence of competition. Marx's theory turns the mainstream analysis of competition on its head.

Since competition arises from the inner nature of capital, "capital exists and can only exist as many capitals, and its self determination therefore appears as their reciprocal interaction with one another" (Marx 1973: 414). Capital as a whole necessarily appears as many capitals. What appears as many is actually one, and capitalism without competition is a contradiction in terms.

This analytical conclusion has been subject of intense debate among Marxists and socialists since the turn of the twentieth century. V.I. Lenin and Karl Kautsky, one the leader of the world's first socialist state, the other the leader of the reformist social democrats of his day, exchanged polemics over precisely this issue. Kautsky argued that capitalist development tended toward a "single world trust" in a world of "ultra-imperialism" and, in such conditions, competition would be dramatically reduced (Kautsky 1914). The political implication for Kautsky was that inter-capitalist wars, generated by competition for markets, would also be eliminated. Lenin attacked this analysis on the grounds that competition and conflict intensified as capitalism developed (Lenin 2000).

The Marxian insights into competition reverse another aspect of mainstream analysis. As noted, many writers look back to a golden age of competition, when competitors were many, production units small and competition free. This follows logically from a theory of competition that places emphasis on the number of competitors. This view is ahistoric. Competition, since it derives from the inner nature of capital, develops and intensifies as capital develops. When competitors were small and many, competition was primitive and embryonic. With the development of capital in its more advanced forms, competition develops into more sophisticated manifestations (Marx 1973: 651). To be concrete, in the early development of capitalism, England during 1750–1850 for example, competition was underdeveloped because there remained precapitalist fetters on its expansion, especially but not only in agriculture (Byres 1996). The incomplete development of financial institutions made it difficult for capitalists to obtain sufficient money capital to enter other sectors of industry. In this early phase of capitalism, competition took the primitive form of the struggle among capitalist enterprises within a sector. Credit institutions grew in importance and capitalist competition reached a more sophisticated form. Competition increasingly manifested itself in the flow of capital across sectors of industry, which themselves may be temporarily monopolized.

> In practical life we find not only competition, monopoly, and the antagonism between them, but also the synthesis of the two, which is not a formula, but a movement. Monopoly produces competition, competition produces monopoly. Monopolists compete among themselves; competitors become monopolists … *The synthesis is such that monopoly can only maintain itself by continually entering into the struggle of competition.*[23]
>
> (Marx and Engels 1976: 197)

In the course of the twentieth century, facilitated by two global wars, capitalist competition had burst through the confines of sectors and countries, to rage on an international scale (Rothschild 1947). Closely related to the process of competition among capitals, Marx developed an analysis of the uneven development of capitalism, considered in detail in the next two chapters. Uneven development refers to the tendency under capitalism for the forces of production to develop unevenly among enterprises in the same sector, across sectors, between regions and countries.

One of the most important aspects of competition is the pressure it generates for the development of the productive forces. Marx argued, and I argue in the next two chapters, that technical change generates crises in capitalist societies. Since the contradiction that forces development of the productive forces upon capital is competition, the theory of crises derives in part from the analysis of competition.

This chapter analyzed why competition is internal to social capital as a whole. The existence of competition is assumed, nor is its existence an empirical question, though its manifestations are subject to empirical inspection. Competition is a fundamental internal contradiction of capital as a social relation. Competition develops and intensifies as capitalism develops. With the development and maturing of capital, all the contradictions of this mode of production develop and intensify, as starkly demonstrated in the global financial crisis of 2008.

Competition and the movement of capital

The rate of surplus value is a social aggregate, whose existence is independent of any particular industry or capitalist employer. It is incorrect to consider the rate of surplus value to vary across sectors and the aggregate to be the weighted average of rates across sectors. Each capitalist exploits her or his workers, but the rate at which surplus value is extracted is determined in the aggregate. Aggregate surplus value is the hidden source of profit which appears only at the enterprise level as the return to capital.

For any specific enterprise, the rate of profit is the ratio of surplus value realized as profit to capital advanced. For an enterprise profit presupposes the competitive interaction of capitals. The price calculation of one capitalist enterprise can be written as follows:

$$P_i = (1 + \pi)(\Sigma a_{ij} P_j + wn)$$

where P_i = price of commodity i measured in units of the money commodity, π = rate of profit of the enterprise, a_{ij} = physical amounts of the means of production consumed in the production process, where i refers to the specific commodity being produced and j denotes a specific production input, P_j = price of commodity input j measured in units of the money commodity, w = the wage rate in units of the money commodity and n = the amount of current or living labor per unit of output.

If the value of labor power is given (w fixed), the profit earned by a particular enterprise depends on the prices paid for the means of production (the P_j) and the efficiency with which those means of production and labor power are consumed. Prices are determined by the movement of capital. Beginning counterfactually with exchange values equal to values, unequal rates of profit across sectors are implied. This must be the case because the rate of surplus value is the same for all industries and enterprises, and the ratio of constant to variable capital differ. Given the a_{ij}s and n s, the aggregate rate of profit is generalized by changes in prices.[24]

Price changes result in the redistribution of surplus value among industries, and in an idealized outcome this process ends when the same rate of profit prevails in each industry. In a two-industry case, this must involve prices rising in the industry that has the higher ratio of constant to variable capital, and prices falling in the other. In the case of many sectors it is not possible to predict the direction of price movement for any given industry from knowledge of the composition of capital measured in commodity values (Sraffa 1960).

Competition is the mechanism by which capital as a whole devolves into its component parts (Marx 1971a: Part II). As it generalizes the aggregate rate of profit to each sector, the movement of capital appears to determine profit rates. This same process, which transmits a general rate of profit across sectors, brings about uneven development within sectors. One can conceive of the movement of capital among sectors with no change in production techniques (a_{ij}s and Ls unchanged). However, in practice the movement of capital brings the introduction of new techniques. The invasion of a capitalist enterprise into another branch of industry because the profit rate is high transforms the productive forces in that sector. This creates a stratification or hierarchy in each sector of production costs and unequal profit rates across enterprises in the sector, as the more efficient producers capture a larger share of sales and the surplus value devolved to that sector.

The process of the equalization of the rate of profit among sectors is simultaneously the process of uneven development and stratification within sectors. Competition tends to equalize returns across sectors while generating unequal returns within industries. Competition is not the equilibrating and harmonious force of neoclassical economics, nor is it the beneficial mechanism of popular mythology. It does not establish a stable, sustainable relationship among capitals. It is the mechanism for equalizing returns across sectors and unsustainable inequality within sectors. The tendency for the rate of profit to equalize hides a fiercely competitive struggle within industries between the strong and the weak.

The law of value predicts a tendency for profit rates to equalize among industries. It shares this prediction with almost all other theories of value and price. By ignoring stratification of capitals within industries, other theories treat this tendency as establishing a stable and harmonious general equilibrium.[25] In Marx's value theory and in reality the tendency for profit rate to equalize is a mechanism of disequilibrium, creating an unstable, fragile, uneven development among competitors. This aspect of the law of value is central to the analysis of crises.

9 Fixed capital and circulation

Circulation of capital

This chapter treats one of Marx's most important theoretical contributions, a contribution frequently overlooked or not appreciated for its radical nature. As explained previously, the circuit of capital has three moments, associated with three forms of capital; money capital, productive capital and commodity capital. Marx demonstrated that this circuit is simultaneously the realization of value and the replacement of use value. Indeed, the reason Marx used his famous M→C→M′ representation of capital was because of the simultaneity of the movement of value and use value. Their interaction and the contradiction between the circulation of value and the circulation of use values proves to be the source of crises.

The circuit of capital is the general circulation of commodities. The initial moment in the circuit, M→C, represents a historically unique way of uniting the means of production with labor. The sale of labor power gives the mode of production its particular character. It is followed by the moment of production, which is capital as function. The moment of production is not unique to capitalism. Human effort and the objects of labor are combined for production in all societies to create the products with which society is maintained. The specific manner in which laborers and their tools enter production stamps the productive forces themselves as capital.

During the production process new value is produced in material form, use values. Once produced, these use values must be transformed into money, C′→M′. Failure to do this necessarily implies that the circuit cannot be renewed at the same or an expanded level. After realization capital returns to its purely social form (money), the form in which it is again a general claim on commodities.

The circuit of capital is a circuit of replacement. First, it is the replacement of the specific with the general, exchange of use values for money; then the replacement of the general with the specific, purchase of labor power and other ingredients of production to initiate production again. In this chapter I consider the process of replacement and reinitiation in detail.

Fixed and circulating capital

To initiate production capitalists advance money in two parts, constant capital and variable capital. These two categories of capital correspond to two functions in the production process. Constant capital exchanges for the means of production, those commodities whose value is transferred in the production process from one material object to another. The means of production are called "constant" capital for the literal reason that their value remains constant in production.

A certain amount of steel, coal, machinery, etc., enters production representing a certain value. After production occurs, the value of means of production is embodied in newly produced commodities. Labor power also enters the production process with a predetermined value, and its use in production results in expanded value. The money exchanged for labor power is variable capital, in that the value that labor creates varies from the value of labor power. Variable capital is "variable" in another sense, which reflects the domination of capital over the production process. For example, when a capitalist buys steel the consumption of that steel is determined by the techniques of production; a certain amount of steel can produce a certain number of nails of a given quantity and size and no more.

This fixed input–output relationship does not apply to workers. A capitalist may purchase the capacity to work of a given number of laborers for a specific length of time, but the intensity of work is not determined until production occurs. Capitalists, or their supervisory agents on the shop floor, can obtain varying amounts of effort from workers. Anyone who has ever worked in a factory or office knows that the intensity of work, like the length of the working day, is the product of day-to-day negotiation and struggle. In the early stages of capitalism, oppression and coercion in workplaces played a major role determining the intensity of work. While this oppression continues as capitalism matures, the introduction of machinery brings the work process increasingly under the direct control of capital and less susceptible to negotiation by workers, who are increasingly deskilled within machine-paced production processes (Bravermann 1974).

The constant/variable distinction clearly identifies the source of surplus value. It is a distinction based on the way value is produced, a distinction central to the understanding of value and surplus value, but no consequence to capitalists. From the vantage point of operating capitalists, all costs appear the same, and reducing constant capital costs appears as much a source of profit as reducing labor costs.

Precisely because the effort that can be extracted from workers varies and that from means of production does not, labor continuously suffers from the efforts by capital to reduce costs of production. It is for this reason that cost-cutting by capitalists, sometimes euphemistically called "downsizing", always focuses on labor, increasing the intensity of work while reducing the number of workers so that the remaining workers produce more than they did previously. Increased political and economic strength of trade unions in the United States, Japan and

Western Europe in the decades immediately after World War II severely limited the ability of capitalists to employ this primitive tactic. However, falling union strength, especially in the United States and the United Kingdom, provided capital with the opportunity to reinstate workplace repression as a central feature of accumulation.

When one moves from the analysis of production to the circulation, the constant capital/variable capital distinction becomes obscured. After production has occurred, constant and variable capital are two component parts of the value of a commodity distinguishable only in an accounting sense. The two great economists of early capitalism, Adam Smith and David Ricardo, devoted most of their analysis to the circulation of value, and found no necessity to employ the constant/variable distinction in their treatment of capital. Their emphasis on circulation led them to an alternative distinction, fixed and circulating capital.

Circulating and fixed capital identify the manner in which the realization of value occurs ($C' \rightarrow M'$). Circulating capital includes all of those elements of production that are completely consumed in the production process, and, consequently, whose value circulates with the newly produced commodities. These elements are labor power, raw materials and intermediate commodities. Fixed capital is that part of the means of production that is not completely consumed during the current production period. These fixed means of production remain embodied in non-circulating material objects such as machines and buildings.

The fixed/circulating distinction disguises the value-creating process, because the source of expanded value, labor power, is lumped together with non-value-expanding means of production. This does not invalidate the distinction; it points to its specific and limited usefulness. Fixed and circulating are categories for the analysis of the circulation of value. They enter the analysis after production has occurred, presupposing the production and the constant/variable division of capital. Once the analysis of the production of value has been made, the concepts of fixed and circulating capital allow consideration of the problems arising in the circulation and realization of value.

The similarity of fixed capital to the neoclassical concept of "capital" is purely superficial. In neoclassical theory capital comes into existence by deferring consumption and need not be durable or productive. A tool that is produced in one period, then used and exhausted in the next period is not durable, but is neoclassical capital because the time spent making it could have been applied to an article for immediate consumption. An example of non-productive neoclassical capital is the proverbial forest (Baumol 1961).[1] The trees in the forest are capital because there is a waiting period for them to mature and be cut, during which time they could be felled and sold for less revenue to buy articles of immediate consumption. The example of a forest provides an excellent demonstration of the logical fallacies in the neoclassical concept of capital, with its confusion between function (productive use) and ownership (claim on property).

Fixed capital has two characteristics important for the circulation process. First, the use value of fixed capital does not circulate, only its value does. Unlike other means of production, fixed means of production undergo no change of material form in the production process. Part of their usefulness is exhausted, but not as a consequence of the material objects being altered. The value of fixed capital is transferred to the commodities it is used to produce, not any part of its use value. This characteristic has an extremely important consequence. All commodities that are inputs to production are bought, then their value replaced though the sale of what they are used to produce. Circulating capital is consumed entirely in one production period and its value completely replaced for the next. Fixed capital is only partly consumed during a production period, so its value must be replaced over several production periods. To state the difference another way, circulating capital is consumed and replaced during one circuit of capital, and fixed capital is used over several circuits, replaced all at once.

Second and obviously related to the first, fixed capital imparts its value to commodities over several production and circulation cycles, over several circuits of capital.[2] As a consequence, a portion of the value of fixed capital does not circulate, but remains fixed in material form. Assume that a capitalist purchases a machine for $1000, that it has a productive life of ten years and operates at a constant rate over that time. In order to replace the machine, in the simplest case, the capitalist would plan to recover one-tenth of the purchase price of the machine each year through the sale of the commodities produced with that machine. The value which remains of an item of fixed capital at any point in its operating life I call its "retained value". Thus, the machine in the example has a retained value of 90 percent or $900 after one year.

This second characteristic lends a specific aspect to the circulation of fixed capital. Means of production are purchased for use in production and when their usefulness is exhausted they must be replaced through another purchase. This implies that they are commodities whose value is continuously transferred to other commodities, but they are replaced all-at-once with one purchase.[3] The difference between function (value transfer through production of other commodities) and replacement (acquired by a single purchase) reflects the twofold nature of commodities manifested in fixed means of production. As values, they decline with their material exhaustion, and this declining value implies the need for a hoard of money for their replacement that is accumulated bit by bit. As use values, they are replaced all at once.

In summary, the transformation of fixed means of production from productive capital to money capital occurs continuously (C′→M′) through the realization of newly produced commodities. However, the transformation of money capital into productive capital for these fixed means of production is a separate, discontinuous process. Realization of value and replacement of use value are separate processes.[4] It might seem that I stress an obvious point, but the implications of this separation of realization and replacement are central to capitalist crises.

Replacement of fixed capital

The contradiction between the realization of value and the material replacement of the means of production generates economic crises. Central to these crises is the inability of capital as a whole to realize the retained value of fixed means of production. This realization problem is different in practice from the inability to sell all newly produced commodities, so-called aggregate demand failures (see appendix to this chapter). The difference is fundamental, because complete and successful realization of the full value of newly produced commodities results in the failure to capture the retained value of fixed capital. Sufficient aggregate demand is the basis for the failure to realize the value of fixed capital.

This apparent absurdity, that failure to realize the value of fixed capital occurs when commodity value is fully realized is yet another example of the brilliance of Marx's critique of capitalism. Going back at least to Malthus, many have argued that market economies suffer from the problem that occasionally or frequently capitalists cannot realize the value of their production, cannot sell all they produce. Without exception these writers attribute difficulties in realization of value to lack of aggregate demand, usually attributed to inequality in the distribution of income or systemic instability of investment.[5]

Both types of explanations, based on inequality of distribution and volatility of investment qualify for what Marx called "vulgar" analysis, theory that elaborates the obvious. It is no insight to point out that capitalism generates extreme inequalities, nor to assess investment decisions as volatile and a source of instability of demand. More important than these obvious characteristics of capital is that they have not over more than two centuries prevented capitalism from expanding throughout the world and transforming the societies everywhere after its own image. The analytical power of Marx's analysis shows itself by explaining the limits to capital not in its weakness, but in its strength.

In precapitalist societies, competition for power within the ruling class occurred in the political sphere. While capitalists struggle over political power, this is derivative from a directly economic competition. Competition in the economic sphere takes many forms, all of which have their basis in the cheapening of commodities, and it is through the cheapening of commodities that capital creates the limits to its accumulation. Commodities are cheapened through technical innovations, which increase the amount of output a worker produces per unit of time. Except in trivial cases, the productivity of labor is raised by providing workers with new fixed means of production. The continuous introduction of new methods of making products implies that existing means of production are continuously rendered obsolete.

The introduction of a new and more efficient way of making computers need have no impact upon the material usefulness of older methods.[6] To the extent that older equipment is not materially exhausted, it can remain capable of producing use values (e.g., computers). The introduction of new production methods affects the potential of the old equipment to pass on its retained value, to have that retained value realized in money form (C′→M′). The innovation renders the old means of production less effective in the competitive struggle among capitals, makes that machinery and equipment "socially obsolete".

If the pressure of competition allows, capitalists with socially obsolete means of production would stretch their use to the limit of their material life. Even if successful in doing so, these capitalists will not be able to realize the original value of those means of production, i.e., the value that determined the price at which they were purchased. The introduction of new techniques, by reducing the value of commodities, at the same time reduces the retained value of existing means of production.

Marx called this process the "moral depreciation of capital", referring to the social process by which useful equipment is rendered socially less useful. The material usefulness of equipment is unchanged by innovation. Innovation makes the equipment less useful as capital, less useful to produce surplus value. When rapid technical change occurs and commodity values fall rapidly in an industry, materially useful means of production can be rendered socially useless, because they cannot produce commodities at low enough values for those commodities to be profitably sold.

The stratification of capitals in an industry, discussed in the analysis of competition in Chapter 8, corresponds to the "moral depreciation" of fixed capital. Devaluation of fixed capital is the consequence of the lower values of commodities that fixed capital produces. The lower values of the circulating commodities imply that enterprises with older equipment may not realize the surplus value that would accrue to them if they were not burdened with socially obsolete means of production. The failure to realize the value of fixed capital is not because it generates commodities that cannot be sold, but because technical change lowers the values of those commodities and, therefore, the value of the equipment that produced them. The problem is not insufficient demand; the problem is the uneven development of capital at the level of production.

In all societies people have worked with means of production that had a lifespan longer than the use values that could be made with them. This is the material basis of the difference between fixed and circulating capital. The specific difference in capitalist society is the manner by which value is transmitted. For circulating capital, value is transmitted completely and replaced immediately upon resumption of the labor process. For fixed capital, value is transmitted incrementally and replacement deferred. This difference does not appear in precapitalist society, because the means of production are not bought and sold. The transmission of value and the replacement of use values create the possibility that conditions may change such that the transmission of value cannot quantitatively correspond to the realization of that value. Competition among capitals realizes this possibility.[7]

Fixed capital is fixed because a part of its value does not enter the circuit of capital, while another part of that value is imputed to the commodities it produces and circulates with them. The circulation of commodities determines the conditions for realization of fixed capital, and these conditions can render the retained part of fixed capital value unrealizable in whole or part. Incomplete realization arises from the contradiction between the process of production (value transmission) and process of circulation (value realization).[8] In times of economic crisis, this contradiction can bring about a catastrophic "moral depreciation" of capital, and intrinsically useful objects become socially useless.[9]

The realization of value, C′→M′, makes a quantitative match of commodity capital to money capital, matching supply and demand. Difficulties fulfilling this match at the aggregate level are manifestations of qualitative changes in the process of production. Commodities reach the market with their value determined, which creates the illusion that their realization is determined in circulation. In other words, it creates the false impression that the level of aggregate sales is determined by the level of aggregate demand. The macroeconomics of Keynes derives from this illusion.[10]

Were there no fixed capital, realization of value would be a purely quantitative matter. Capital advanced for production would circulate in its entirety in commodities, and the realization of these commodities would be the realization of capital advanced for any circuit of capital. Realization of value, in part or whole, would correspond to the money exchanged for commodities. In this case the circulation of value would proceed smoothly. Any interruption of this circulation would be explained by factors influencing the moment C′→M′ itself, not by the moment of production. In effect, this would be simple commodity circulation, discussed in the appendix to Chapter 4 and again in the appendix to this chapter.

But the existence of fixed capital introduces qualitative changes into the analysis of circulation. Superficially, the realization of circulating capital can be considered as a quantitative process, for the sale of commodities at their values assures the conversion of the circulating value into money. However, because technical change reduces the values of commodities, an equality of value produced and value realized does not ensure realization of the value of non-circulating capital, fixed capital. The relationship between this, Marx's analysis of realization and crises, and mainstream theories of "demand failure" are treated in the appendix to this chapter.

Durability of fixed capital and the development of capitalism

The intention of capitalists in introducing technical changes is to lower the unit cost of production and increase profit. As explained earlier, Marx termed the sum of constant and variable capital, CC+VC, the "cost-price". For a capitalist, this sum is a benchmark, the minimum selling price at which the capital advanced will be replaced by money. The sum (CC+VC) appears as the basis of price to capitalists, rather than a component part of the value of the commodity.[11] In this simple cost calculation, "the extortion of surplus labor loses its specific character" (Marx 1967: 45). As explained in Chapter 3, surplus value is distributed on the basis of capital advanced, so it appears that constant capital (dead labor) is as much a source of profit as variable capital (living labor). This illusion equates the calculation of profit with the source of profit.[12]

The inclusion of fixed capital requires an expansion of the cost price formula in order to analyze the two qualitatively different aspects of constant capital, i.e., $[(CC_1+CC_2)+VC]$, where CC_1 represents the transfer of value from fixed means of production and CC_2 the transferred value of raw materials and intermediate commodities. The term CC_1 represents a transfer of value with transfer of material form, while CC_2 involves a transfer of value corresponding to material transformation of means of production.

In capitalist society, the introduction of technical innovations is determined by their impact on the cost price calculation of capitalists. The innovations change the production process, and the analysis of this change provides the basis to understand the transfer of value. The means of production at their disposal determine the ability of people to produce use values, both in quantity and quality. Increases in the number of use values produced per unit of time are achieved through increasing the fixed means of production employed by labor.

This increase in what Marx termed the technical composition of production, the ratio of the number of workers to number of machines in a simple case, comes about through the division of labor.

Adam Smith based his analysis of technical change on his observations of the division of labor in the production process.[13] Marx's contribution was that he related the division of labor to the introduction of machinery in the production of value under capitalist relations. The division of labor within production is achieved by the introduction of machinery, which reduces and simplifies the tasks performed by each worker, which is a process of the deskilling of the proletariat (Marx 1971b: Chapter 15). The concrete skills of the laborer become increasingly reduced and irrelevant, so that the formal abstraction from concrete labor in exchange approximates a real abstraction in production. Through the division of labor, tasks become trivialized to the point that each worker is a near substitute for every other in production as he or she is in exchange.

The process of technical change involves providing each worker with more fixed means of production. This is a controversial conclusion, attacked by critics of the labor theory of value, who argue that technical change can be "capital saving", by which they mean "fixed capital saving". If one completely abstracts from the material aspect of the production process, it is possible to formulate such an outcome. The cost price has two elements, CC and VC, and if one ignores how technical change occurs in practice, innovation can either decrease constant capital ("capital saving") or variable capital ("labor saving").

The "capital saving" argument embodies several fundamental mistakes, the most important being the failure to distinguish between value and use value. An increase in productivity is by definition an increase in the quantity of output a worker can make per unit of time. If the intensity of work does not change, more output per unit of time requires more machinery. Machines are complicated mechanisms that carry out simple tasks. Their introduction requires a work process to be divided into a series of simple tasks.

If other things remain unchanged, the introduction of more machinery will raise the composition of capital measured by both values and prices; i.e., raise the composition of capital. Because living labor is the source of expanded value, this one might be tempted to conclude that this would reduce the rate of profit. This conclusion is incorrect. The condition that an innovation reduces the cost price of a commodity ensures that the innovation raises the rate of profit.[14]

One important way by which fixed constant capital is reduced is by increased longevity of means of production. By lasting longer, the portion of the value of fixed means of production transferred to commodities during any production period is reduced. A technical change that involved nothing more than increasing the material lifespan of fixed means of production while allowing the same number of commodities to be produced each production period would reduce the fixed constant capital portion of the cost price (though not the circulating constant capital).

Increased durability of fixed means of production is in direct contradiction with the competitive struggle, which forces the shortening of the value life of fixed means of production.[15] To counteract downward pressure on profitability, capitalists seek cost reducing innovations that extend the material usefulness of fixed means of production. This extended material life of machines and equipment comes in conflict with the "moral depreciation" of capital that shortens the social lifespan of fixed means of production. This confrontation can intensify as capitalism develops, and is perhaps the clearest example of what Marx identified as the general conflict between the development of the productive forces, on the one hand, and the relations of production, on the other. The contradiction generates devaluation of socially obsolete fixed capital, making its conversion into money capital (realization) quantitatively incomplete.

Capitalist competition induces the longevity of fixed capital and, at the same time, contradicts that longevity by devaluing fixed capital. This devaluation, which is the result of accumulation itself, makes economic crises inherent in capitalism. During these crises the devaluation of fixed capital brings on the general devaluation of commodities. I analyze this process of crisis in the next chapter.

Appendix

Marx and demand failures

A common interpretation of Marx, especially in North America, is that his theory of capitalist crisis was based on an analysis of systematic demand failures affecting either final consumption or investment or both.[16] Those who hold this view are frequently termed "under-consumptionists". This is an inaccurate term, because in the net product framework that such theories use, a lack of sufficient consumption demand derives from a lack of sufficient investment.[17]

With minor exceptions, all modern theories that explain crises as caused by insufficient demand are derivative from the work of Keynes, the greatest economist of the twentieth century. Keynes developed this theory of macroeconomics in an attack on his mainstream contemporaries, whom he called "the Classicals". The neoclassical and Keynesian equivalent of aggregate realization of commodity value is general equilibrium. In Classical/neoclassical analysis this is a general equilibrium with full employment. In Keynesian analysis the general equilibrium is associated with varying degrees of unemployment, which is why Keynes called his theory "general".

The Classicals argued that if competition is perfect, market economies automatically generate through price adjustments the necessary money demand to match monetized supply, with the three most important prices being the interest rate, the wage rate and the aggregate price level. This automatic adjustment would always bring aggregate demand equal to aggregate supply with the labor force full employed (full employment general equilibrium, discussed in Chapter 8). Because Classical macroeconomics assumed that the economy had only one product, which continues in the neoclassical resurrection of the Classicals, the "price level" was the price of the single composite commodity, and the real wage was the money wage divided by that price.

Keynes and his successors pointed out many internal inconsistencies in the Classical model of automatic adjustment, and two stand out for discussion of Marx's treatment of aggregate realization, adjustment of the price level and the definition of time in the model. If one begins a Classical/neoclassical analytical sequence with unemployment, adjustment to full employment cannot occur even in theory by the adjustment of the wage level. In the simplest case of a one commodity system with unemployment, a fall in the money wage will not bring full employment. As the money wage falls, perfect competition will cause the price level fall at the same rate to maintain what the neoclassicals term "normal" profit. The fall in the price level prevents the necessary decline in the real wage. Neoclassical theorists have offered solutions to this analytical difficulty, but none have proved satisfactory.[18]

The most effective Keynesian critique of neoclassical macroeconomics is of its treatment of time in the full employment adjustment process. As explained in Chapter 8, the neoclassical model achieves a general equilibrium at full employment by assuming that all exchanges occur simultaneously. When exchanges occur across many markets sequentially, the economy does not achieve a general equilibrium at full employment. While apparently simple and obvious, this critique is theoretically devastating.[19] The difference between the neoclassical models and Keynesian models is that the former are consciously designed as purely mental creations with idealized economic behavior, while the latter are constructed to have a correspondence to actual economies.

Marxist or non-Marxist, theories of demand failure are explanations of unemployment not crises. A lack of sufficient aggregate demand cannot result in a continuous fall in output. If capitalists cannot sell all they produce, they will react to this excess supply of commodities by producing less. The decrease in output will cause a decrease in income payments, including wages. This is the "multiplier" process of Keynes, which results in a fall in income to a stable level, an equilibrium with unemployment, which is lower than the original by a multiple of the initial excess supply of commodities. Insufficient aggregate demand provides an explanation of unemployment and stagnation, and in general aggregate demand explains the level of output.

The difference between a theory of employment and a theory of crisis is that the latter has a mechanism that causes output to decline irreversibly from a stable level, which requires a qualitative transformation of the model from stability to instability; and a second mechanism that brings the irreversible decline to a stop. Keynes, unlike Luxemburg (Tarbuck 1972), recognized that a theory of insufficient demand could not by itself provide an explanation of crises, and focused on the "secular stagnation" implied by his analysis.[20] The same is true for the much misunderstood "tendency of the rate of profit to fall" hypothesis. If this is interpreted as a long run tendency for capital as a whole, it would, if correct, be an explanation of unemployment and stagnation as it was for Adam Smith and David Ricardo.[21]

Because crisis theories require an economy to make a discontinuous divergence from a stable position, they are logically inconsistent with the neoclassical method. As a result, non-Marxist attempts at crisis theories, usually termed theories of the "business cycle" or "trade cycle", have been by Keynesians. A partial exception to this generalization is the purely mechanical "multiplier-accelerator" algebra of Samuelson,[22] which inspired several non-financial crisis models (Gordon 1986). The limited insight provided by these models suggests that seeking explanations of crises in the "real economy" without reference to financial capital is an analytical dead end. This conclusion also applies to Marxian attempts.

John Stuart Mill may have been the first non-Marxist to propose a coherent discussion of crises arising from financial instability,[23] which became a major theme during the twentieth century.[24] While many twentieth century writers provided important insights into the inherent instabilities arising from financial capital and how these serve as mechanisms to trigger crises, none developed a theory of the cause of crises in capitalist economies. Whether correct or not in his analysis, and I argue that he was, Marx holds distinction of having the only analysis of capitalism that develops a theory linking disruptions in production of commodities (the "real sector") via financial instability to crises.

Having briefly reviewed non-Marxist treatments of demand failures, I can consider the analysis of Marx in relation to them. Marx's theory of value is completely inconsistent with neoclassical general equilibrium. He considered absurd the hypothesis that price adjustment would bring stability to markets. Moreover, his explanation of unemployment was fundamentally different from that proposed by Keynesians. Unemployment in Marx's analysis is the result of the "general law of capitalist accumulation", which is explained in the next chapter. Prior to treating the General Law, I focus on the simpler issue: does the analysis of Marx support or reject the hypothesis that the expansion of capitalist economies is constrained by the level and growth of demand? The answer is (1) in his analysis Marx placed great stress on the instability of capitalism, (2) he argued that recurrent moments when aggregate demand is insufficient (demand failures) are the symptoms of that instability and (3) the cause of the demand failures arises from the capitalist nature of the production process. These points are developed in Chapter 10.

10 Accumulation and crises

Economic crises

Capitalist society is based on historically unique relations of production and these social relations manifest themselves in unique forms. Even those that are older than capitalism, money and commodities, for example, take on new and qualitatively different significance in capitalist society. All phenomena I have treated to this point, value, profit, money, credit, competition and fixed means of production, present themselves as part of the circulation of capital. These phenomena interact to generate the most grotesque manifestation of the historical uniqueness of capitalism, economic crises.

An economic crisis is a disjuncture in the process of social reproduction that prevents complete reproduction of the circuit of capital. The term economic crisis is synonymous with capitalist crisis, or a crisis of capital, because the category "economic" presupposes capitalist society and capitalist social relations. The division of social life into the economic and the non-economic reflects the twofold nature of commodities: labor performed for exchange becomes subject to objective regulation in the phenomenal form of monetary costs. It becomes formally separated from labor that is not performed under the domination of capital.

This separation remains incomplete until labor power itself is a commodity, in which case each working person's life is institutionally divided between work (the economic) and leisure (the non-economic). From this division emerge the categories of bourgeois society, wages and profit, for example, which are the superficial expressions of capital's domination of social production. The term "economic crisis" presupposes these categories, just as the phenomenon to which it refers presupposes the circulation of capital.

One could use the term "economic crisis" to describe disruptions in other modes of production. For example, it could be used to describe the consequences of the Black Death in medieval Europe, because the plague resulted in decline in production, widespread dislocation of population and famine. To do so would be a usage so broad that it would rob "economic" of meaning, as well as contradict what is generally understood by identifying a crisis as "economic". At least since the time of Ricardo,[1] economic crisis referred to the phenomenon of overproduction, a situation in which use values pile up idle, unused and unusable due to relations of ownership. Crises of overproduction necessarily involve overproduction of value, in which some commodities cannot be sold, and realization is the necessary condition for their consumption as use values. Overproduction of value implies overproduction of capital, since commodities, the carriers of objectified labor, are commodity capital.

When products do not circulate as commodities and are produced directly for consumption, overproduction of use values is impossible.[2] Interruptions in social reproduction in precapitalist society took the form of underproduction of use values, resulting in famine and social upheavals, and were themselves the result of plagues, warfare, natural disasters or direct class conflicts that undermined the relation of the exploited to the exploiter. All meaning of the term "economic" would be lost if such crises are categorized with the form of social disruption unique to capitalism, general overproduction of use values.

Any theory of capitalist reproduction with pretension to be seriously considered must account for economic crises.[3] Marx's mature writings were devoted to explaining economic crises, and his theory of crisis is inseparable from his theory of accumulation. In the process of accumulation, all of the tensions and contradictions of capitalist production and circulation are intensified, and economic crisis is the predictable outcome of the accumulation process (Marx 1971a: Chapter 15). All economic crises have a common root cause, based in the production of value, not in its distribution or realization.

Accumulation and value formation

Capitalist accumulation is a particular historical form of society in which the material reproduction of the means of production and means of human subsistence creates a specific form of class rule and a specific form of exploitation of the direct producer. Accumulation is fundamentally the replication of the capital–labor relationship on an expanding scale. Marx emphasized this by at one point defining accumulation as the growth of the proletariat (1970b: 576). In countries with substantial precapitalist sectors, accumulation involves the qualitative transformation of direct producers from servile and petty commodity production relations into proletarians. In advanced capitalist countries, the growth of the proletariat is achieved by the replenishing and depletion of the industrial reserve army, a process which Marx called "the general law of capitalist accumulation".

Because living labor is the source of value, the growth of capitalist employment implies the expansion of value, and capitalist accumulation is the accumulation of value (ibid.: Chapter 25). The accumulation of value appears to be a quantitative phenomenon, $M \rightarrow C \rightarrow M$, $M' > M$. It is not uncommon for accumulation to be treated as if this were its essential character, rather than its appearance. For some purposes it is useful to analyze the purely quantitative aspect. When doing so the subject of investigation is expanded reproduction, which abstracts from technological change and its effects.

Expanded reproduction is the framework Marx used to analyze realization, which is not a simplified model of accumulation. Expanded reproduction is an idealized analytical device to demonstrate the quantitative aspects of the circuit of capital. The mechanics of realization are demonstrated, and then the analysis can consider accumulation because realization has been eliminated as a cause of the interruption of accumulation.[4] After analyzing the conversion of commodity capital into money capital, one moves problems of realization from the category of cause to category of consequence. Theories that assign the cause of crises to the realization of value fail to appreciate the distinction between expanded reproduction and accumulation. The most extreme manifestation of this failure is the formal theoretical separation by mainstream economics of expanded reproduction and accumulation under the categories "short term" and "long term".

Accumulation is simultaneously the process of value expansion and the process of value formation. The first can be considered in terms of capital as a whole, while the latter involves the interaction of many capitals. Marx first analyzed accumulation by abstracting from competition among capitals, which implies that commodities exchange at their values. The basis for accumulation is the production of surplus value, which arises from the competition between the two defining classes of capitalist society, capitalists and the proletariat. This competition or class struggle underlies the quantitative expansion of capital. The qualitative developments within this quantitative expansion arise from the competition among industrial capitals and between industrial and financial capital. As the analysis proceeds it becomes clear that the quantitative dynamics resulting from the class struggle drive capitalism, and the qualitative dynamics arising from capitalist competition undermine it.

Inherent in the capital relation is competition among capitals, the fragmentation of total capital into formally autonomous parts. This competition manifests itself in the cheapening of commodities through technical change. Technical change is perhaps the aspect of accumulation most mystified by mainstream economics. The mystification has two parts. Conceptually, it is mystified by being treated only from the value side, which I discussed in the context of fixed capital. A second part of the mystification is the manner in which technical change is viewed in relation to time. It is characteristically treated as a "long run" influence, whose consequences can be ignored in the "short run". The "short run/long run" distinction in neoclassical theory does not refer to the passage of time, but refers to abstract analytical categories.[5]

In real economies at all moments some enterprises introduce new production techniques. While they may be bunched in periods of rapid technical development, introduction of new techniques occurs continuously and their impact is continuous. Long time periods consist of the accumulation of small time periods, making it contradictory to ignore technical change during the latter and consider it during the former, since the one is the sum of the other. As we shall see, this metaphysical temporal distinction results in a misunderstanding of Marx's famous (or infamous) tendency of the rate of profit to fall.

As accumulation proceeds, the competition among capitalist enterprises prompts the introduction of new techniques to reduce unit costs of production.

This results in a fall in the concrete labor time necessary to produce commodities in those production units where the new techniques have been introduced. Technical change creates a temporary quantitative indeterminacy in the value of commodities. In each sector technical change creates a situation in which the same commodity is produced across enterprises with different amounts of concrete labor.

If the analysis were based on the embodied labor view of value (Chapter 1), the concept of value would break down, because commodities arrive in markets after being produced with different amounts of concrete labor.[6] Marx's theory of abstract labor resolves this apparent contradiction. In practice the interaction of capitalist enterprises must generate a common selling price out of a diversity of labor processes for the same commodity. In the circulation of commodities, some of the enterprises discover that part of the concrete labor consumed in production is not socially necessary, it is not value creating.[7] Capitalists make this discovery through what neoclassicals call the "signal" given by the market price of the commodity. The process of value formation provides the concept to resolve the problem of establishing a common value from the common price, abstract, objectified labor.

The value of a commodity is not determined by the concrete labor consumed in its production in a particular labor process. The concrete labor of all labor processes for one commodity is transformed into abstract (objectified) labor by the interaction of many capitalist enterprises through exchange. In the process of accumulation the circuit of capital begins with a set of values and a new set of values confronts capitalists at the end of the circuit. The moments of circulation, M→C and C′→M′ force the changes in the material process of production to manifest themselves as changes in values. What appears as purely quantitative, M→C ... P ... C′→M′, is the phenomenal form of continuous qualitative change. The change of form of capital (money capital to productive capital to commodity capital) is the process of the formation of new values.[8] This necessarily implies that the circulation of capital affects the amount of surplus value that can be realized as profit; value arises from the interaction of production and circulation.

The impact of the formation of a new value for a particular commodity is not limited to the sector in which it is produced. If the commodity is a means of production, a decline in its value directly cheapens the constant capital in every sector using that commodity as an input. This reduces the values of the commodities in all those sectors. If the commodity is an element of workers' consumption, a decline in its value reduces the value of labor power and may cheapen variable capital.[9] Technical change, even were it restricted to a few commodities, results in a general reduction in the value of commodities during the process of accumulation.

The formation of new values, subsumed within accumulation, involves the process of the redistribution of capital (centralization) as well as the growth of existing capitalist enterprises (concentration). In consequence, analysis of accumulation requires treatment of credit as part of the process of competition.

The introduction of new technology involves an increased division of labor, requiring production on an expanded scale. The growth of credit and purely financial obligations accompanies accumulation and the formation of new values.

The process of accumulation brings together all the aspects of capitalism considered previously: formation of values, division of money into its functions as means of circulation and means of payment, intensification of competition, and the contradiction between the value life and material life of fixed capital. Technical change is the basis of the interaction of these elements through the development of the productive forces. This material process occurs in the context of the production of value, and the source of economic crises lies in the opposition of the material and value aspects of production and circulation,[10] which finds its expression in the tendency of the aggregate rate of profit to fall.

The tendency of the rate of profit to fall

Marx considered the law of the tendency of the rate of profit to fall the key to unlocking the concrete workings of a capitalist economy.[11] In *Capital* he does not present the law until well into Volume III, but it is implicitly part of the discussion of accumulation in Volume I where the elements of the tendency are considered (Marx 1970b: Chapter 25). The tendency is not pursued in the first volume because its implications could not be elaborated until he considered the circulation process. The tendency arises in production, the subject of Volume I, but the analysis of production is insufficient to explain it.[12]

An initial exposition of the tendency requires abstraction from circulation, or its operation becomes lost in the confusion of its consequences. The tendency of the rate of profit to fall is the direct consequence of the development of the productive forces; it is the consequence of the dynamism of capitalist society. It is a tendencial law of accumulation, not of simple or expanded reproduction.

The circuit of capital is initiated by the exchange of money for the elements of production, $M(CC+VC) \rightarrow C$. The money advanced is divided into constant and variable capital, and this division is quantitatively determined by the physical amount of the means of production required in relation to the labor power required, and the value of these. For simplicity of presentation, I assume that there is only one means of production, only one type of labor and only one commodity that workers consume. In symbols for capital as a whole,

$$CC = A\Lambda_1$$

$$VC = w\Lambda_2 N$$

where, A = the quantity of means of production in units, Λ_1 = the unit value of the means of production, Λ_2 = the unit value of the commodity workers consume, N = the number of workers employed for a given time period and w = the amount of the commodity which workers consume that one worker can purchase.

The ratio A/N is the technical composition of capital, the ratio of physical quantities of means of production and to the number of workers. This is technical in the strict sense of a ratio of material quantities. Its determination is not exclusively technical, because the techniques of production utilized in any society reflect a process of class struggle. This is especially true in capitalist society, in which the ruling class seeks to establish its direct control over the process of production.

When expressed in terms of values, the ratio $[A\Lambda_1/w\Lambda_2N]=CC/VC$ measures the value composition of capital. The tendency of the rate of profit to fall results from the interaction of the technical and value compositions during the process of accumulation. The relationship between the two is quite complex. Technical change raises the material productivity of labor, so that a given number of workers in a given time period processes more products. This must increase the technical composition of capital as a result of two separable processes. First, increased productivity is achieved by a further division of labor within the work process, as more and more machines each do smaller and more detailed tasks. This process involves a rise in the ratio of fixed means of production to the number of workers. As a consequence of this subdivision of the labor process, the number of products produced by a given labor force increases, which requires that the circulating means of production that a worker transforms during a given time to increase. Thus, the technical composition of capital rises because of a relative increase in fixed means of production (the cause of productivity increases), and a relative increase in circulating means of production (the consequence of productivity increases).

Whether the value composition of capital rises depends on what happens to A/N and changes in the values of commodities. The analysis proves complex because the same process that increases A/N decreases both the values of both types of commodities (Λ_1 and Λ_2). The complexity has a time dimension, because the immediate impact of technical change is to increase A/N, and the adjustment to new (and lower) values comes later in the process of circulation. This difference creates an ambiguity in the definition of the value composition of capital. In the phase M→C, labor power and the means of production have been purchased at some initial set of values. In the subsequent phase of production the labor process is altered by technical change, so that when the new commodities arc realized, C′→M′, a new set of values emerges from circulation. Which set of values should be used to aggregate A/N when there is more than one type of input? To deal with this ambiguity, Marx introduced the concept of the organic composition of capital, which he defined as the value composition measured prior to the establishment of the new values that are implied by technical change but not objectified in exchange.[13]

The distinction between the value and organic compositions is fundamental to accumulation and crises. The distinction refers to the process of forming values and market prices, not merely which set of values to use to convert the technical composition into a value ratio. At one moment in the circuit of capital a set of value relations has been established in the market. A change in the technical composition will result in a fall in the value of commodities following the competition among capitals. Conceptually, moving immediately to the new values presupposes the process of value formation without analyzing it, treating is as an instantaneous shift between positions of equilibrium.

The circuit of capital is initiated by the exchange of capital for labor power and the means of production. The values of these were set by the techniques prevailing in each sector of the economy prior to the exchange. I call these the "initial" values, associated from the initial techniques of production. Those means of production and labor power are consumed by some capitalists using newly introduced techniques, which implies lower values in the future. The commodities produced then circulate, C′→M′, in a competitive context that brings their values below the initial values at which they entered the circuit of capital. The technical change necessarily involves a rise in the organic composition of capital, because the organic composition is the technical composition valorized by the old set of values. On the basis of the old values, the rate of surplus value is unchanged, but the ratio of CC/VC has risen. This implies a fall in the rate of profit.[14] Marx called this "the law as such" (1971a: Chapter 12).

The "law as such" does not mean that a rise in the organic composition results in a fall in the aggregate rate of profit. The law of the tendency of the rate of profit to fall is an alternative way of identifying the expelling of living labor from the production process, which Marx called "the general law of capitalist accumulation". Whether the tendency results in an actual fall in the aggregate rate of profit, and the aggregate in a fall in the general rate of profit, and, finally, the general in a fall in the rate of industrial profit (e.g., deducting for interest) cannot be answered at this level of abstraction. The movement from the abstract tendency through all the steps to an actual fall in profit rates involves the analysis of value formation, which occurs at the level of many capitals.

Marx was aware of the tendencial and abstract nature of "the law as such", and set alongside it a process that refers to value adjustment, "the law of the counteracting tendencies to the tendency of the rate of profit to fall" (ibid.: Chapter 14). This "counteracting" law brings about the adjustments of the value formation process. Changes in the labor process reduce the labor time required to produce commodities. Through the interaction of capitals, this reduces the abstract necessary labor time (value) of commodities. A fall in the value of commodities, given the standard of living of the working class, reduces the value of labor power. If the working day remains unchanged, this results in a rise in the rate of surplus value.

Surplus value is thereby raised relatively, defined as a fall in necessary labor time with the length of the working day unchanged. This rise in the rate of surplus value counteracts the tendency of the rate of profit to fall. The counteraction may be reinforced if the values of the means of production fall more than the values of the commodities workers habitually consume. If this occurs, then the value of constant capital may fall relatively to the value of labor power, reducing the value composition of capital. If the standard of living of workers does not change, a general fall in the value of commodities will raise the rate of profit.

The major consequence of the law of the counteracting tendencies to the tendency of the rate of profit to fall is an increase in the rate of surplus value.

The two laws are interrelated: the law as such gives rise to its counteracting tendencies. The rise in the technical composition of capital increases labor productivity and lowers the values of commodities. However, the laws operate at different levels of abstraction. The law as such arises in production and can be developed for capital as a whole. Because consideration of capitalist production presupposes capitalist relations, the law as such reflects changes in the forces of production. The counteracting tendencies involve the interaction of capitals, and the operation of the relations of production (competition, money and credit). The interplay between the tendency and the counteracting tendencies is a specific example of the relations of production confronting the forces of production.

It is wrong to interpret the law as such as a "long run" phenomenon, because that would confuse the technical composition with its value counterparts. The historical tendency of capitalist development is for the technical composition of capital to rise. This indicates nothing more than the development of the productive forces under capitalism. It is another way of saying that labor productivity rises. The law as such and its accompanying familiar, the law of counteracting tendencies, are laws of the accumulation process, at work in each circuit of capital. If they must be placed within a time dimension, then they should be defined as "short run" laws of value formation.[15]

Understood as part of the process of accumulation, the law as such provides the key to unlock the dynamics of capitalist crises. If it is interpreted as a relationship between static states, it collapses both as an analytical mechanism and a descriptive tool. As a consequence, critics of Marx have sought to present the law statically, as have some defenders of Marx. The law of the tendency of the rate of profit to fall can be refuted in a static context because between static states there can be no tendencies, only outcomes. When treating the law as such, critics characteristically omit the word "tendency", referring instead to the law of the falling rate of profit, a phrase that implies that a prediction has been made as to the actual movement of the rate of profit.[16]

The law as such and the counteracting tendencies to it are not laws of long run development, but laws of accumulation. They come into play as a result of a dynamic process of uneven development and disappear when one considers static positions. To try to refute or defend the law of the tendency of the rate of profit to fall by reference to situations in which commodities exchange at equilibrium values is similar to an attempt to analyze the acceleration of bodies by gravity when they are lying at rest. The phenomenon is defined out of existence.

One of the most common formulations of the "falling rate of profit" hypothesis that the rate of profit will fall if the organic (*sic*!) composition of capital rises more than the rate of surplus value as the result of technical change. This is also static. First, if one abstracts from fixed constant capital the rate of surplus value always rises more than the value composition of capital. Second, the two changes (in CC/VC and SV/VC) are part of the same process of value formation, and are therefore related to each other in a strict and determinate way, so that the statement collapses into "the rate of profit will fall if the rate of profit falls". Marx considered in detail the relationship between the rate of surplus value and the composition of capital, but did so by use of the distinction between the value composition and the organic composition, which renders the analysis dynamic.[17]

The tendency and value formation

The tendency of the rate of profit to fall manifests itself in an actual fall in the aggregate rate of profit as a result of the process of value formation. The actual fall results from quantitative difference between the values that prevail when capital is advanced and those that will prevail in the future. The contradictions of commodity production reach their most intense manifestation in the tendency of the rate of profit to fall.

The explanation of this process requires clarification of why the general rate of profit would fall along with why it would not fall. If the rate of profit always fell, it would not be a tendency, but an obvious trend about which there would be no controversy. The rate of accumulation would be closely constrained, for in each circuit of capital, the ratio of surplus value to capital advanced would fall. Because accumulation is the result of capitalized surplus value, a falling rate of profit would imply a secular slowdown in accumulation in all capitalist countries. The task is to explain why the rate of profit does fall and why under some circumstances it does not. A theory that always predicts one or the other is no guide to understanding reality, where both occur.

The process of accumulation can be summarized as follows:

1. Accumulation is initiated by the advance of capital, and the elements of production are purchased at prevailing values.
2. Production follows by workers employing a quantity of fixed means of production purchased at a set of values that prevailed in some previous period.
3. Technical change reduces living labor relatively to the means of production, raising the organic composition of capital. Because technical change occurs unevenly, different enterprises take the same commodities to the market after using different quantities of concrete labor in their production.
4. Once the production process is completed, the produced commodities must be realized. In the process of realization, new values are objectified in these commodities, lower than before.

This process has two major consequences. First, within each sector of industry, a redistribution of surplus value occurs. Those capitalist enterprises unaffected by technical change will have higher cost prices than those that introduced the new technique. At the uniform selling price, the non-innovators will realize less surplus value as profit than the innovating enterprises. For the enterprises with higher unit costs, the rate of profit will fall. The fall in the rate of profit for these capitals is the result of initiating the circuit of capital at one set of values and realizing their commodities at a lower set of values. This is also true of the innovating capitals, and leads to the second effect. For all capitals, the values at which the commodities were realized are below the initial values. The capital advanced, denominator of the profit formula, is calculated upon the initial values, which were higher than the values that determine the amount of surplus value realized. The greater the increase in the productivity of labor, the greater will be the quantitative difference between these two sets of values.

During this process, the organic composition of capital is relevant, because the new and lower set of values does not affect capital advanced until the next circuit of capital, at which point it enters the profit calculation. Even at that point, the new values affect only the increments of fixed capital, because fixed capital does not circulate in its entirety; part remains fixed in the machines and other equipment. The problem for capital is to realize the value of existing means of production in the context of the progressive devaluation of those means of production.[18] This problem affects those capitals using new means of production as well as those using socially obsolete ones. For each enterprise means of production and labor power are purchased at one set of values and realized at another. The difference between enterprises is that for those using new means of production the devaluation of the capital advanced is offset in part or in whole by the reduction in the cost price of the realized commodities.

In this process of accumulation and value formation the rate of profit will fall for some capitals, those using old means of production. As the circuits of capital repeat themselves, each time with technical change reducing the concrete labor consumed in the production of commodities, the stratification of capitals increases. The proportion of capitals experiencing a fall in the rate of profit depends upon the intensity of the competitive struggle.

To this point, no mention has been made of crises. The analysis has demonstrated that technical change, by devaluing existing means of production, can under certain circumstances result in an actual fall in the rate of profit, affecting capitalist enterprises to varying degrees. This process is the consequence of the simultaneous existence of means of production of different efficiencies in use of concrete labor, of different "vintages" to use the neoclassical term. If we abstract from this stratification of capitals and consider only equilibrium situations, and the same values prevail when capital is advanced and when commodities are realized, no fall in the rate of profit occurs, general or specific. This would be the analysis of expanded reproduction, not accumulation.

Crises and the tendency of the rate of profit to fall

Capitalist reproduction is an integrated process of social production and circulation, and its repetition involves the unity of these two moments. A crisis in such a society manifests itself as separation of these two moments. The possibility of such a separation is inherent in the unity itself, since the unity is an antagonistic one.[19] This antagonism manifests itself at the most abstract level in the metamorphosis of the commodity itself, C→M. This metamorphosis expresses that a commodity is produced for its exchange value, which creates the possibility that once produced it may not be exchangeable at all or at sufficient profit.[20]

Circulation provides the possibility, not the explanation, of crisis. In most circumstances commodity realization occurs without difficulty. The analytical task is to explain the moments when difficulties appear. The exchange itself cannot do this. Unsold commodities announce the difficulty after the fact.[21] The realization of commodities occurs as part of the circuit of capital, and it is in the circuit of capital that the explanation of crisis lies.

The process of accumulation reallocates labor across sectors of production. This reallocation of labor implies a redistribution of surplus value, so that enterprises may expand beyond the limit set by their realized profit. This, the socialization of capital, is facilitated by the credit mechanism. With the growth of credit, a division emerges between money as means of circulation and means of payment. During accumulation, credit serves the first function, and commodities circulate on the promise of future payment. Buying on credit adds a further dimension to the metamorphosis of commodities, allowing for their circulation and shifting their realization as money to the future.[22] Deferred payment creates the possibility that at some future point the demand for the money commodity will exceed the demand for all other commodities to an extreme degree.[23] Were widespread cancelation of the pyramid of debt demanded by creditors, an amount of money would be required to realize not only all currently produced commodities but also all those previously circulated by credit.

The growth of credit, which facilitates the centralization of capital, is the financial side of the development of the productive forces. The development of the productive forces creates a quantitative difference between the value of commodities at the outset of the circuit of capital and at the moment of realization. This quantitative difference can transform the tendency of the rate of profit to fall into actual decline. With an actual decline some enterprises can no longer meet their debt obligations and collapse financially. If many capitals are thus affected, a general credit crisis results. The general credit crisis provokes a crisis of realization, and commodities go unsold. The credit crisis becomes a crisis of overproduction.

A credit crisis, like a fall in the rate of industrial profit, is activated by the interaction of capitals and cannot be analyzed or theoretically established at the level of capital as a whole. The interaction of capitals is not an interaction of equals, but of the strong and the weak, of the more and the less efficient. In general, the less efficient capitals will suffer more in the credit crisis. The larger capitals will also be threatened with financial collapse, since they, too, have entered into credit buying; indeed, it is through growing indebtedness that the larger capitals have become larger. The credit collapse imposes itself upon the strong, the weak and all between.

The process of accumulation and crisis is summarized as follows. The necessity to realize commodities as money creates the possibility of crisis, a possibility historically specific, predicated upon general commodity production, which itself is created by labor power being a commodity. The specific form of crisis derives from the separation between money as means of circulation and as a means of payment, which creates growing indebtedness. This separation derives from the restructuring the division of labor.

The cause of capitalist crisis is the tendency of the rate of profit to fall, a tendency arising from technical changes in the sphere of production, forced upon capital by competition. This tendency finds expression through the formation of new values. A fall in the rate of profit is the qualitative change that activates the developing tensions in the accumulation process. First, it implies a slowdown in accumulation, as for many capitals there becomes relatively less surplus value to convert into new capital. Second, it bankrupts inefficient capitals, setting off a credit collapse. The inability to realize value because all commodities cannot be sold or not at their values is the crisis itself.

Marx stated the process as follows:

> The general *possibility* of crisis is given in the process of metamorphosis of capital itself, and in two ways: in so far as money functions as *means of circulation*, [the possibility of crisis lies in] the separation *of purchase and sale*; and in so far as money functions as *means* of payment, it has two different aspects, it acts as *measure* of *value* and as *realization of value*. These two aspects [may] become separated. If *in the interval* between them the value has changed, if the commodity at the moment of its sale is not *worth* what it was *worth* at the moment when money was acting as a measure of value and therefore as a measure of reciprocal obligation, then the obligation cannot be met from the *proceeds of-the sale of the commodity.*
>
> ...[I]t is quite clear, that between the starting-point, the prerequisite capital, and the time of its return at the end of one of the periods, great catastrophes must occur and elements of crises must have gathered and developed.[24]
>
> (1968: 513–14, 495)

The separation of moments of circulation by production results a change in values between the two moments, and as a result, the "elements of crises must have gathered and developed" (ibid.: 513). The crisis itself can cause a general fall in the exchange value of commodities when they all cannot be realized, accompanied by the "moral depreciation" of existing means of production. Bankrupt enterprises liquidate their material assets, selling to the surviving, more efficient capitals. The market devaluation of the existing means of production raises the rate of profit on this fixed capital and extends its useful life as part of the value-producing process.

The crisis was caused by the fall in the rate of profit that resulted from the implicit devaluation of means of production by technical change. In the crisis, the devaluation becomes explicit. Old means of production are forced to circulate in their entirety as the result of financial failures, to be sold off in mergers, takeovers and bankruptcies. What was latent during accumulation, the inability to realize fixed capital at its original value, becomes an actual failure when these means of production are liquidated in order to meet credit obligations.[25] This collapse of capital values momentarily resolves the contradictions in the process of value formation, laying the basis for a higher rate of profit and renewed accumulation.[26]

In a credit crisis collapse in the value of fictitious capital (financial assets) can be reduced by the devaluation of commodities, which increases the value of money. Part of this process is the devaluation of the means of production, forcing the circulation of their value, part of which remained fixed in place in the period of expansion. The economic crisis in its full development involves the devaluation of capital accompanied by the growing unemployment of the labor force.[27]

In the crisis, the process of devaluation converts the organic composition of capital into the value composition. The process of value formation, which proceeds by incremental steps during accumulation, is sharply accelerated during the crisis, and values rapidly approach the level implied by the most advanced forces of production that are in use. The process of accumulation is a process of dynamic uneven development, during which technical change repeatedly lays the basis for new sets of values. This uneven development generates its compensating force, the economic crisis. During the crisis, socially obsolete means of production are physically discarded and socially devalued. The new values latent in the new productive forces emerge to rule exchange. As a consequence, the valorized composition of capital may fall (CC/VC) and the rate of surplus value rise (SV/VC), the latter occurring as a result of a fall in the value of the commodities workers consume. A new and higher rate of profit is established by the combination of devalued fixed capital (in the denominator of the profit formula) and a rise in the rate of surplus value (in the numerator).

The "inevitability" of crises

The elements giving rise to economic crises are inherent in the accumulation process. Capitalism is a mode of production that generates continuous change in the forces of production. This dynamic characteristic of the capitalism sets the limits to accumulation, because the development of the productive forces undermines the basis on which surplus value is realized at any moment. As a consequence, crises are part of the accumulation process; they are inherent in capital.[28]

This cyclical repetition does not result in a simple repeating of cycles of expansion and contraction. The development of capitalism is contradictory, in that social relations change to facilitate and to block the rejuvenating effects of crises. The credit system grows more sophisticated, making the centralization of capital easier, but also making it more unstable and displacing capital as function with capital as ownership. The development of the credit system coincides with an increase the centralization of capital, so that each cycle of accumulation and crisis occurs in the context of a social system dominated by larger and more powerful capitalist institutions.

These powerful economic institutions cannot be restructured or eliminated by economic processes alone, as the financial crisis of the late 2000s demonstrated. With so-called globalization, capitalist production becomes controlled by immense financial institutions that can invoke the aid of the state to prevent their disintegration in face of competitive pressures. As a consequence, the function of economic crises is partly undermined, and the necessary attrition of the inefficient capitals is blocked. The role of the state in mitigating crises is considered in the final chapter.

No discussion of economic crises is complete without stressing their grotesque nature. In last book of the Christian Bible, the Book of Revelation of Saint John the Evangelist, there is a scroll with seven seals, and the breaking of the first four seals unleashes the four horsemen of the apocalypse, pestilence, war, famine and death. All too often a fifth horseman has wreaked comparable misery, capitalist crisis.

11 First crisis of the twenty-first century

Escaping production

In 2005 at a conference in Beijing of radical scholars, a prominent North American Marxist told those who would listen that there would be no more major crises of capitalism. The end to crises was because financial capital had developed the means to ensure itself against all forms of risk and uncertainty. This spectacularly wrong embracement of the propaganda of financial capital required one to discard common sense, as well as Marx's theory of value. That Marxists might take seriously the possibility that capitalist crises were a thing of the past is a tribute to the powers of obfuscation generated by the production and circulation of commodities.[1] Capital can, indeed, insure and protect itself against many disasters, but those arising from its own international contradictions are not among them.

The theory of value provides an explanation of the financial upheaval in 2008 that few mainstream commentators anticipated and almost none understood.[2] The common misunderstanding was that the crisis as the consequence of irresponsible lending by financial institutions, combined with new forms of financial assets that removed lenders from any direct responsibility of what their lending had financed. This interpretation mistakes outcome for cause. The apparently reckless lending and the proliferation of financial "products" are predicted from Marx's theory of value and money. They are the expected consequences of the contradiction between the forces and relations of production. This chapter takes that general statement of contradiction and applies it concretely to the *début du siècle* crisis that burst forth in 2008.

The fundamental dilemma that continuously plagues capital is that its *raison d'être* is profit that arises in production, but the production process is the fundamental source of its difficulties. In a paradox, it is for exactly this reason that capitalists attempt to distance themselves from production. The most obvious reason that individual capitalists seek to escape production is to avoid the disruptions that potentially arise from the competition with labor over control of the production process. Throughout the 250 year history of capitalism workers have used a variety of actions to contest control by capital over production process, with strikes one of the most disruptive from the perspective of capital.

However, the pressure for capital to escape from the confines of production goes beyond the potential disruptions arising from the class struggle, it comes from the inter nature of capital, the contradiction between value in exchange and value in use. Production is a material process whose expansion was material limits, the potential labor force, the available means of production and prevailing skills and technology. In contrast the expansion of value appears as unlimited, the apparently magical process of converting a quantity of money into a larger quantity of money. Financial capital is the pursuit of this magic, the discovery of a financial Philosopher's Stone that converts money into more money, value into more value, without production. Just as some great thinkers in the middle ages devoted themselves to alchemy,[3] similarly in the realm of finance capital men and women devote themselves to the pursuit of the absurd, converting money into money without production. However, these modern alchemists are revered as brilliant of mind, bold of spirit and are rewarded for their semi-criminal behavior beyond dreams of avarice.[4] If not the capitalist fifth horseman of the apocalypse, they are among the stable hands.

Finance to speculation

The twofold nature of commodities gives rise to money, which is a synthetic abstraction from that contradictory nature. This, the first step or first degree of abstraction, results in a second degree abstraction from money to credit, then successive abstractions with fictitious capital assuming increasingly exotic forms, each further from the production process. In the early period of capitalism, the owner-operator holds direct title to the productive apparatus of the enterprise and its output, direct ownership of use values. With the shift to "public limited companies" in the nineteenth century ("incorporated companies" in the United States) the capitalist owns financial paper ("stocks"), which provides a claim on profit.

Stocks represent the abstraction from capital as function to capital as ownership. This aspect of abstraction continues as claims on ownership are replaced by claims on the valuation of that ownership. These claims are then traded, becoming the abstract and mobile representations of the concrete and immobile. The trading of stocks results in a fundamental break with the concrete. Were they traded for the income they generate, their claim on current profit, they would be relatively mundane financial instruments serving no more than a minor distribution function.

However, their usefulness to those who trade in them lies in their potential to appreciate in exchange value. Indeed, financial markets throughout the capitalist world traded in stocks that generate no income themselves, transforming stockholders from *rentiers* to speculators.[5] This transformation is of singular importance for the stability of capitalism. It implies that the role of finance capital changes from facilitating the concentration and centralization of capital to the redistribution of surplus value through speculation. The development of the power of finance over production, ownership over function, takes a qualitative leap to the dominance of speculation over finance itself. As a result, the financial sector becomes the embodiment of instability.

In place of purchasing a nominal claim on corporate ownership, money can convert into a claim on someone else's claim on nominal ownership.[6] These claims without ownership consist of collections of stocks selected by financial institutions and sold in units. In the first abstraction from ownership stocks are associated with specific capitalist enterprises, such as Microsoft. In the further abstractions the link to enterprises consists at most of a list of the companies whose stocks are part of the collection. And the purpose of the abstraction is speculation not finance.

This abstraction from capital as ownership and then from capital as finance implies more than the separation of ownership from control, an aspect of corporate governance analyzed in the 1930s.[7] In capitalist society the purpose of production is exchange, not use, and the purpose of exchange is profit. It would appear that the next logical statement is that profit determines the market value of an enterprise, and therefore the market value of its stock. However, in the last decades of the twentieth century in the United States the process of abstraction went far beyond this. The market value of the stock of a capitalist enterprise came to reflect its place in a system of financial speculation whose relationship to the real wealth of society was so esoteric and complex as to be beyond the immediate understanding even of financial "experts" themselves. The buying and selling of commodities themselves becomes a minor sideshow of capitalism compared to the buying and selling of representations of the anticipated value of enterprises in which those commodities were nominally produced.

Capitalist risk

Credit provides a powerful mechanism for the acquisition of fictitious capital, serving as a means of exchange with deferred payment. A quite early mechanism to multiply the power of finance was the practice of "buying on margin" or "leveraging". This technique, which developed into increasingly complex forms, involves the purchaser paying a fraction of the money value of a transaction with a promise of full payment at a specified future date. The infamous financial "derivatives" represent various forms of leverage whose complexity came from the nature of the underlying asset on which they are nominally based, the contracted dates that defined them and what the holder had to deliver on those dates.[8]

The proliferation of financial derivatives at the end of the twentieth century prompted a fiction that capitalists had discovered the mechanism by which they could protect themselves from economic contractions. This capitalist Philosopher's Stone gave birth to the concept of the "new economy" that would enjoy continuous growth immune from "boom and bust".[9] This immunity would be achieved by the proliferation of financial "products" that could eliminate risk. The logic of the argument, an invalid syllogism, went as follows: capitalist crises result from the economy suffering shocks when risks are realized in practice; by use of derivatives it is possible to insure against risk; therefore, it is possible for capitalism to be free of crises.

The risks against which capitalists seek to protect themselves are not the source of instability and crises, but the contrary. It is instability and crises that create the risks against which capitalists seek to protect themselves, and the mechanisms designed to achieve this protection create the illusion that such protection is possible. As capitalism develops, capital as ownership supplants capital as function, and capital as ownership becomes subsumed within capital as finance, with capital as finance becoming capital as speculation. The function of the arcane representations of fictitious capital is the same as fictitious capital itself, only divorced from the vestiges of what created the ownership function, the redistribution of surplus value.

In capitalist society the term "risk", like all terms arising from the circuit of capital, has an historically specific meaning. Risk is the possibility that a capitalist enterprise may not be capable of meeting its financial obligations.[10] Except as an occasional and marginal social phenomenon, this risk is unique to capitalism. An early manifestation of the general financial crisis of late 2008 was the foreclosures on housing loans in the so-called sub-prime mortgage market. These foreclosures and the associated collapse in the value of financial assets occurred not because the borrowers were a bad risk; they occurred because housing was a commodity in a society characterized by high inequality. The asset collapse in this market was a spectacular but minor aspect of the general financial disaster to come.

The risk against which capitalists seek to insure themselves reflects the division of social capital between capital as function and capital as ownership, and between capital as ownership and capital as a claim on surplus value. Credit extended to facilitate the expansion of an enterprise beyond its profit involves risk because of the competition among enterprises to achieve that expansion simultaneously. The competition for credit can prompt productive enterprises to undertake investments that are intrinsically risky in the universal sense of technological uncertainties. However, at the level of capital as a whole, expansion involves no financial risk. It is the struggle among capitals over the distribution of surplus value that creates financial risk.

The transformation of financial capital from a function that was primarily financial in the strict sense of lending to industrial capital to a predominantly speculative role fulfilled the parasitic potential of money capital. When its primary function was to finance the concentration and centralization of industrial capital, its activities were unproductive because these did not themselves create value or surplus value. Though unproductive, these activities were supportive of the accumulation process. Like the policeman who guards the property of capital or the lawyer who writes its contracts, the banker could claim the distinction of making a necessary contribution to accumulation, though not a productive one. Once speculation replaces finance as the principal activity of money capital, the banker and colleagues remain necessary, but increasingly dysfunctional. Therein lies the nature of the first economic crisis of the twenty-first century.

Formal subsumption of productive capital

Competition among financial capitals differs fundamentally from competition among productive capitals, because the latter produces surplus value while the former only distributes it. Two levels of appropriation occur: the industrial capitalist appropriates the unpaid labor of workers, and the financial capitalist appropriates a share of the spoils taken by the industrialist. Financial capital is a parasite, while industrial capital is an exploiter. Productive capital can increase profit by raising the productivity of labor, in contrast to financial capital that is restricted to intensifying work or finding more effective parasitic mechanisms.

The initial impact of the introduction of an innovation in an industrial enterprise is to lower production cost and increase profit. Other industrial enterprises producing the same commodity will be under pressure to adopt the same innovation. As they do so, the average profit rate in the sector will rise, attracting an inflow of new competitors, which will lower the price of the commodity. If the commodity the sector produces is bought by workers or used as an input for commodities workers buy, the value of labor power will fall and the rate of surplus value will rise. This analytical sequence implies that if an innovation is productivity increasing for one enterprise, the process of competition renders it productivity increasing for capital as a whole (see Chapter 3).

Financial capital costs can be lowered but the aggregate amount of surplus value is unaffected. Because financial capital does not contribute to the creation of surplus value, competition among financial institutions focuses on two processes: (1) attempting to extract profit from productive capital and (2) the struggle within finance over that extracted profit. The increasing financial instability in the last decades of the twentieth century was the result of these two processes.

The concrete consequence of the first redistribution process is shown in Table 11.1, which reports the value added going to the financial sector in the United

Table 11.1 Financial value added in GDP and GDP growth by decade, United States, 1920–2007

Year	*Financial sector/GDP*	*GDP growth by decade*
1920–1929	3.6	
1930–1939	4.9	
1940–1949	3.4	
1950–1959	2.9	3.5
1960–1969	3.7	4.4
1970–1979	4.1	3.3
1980–1989	4.7	3.1
1990–1999	6.0	3.1
2000–2006	7.4	2.6
2007	8.0	

Source: http://pages.stern.nyu.edu/~tphilipp/papers/finsize.pdf and Council of Economic Advisors (2010).

Note
The final sector share refers to the beginning of the decade except for 2007.

States. Following World War I mechanisms of speculation developed substantially in the United States, and the financial sector increased from less than 4 percent of GDP to almost 5 percent. Strict regulation of financial institutions in the 1930s resulted in a decline in 1940 to the level of twenty years previously, where it remained into the 1970s.[11] The repeal of Roosevelt's New Deal regulations, beginning in the 1980s and culminating at the end of the 1990s, brought a dramatic rise in the income share of the financial sector, to 6 percent in 1990 and 8 percent in 2007. The second column of Table 11.1 suggests that this rise in financial income was not associated with more rapid economic growth. The quantitative growth of finance relative to the aggregate economy indicates the parasitic function of finance, to allocate surplus value to itself, the abstract form of capital, capital removed from both function and ownership.

Toward the end of the twentieth century in the United States and the United Kingdom industrial capital countered the growth of financial profit by a partial conversion of itself into its opposite, financial capital, funding expansion with new stock sales.[12] Inherent in this method of corporate finance was the probability that the production and sale of commodities might prove incapable of generating the cash flow consistent with maintaining the expanded financial value of the enterprise (Wray 1994). By partial financialization of itself, productive capital opened itself to the vulnerabilities that plague money markets, while simultaneously financial institutions developed increasingly complex "products" to generate the income to compensate for the lending lost to equity sales.

In the circuit of capital money serves several functions, means of circulation, store of value and means of payment. As means of circulation it can assume many forms, manifested in the proliferation of financial derivatives. This proliferation creates a source of weakness in the financial system, increasing its potential for instability. The fundamental cause is the process of abstraction discussed in the opening part of the chapter.

As capital as a whole seeks to escape the limits dictated by the sphere of production, the link between market values and commodity value grows more tenuous. This weakness is magnified when financial capital asserts itself from facilitator to manipulator of productive capital, and infects productive capital with the contradictions specific to it.[13] In the twenty-first century, capitalism in the United States had moved even beyond financial capital manipulating productive capital. What appeared to be productive capital had not been "taken over" by financial capital, but had been subsumed within financial capital and lost its identity as productive capital. The much commented upon shift in perspective from the long term to the short term by corporate management is a manifestation of this loss of identity.[14]

Financial collapse in the twenty-first century

General crises such as that at the beginning of the twenty-first century that provoke the collapse of production and unemployment do not arise from antagonism between factions of capital, serious as they are. Their cause lies in the sphere of production, the contradiction between the development of the productive forces and the social relations that manifest that development. The subsumption of industrial capital to financial capital lent to this crisis its specific characteristics. In this case the most striking aspect was the general collapse in the value of financial assets in most of the advanced countries, facilitated by the reduction in regulatory constraints of the previous thirty years, especially in the United States.

The rapid ascendancy of finance capital is shown in Figure 11.1, which provides an index of the Standard & Poor's measure of the value of stocks on the New York Stock Exchange (NYSE) for 1975–2010. This time period is chosen because it is after the US government ended its commitment to a fixed price of gold and after the first boom in petroleum prices, both of which had a temporary distorting effect on inflation rates. From 1975 through 1993, stock market valuation rose at 9.8 percent per annum in current prices and 3.8 percent when deflated by the wholesale price index. The latter, a constant price valuation, was only slightly higher than the growth in output of corporate GDP, which was 3.3 percent.

Coinciding with the deregulation of the US financial sector, from 1993 through 2000 the NYSE index rose at a phenomenal 19 percent per year in current prices and at an equally phenomenal 16 percent in constant prices. Over

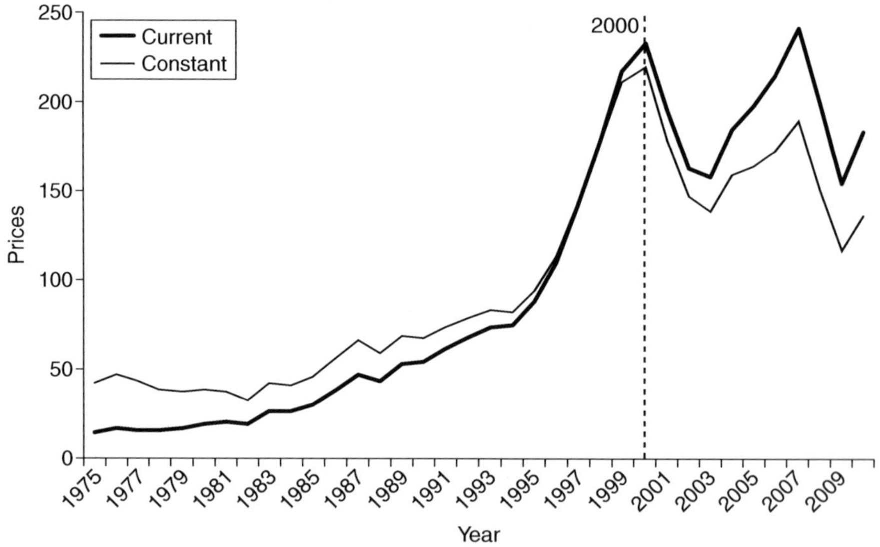

Figure 11.1 Standard & Poor's US Stock Market Index, current and constant prices 1975–2009 (source: the stock market data are taken from the web page of Robert Shiller (2000), www.econ.yale.edu/~shiller/data.htm).

Note
The index is calculated with the period average as the base. The price adjustment is with the wholesale price index.

seven years when corporate output increased by 34 percent in constant prices (4.3 percent annually), the value of financial assets increased by 165 percent. While there are no comparable statistics on the value of fixed means of production, it can be approximated by the increase in output,[15] which would imply that after adjusting for inflation the increase in value of financial representations of corporate assets was five times the increase in the value of fixed capital.

This level of increase proved unsustainable, as any rational observer would have predicted (thought few did). The NYSE index declined by over 35 percent from 2000 to 2003, but this was quickly followed by an increase of one-third from 2003 to 2007. As a result of this stock market volatility, in 2007 less than a year before the financial crisis would strike, corporate financial assets were 225 percent higher than 1993, compared to a likely increase in fixed capital of 142 percent. The sharp decline in market values of stocks during 2000–2003 had achieved a partial alignment of the market value of fictitious capital with commodity value. The financial collapse of 2008–2009 would complete the task and threaten a financial disaster beyond imagination throughout the developed countries.

The instability of fictitious capital value would be transformed into financial collapse through a rush for money to serve as means of payment. This represented an attempt to convert credit money and debt into more secure forms of money and, specifically, commodity money. Figure 11.2 presents the

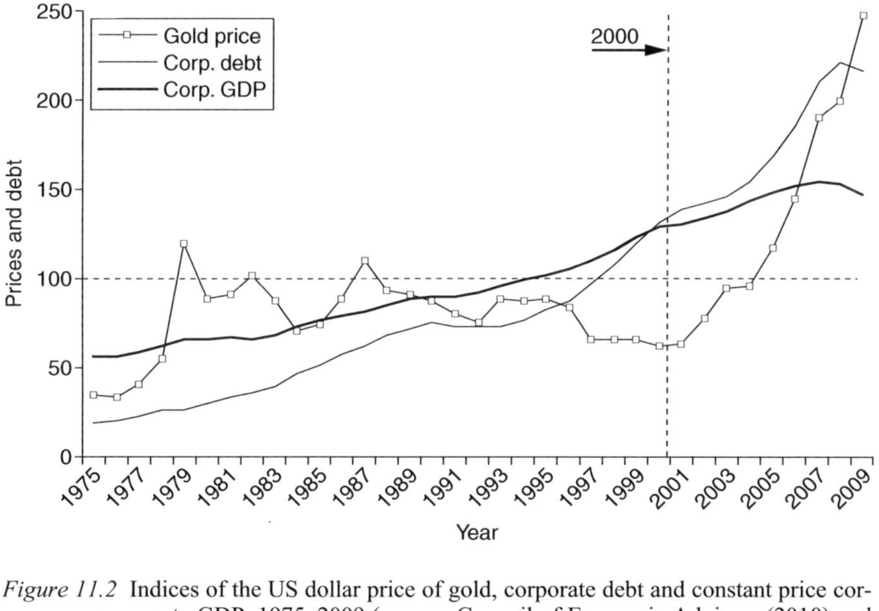

Figure 11.2 Indices of the US dollar price of gold, corporate debt and constant price corporate GDP, 1975–2009 (source: Council of Economic Advisors (2010) and flow of funds analysis of the Federal Reserve system, www.federalreserve.gov/releases/z1/current/).

Notes
Corporate debt is in current prices.

manifestation of this process of monetary conversion and debt cancelation. Over the twenty-five years, 1975–2000, corporate gross domestic product grew in constant prices at 3.4 percent per year, with nominal debt of corporations increasing by 8.5 percent annually. During the first half of the 1980s nominal corporate debt was slightly over 90 percent of corporate GDP, and almost the same during the mid-1990s.

The extraordinary growth of stock values, described above and shown in Figure 11.1, was accompanied by a growing corporate debt-to-output ratio. In 1998 debt was 102 percent output, 112 percent in 2006 and 124 percent in 2007, and over this ten years total debt almost doubled. The analysis of money and its forms in Chapters 5–7 predicted that rapid accumulation of debt would prompt a conversion from valueless representations of money to the money commodity, movement from means of circulation to means of payment. When there are many forms of valueless money and a proliferation of forms of fictitious capital, the concrete manifestation of this conversion is extremely complex. One form it should take would be a rise in the fiat price of the money commodity.

Figure 11.2 verifies this is devaluation of fiat money. Over the twenty years 1980–1999, the price of gold averaged US$370 with a quite low variation, and in 2000 the gold price dropped to a twenty year low of $273. Then, as corporate indebtedness and stock prices increased, the gold price began a rapid rise, to $513 in 2005, an all-time high of $636 in 2006, and a phenomenal $1104 in 2009. Inspection of Figure 11.2 shows clearly that the spectacular rise in gold prices preceded the financial crisis. When the crisis arrived, with a sharp slow down in growth in 2007 and decline in 2008 and 2009, the rush to gold, the manifestation of a rush to money as means of payment and store of value, accelerated.

Those skeptical of analysis based on commodity money might argue that the increase in the price of gold after 2000 was part of a general speculative process that affected most raw materials and primary products. Figure 11.3 shows that this was not the case. From 2000 through 2007 all the commodities reported in the chart display an upward trend. The prices of crude oil, non-precious metals and food and beverages have a pattern typical of commodities that are bought and sold for their value in use. Their prices rise during the years when corporate demand for inputs and household demand for food was expanding, then decline when output contracts. In contrast, gold shows the telltale pattern of a money commodity. Its price continues to rise after contraction of output and the general demand for commodities. This commodity, unlike the others, was being held for itself, for its embodiment of all other commodities. The skeptics might say the increase in the price of gold as the crisis arrived reflected speculators moving to the "safest possible investment", so-called flight to quality.[16] To which Marx would answer, yes, because gold is the money commodity.

A financial crisis is not the same thing as an economic crisis, nor is it the cause. Financial collapse can occur accompanied by relatively small disruptions to the accumulation process. This was the case in the late 1980s. On October 19, 1987, designated "Black Monday" in financial jargon, the NYSE index dropped

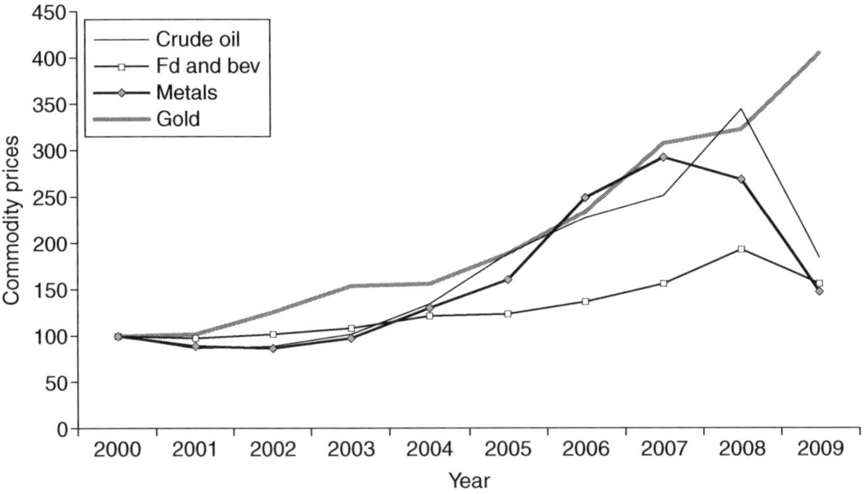

Figure 11.3 Indices of international commodity prices, 2000–2009 (source: IMF (2010)).

Notes
Crude oil: simple average of three major spot prices. Fd&Dev: food and beverages, trade weighted average of tea, coffee and cocoa. Metals: non-precious, copper, aluminum, iron ore, tin, nickel, zinc, lead and uranium.

by almost 20 percent, the largest one day proportional decline in US stock market history. During 1986–1989 corporate output rose in constant prices by at least 3 percent each year, and by over 4 percent in 1988. The exuberance of financial speculation is quite capable of generating its own disruptions within itself that unsettle the exotic abstractions from real wealth. This is never the cause of a crisis of accumulation.

The Great Contraction of the late 2000s resulted from a long period of sustained accumulation that continuously transformed production forces with innovations that have received much comment, most notably so-called information technology. At the end of the twentieth century and into the twenty-first this technical change undermined and unsettled the real structure of capital. Deregulation of the US financial sector during 1981–1998, that allowed for proliferation of fraud and semi-criminal activity, went far to determine the form that the disruption of accumulation would take. But the cause, as in all previous crises, was the uneven development of productive capital, an uneven development that competition among capitals would resolve through the destruction of part of capital. Had the deregulation of finance not occurred, could this crisis have been avoided? I address that question in the final part of the chapter.

Controlling capitalism

The conversion of financial crisis into general economic contraction at the end of the 2000s demonstrated the inherent contradictions in the accumulation process. It also demonstrated the role of the state to mitigate the consequences of those contradictions. When accumulation proceeds vigorously, capitalists praise the virtues of "free markets" in the name of efficiency and demand fewer constraints on their behavior. When accumulation collapses their demands switch to the need for government intervention.

As happened in the 1930s in the United States, the crisis of the 2000s demonstrated that a range of government actions could be effective to rescue national economies from collapse. Perhaps the strongest evidence of the effectiveness of state interventions and controls in stabilizing and maintaining accumulation was the minor impact that the international financial crisis had on China. In 2007 the average growth rate across the six largest developed capitalist countries was 2.4 percent, which fell to less than 1 percent in 2008 and a negative 4.4 percent in 2009.[17] Over the same three years China's state-managed capitalist economy grew at more than 8 percent annually. Many specific aspects of government economic policy in China explain its apparent immunity to the crisis, and they all have one thing in common: they restrict competition. The approach of the Chinese government to capitalism might be summarized as the principle that capitalist accumulation is too contradictory to be left to private capital.

The success of Chinese capital in avoiding the crisis that swept the rest of the capitalist world raises the question of whether similar success in avoiding crises could be achieved by governments in capitalist countries that do not rule by overtly authoritarian means. The experience of the United States and Western Europe after World War II, during the so-called golden age of capitalism, suggests that the answer may be "yes".[18] A closely regulated capitalist economy within a political regime of bourgeois democracy was to a great extent achieved in the post-war period. The achievement was the direct result of the strength of organized labor. The reconstruction of managed accumulation will require the reconstruction of the strength of the working class.

Controlling capitalism in lieu of overthrowing it would require four fundamental reforms, whose purpose would be to restrict severely the economic and political power of capital.[19] First, the financial system would be taken into state ownership to prevent the tendency inherent in money capital to proliferate vehicles of speculation. The governments of the United States and the United Kingdom had the opportunity to do this in 2008 and 2009, and did not, even though a Swedish right-of-center government had provided the model in the early 1990s.[20] By control of the banking system the state would confine capital to capital as function.

Nationalization of the financial system would be essential because state action to reduce the severity of crises would have contradictory results. The uneven development of capital creates the conditions for the uneven development of accumulation, and uneven development via the credit system produces financial or monetary crises, followed by crises of generalized overproduction. The state can act to maintain demand, using monetary and fiscal policy, and this can postpone the crisis of realization. However, this postponement is at the cost of maintaining a fragile structure of stratified capitals. Postponing a crisis of realization prevents the devaluation of fixed capital that would facilitate the reorganization of capital. Control of the financial system provides the state with the vehicle for a guided restructuring of productive capital in place of the catastrophic crisis mechanism.

Second, the state would pursue a purposeful macroeconomic policy. The nationalization of the banking system would be complemented by state management of external trade and capital flows and counter-cyclical fiscal and monetary policy. Management of international transactions would include a fixed exchange rate and strict controls over capital inflows and outflows. The fixed exchange rate would reduce currency speculation to the marginal role it played in the 1950s and 1960s. Effective implementation of a fixed exchange rate requires controls on capital inflows and outflows. Counter-cyclical fiscal policy with an accommodating money policy would provide macroeconomic stability and full employment.

Third, government regulation of labor markets would be based on the principle in the constitution of the International Labor Organization that "labor is not a commodity".[21] The apparent inconsistency between this principle and capitalist wage labor could be resolved by various programs that eliminate unemployment as a form of labor discipline. The most effective of these would be the universal guaranteed minimum income program.[22] A universal income program would not eliminate exploitation, which is inherent in capitalism, but would no longer allow unemployment as a disciplining tool of labor.

Fourth, and the basis for all of the above would be the protection of the right of workers to organize. A program of fundamental reform of capitalism would be based on the political power of the working class, in alliance with elements of the middle classes. This is the bourgeois democratic alliance that brought about major reforms throughout Europe after World War II. An effective reform of capitalism that eliminates capital's economic and social outrages requires a democracy of labor and its allies in which the political power of capital is marginalized.

The economic consequences of this program could be profound, capitalism without severe crises. The political consequences would be even greater. Nationalization of financial sectors would end the profoundly anti-democratic role of capital in dictating economic and social policy through speculation in financial markets. In the twenty-first century it became common throughout the globe for economic policy to be dictated directly by capital in the form of the argument that almost any progressive measure would "unsettle capital markets".

For example, both in the United States and the United Kingdom arguments against the deficit spending that would reverse economic decline alleged that this obviously necessary and sensible policy would result in currency speculation and capital flight. In the case of the United Kingdom, in the summer 2010 the new right wing government of Conservatives and Liberal Democrats successfully used this argument to gain public support for unprecedented reductions in social expenditure. The same argument was made by the leaders of continental Europe. Most absurd of all, the German Chancellor, Angela Merkel, led the rest in refusing to join in the mild fiscal stimulus sought by US President Barack Obama. This refusal was in apparent ignorance of her country's small fiscal deficit and massive trade surplus which were the ideal conditions for an expansion of expenditure.

For large capitalist countries, the United States, Japan and Germany, the suggestion of capital flight in response to mildly progressive policies is pure ideological propaganda by the agents of capital. For smaller countries, Greece in 2010 being an infamous example, the financial holdings of international capital are small enough in relation to their total capital to make "punishing" governments for progressive behavior both possible and effective. Therefore, nationalization of financial capital is essential to maintain bourgeois democracy.

The sufferings caused by the Great Depression of the 1930s, quickly followed by the horrors of World War II, generated a broad consensus in the developed countries of the need for state intervention to protect people against the instability and criminality that results from the accumulation of economic and political power by capital. Franklin D. Roosevelt, four times elected president of the United States, had this dangerous power in mind when he addressed the US Congress in 1938:

> Unhappy events abroad have retaught us two simple truths about the liberty of a democratic people. The first truth is that the liberty of a democracy is not safe if the people tolerate the growth of private power to a point where it becomes stronger than their democratic State itself. That, in its essence, is fascism-ownership of government by an individual, by a group or by any other controlling private power. The second truth is that the liberty of a democracy is not safe if its business system does not provide employment and produce and distribute goods in such a way as to sustain an acceptable standard of living. Both lessons hit home. Among us today a concentration of private power without equal in history is growing.

In the twenty-first century the advanced industrial countries, especially the United States and the United Kingdom, reached the point at which private power became stronger than "their democratic state". This private power of capital was manifested in those financial markets that through the contradictions of value and use value became vehicles of speculation. Even more serious, they became the vehicles for capital to assert a thinly disguised dictatorship that overrrode bourgeois democratic decisions. A radical program such as described above is required to prevent capital's unconstrained power from fulfillment of Roosevelt's warning against fascism.

During and after World War II even prominent non-Marxist economists recognized the dysfunctional and anti-democratic nature of excessive power of capital. In 1947 in the premier English language economics publication, the *Economic Journal*, K.W. Rothschild wrote,

> [W]hen we enter the field of rivalry between [capitalist] giants, the traditional separation of the political from the economic can no longer be maintained. Once we have recognized that the desire for a strong position ranks equally with the desire for immediate maximum profits we must follow this new dual approach to its logical end.
>
> Fascism ... has been largely brought into power by this very struggle in an attempt of the most powerful oligopolists to strengthen, through political action, their position in the labor market and vis-à-vis their smaller competitors, and finally to strike out in order to change the world market situation in their favor.
>
> (1947)

The twenty-first century version of capitalists seeking "to change the world market situation in their favor" is globalization. While history does not repeat itself, it carries lessons. The link between excessive power by capital and reactionary political power is an obvious lesson that capital does not let humanity forget.

For over 200 years a struggle has waxed and waned to restrict, control and eliminate the ills generated by capitalist accumulation: exploitation of labor, class, gender and ethnic repression, international armed conflict and despoiling of the environment. When the great majority has allied, this struggle has brought great advances in social justice and well-being. When capitalists, a tiny minority, have been successful in creating their own anti-reform and counter-revolutionary majority much is lost. The last thirty years of the twentieth century and into the twenty-first was such an anti-reform period, during which capital achieved a degree of liberation it had not enjoyed since before World War II. Capital's self-liberation threatens the existence of the bourgeois democracy that capital itself brought into being.

Notes

Preface

1 My points can be compared to what Marx considered to be the most important points in *Capital*. In 1867 he wrote to Engels,

> The best points in my book are: 1. (this is fundamental to all understanding of the facts) the *two-fold character of labour* according to whether it is expressed in use-value or exchange-value, which is brought out in the very *First* Chapter; 2. the treatment of *surplus-value regardless of its particular* forms as profit, interest, ground rent, etc.
>
> (http://www.marxists.org/archive/marx/works/1867/letters/67_08_24.htm)

2 Samuel Clements, better known as Mark Twain, wrote,

> When I was a boy of fourteen, my father was so ignorant I could hardly stand to have the old man around. But when I got to be twenty-one, I was astonished at how much he had learned in seven years.

The passage is from his article, "Old Times on the Mississippi", *Atlantic Monthly*, 1874.

3 I was fortunate to send the manuscript of *Capital and Exploitation* to have Princeton University Press, allowing me have Sanford G. ("Sandy") Thatcher as my editor.

1 Value as embodied labor

1 A review of theories of value more thorough than in this book is found in Saad-Filho (2002: Chapter 2). This book is the most important work on Marx to appear in English in the last twenty years.

2 On the difference between Ricardo and Marx, see Gerstein (1976); and on Marx and Sraffa, Himmelweit and Mohun (1978).

3 Following Gerstein and Himmelweit and Mohun, I shall use the term "labor theory of value" to refer to the theory that analyzes the form of value, and "the labor-embodied theory of value" to refer to those theories that consider only the magnitude of value. The distinction will become clear below.

4 The German title of Sombart's article is "Zur Kritik des ökonomischen Systems von Karl Marx".

5 Engels' comment is: "So says Sombart; it cannot be said that this conception of the significance of the law of value for the capitalist form of production is wrong" (Marx 1971a: 894). Morishima and Catephores write, "Engels rejected [Sombart's] interpretation immediately". They refer to Sombart's implicit limitation of the law of value to capitalism (1978: 179).

6 This concluding question is buttressed by the assertion,

> [N]ot only does the peasant know the artisan's working conditions, but the latter knows those of the peasant as well ... People in the Middle Ages were thus able to check up with considerable accuracy on each other's production costs ... at least in respect of articles of daily general use.
>
> (Marx 1971a: 897)

7 Engels refers to "this barter on the basis of quantity of labor" (Marx 1971a: 898).

8 And the labor time embodied in money is irrelevant to the exchange. If it is known, then money is no different from any other commodity in the theory. If unknown, this ignorance only affects the producer and exchanger of money, not those who exchange other commodities via money.

9 The argument of Engels about the role of perception is similar to the assumption of "full information" in the analysis of behavior in neoclassical economics. Both imply that money is valueless (Weeks 1989: Chapter 4).

10 Elsewhere Engels seems to argue this: "the introduction of metallic money brought into operation a series of laws which remain valid for all countries and historical epochs in which metallic money is a medium of exchange" (1976: 187). Since metallic money appeared in antiquity, its "series of laws" must have prevailed for several thousand years, co-existent with the exchange Engels analyzes. The only function of money mentioned is as means of circulation.

11 "[T]his high rate of profit, equal for all participants" (Marx 1971a: 902).

12 In *Anti-Duhring*, Engels argues that capitalist private property emerges "in the interest of increased production and of the furtherance of trade – hence as a result of economic causes" (1976).

13 Sweezy argued that landlords switched to wage labor in response to the spread of exchange, since this form of exploiting labor proved more profitable.

14 This is because the movement of capital tends to equalize the rate of profit. Thus relevant for capitalism at the level of analysis of many capitals are "modified values". See Gerstein (1976). Marx considers these "modified values" (prices of production) in the first part of Volume III of *Capital.*

15 See Morishima and Catephores (1975), and the reply by Meek. The critique is also found as Chapter 7 in Morishima and Catephores (1978).

2 Value as a social relation

1 In a famous letter after the publication of Volume I of *Capital*, Marx wrote that his analytical development of the twofold or dual nature of commodities, and especially labor power, was one of "the two best points in my book" (Marx and Engels 1965: 192).

2 Marx comments as follows on this, referring to the eighteenth century American Benjamin Franklin:

> From the outset Franklin regards labor-time from a restricted economic standpoint as the measure of value. The transformation of actual products into exchange values is taken for granted, and it is therefore only a question of discovering a measure of their value.
>
> (1970a: 56)

3 In *Capital and Exploitation* (Weeks 1981) I wrote that in a capitalist society "no division of labor is established by custom or central authority prior to production", which is wrong. Custom affects the division of labor in every society, but in capitalist society it appears to be determined by markets. In capitalist society custom is weakened, but powerful non-market factors such as inherited wealth, sexism, racism play a major role in the division of labor.

4 In Rubin's words, "Productivity of labor–abstract labor–value–distribution of social labor: this is the scheme of a commodity economy in which value plays the role of regulator" (Rubin n.d.: 67). The same schema is used in Gerstein (1976). Some authors, including Marx at points, use the term "private labor" instead of "individual labor". While this term is not wrong, it is subject to misinterpretation. In this context, "private" refers to ownership, not to process. In no society is production literally private and isolated, because each producer at a minimum uses inputs created by another producer.

5 See the comments by Marx on Proudhon's embodied labor theory of value (Marx and Engels 1976: 126ff.).

6 To the extent that money mediates this exchange the determination of prices will become important on both sides, but it will do so for [the buyer] only so far as he does not want to pay too much for the *use value* of labor; not in so far as he is concerned with its value [emphasis added]. The essence of the relation remains unchanged even if this price which begins as conventional and traditional is thereafter increasingly determined economically … nothing is essentially changed thereby, because the determination of prices remains a *merely formal moment* for the exchange of mere use values.

(Marx 1973: 467)

7 Although the direct producer still continues to produce at least the greater part of his means of subsistence himself, a certain portion of this product must now be converted into commodities, must be produced as commodities. The character of the entire mode of production is thus more or less changed. It loses its independence, its detachment from social connection. The ratio of cost of production, which now comprises greater or lesser expenditures of money, becomes decisive.

(Marx 1971: 797)

8 The division of a product into a useful thing and a value *becomes practically important only when exchange* has acquired such an extension that useful articles are produced for the purpose of being exchanged *and their character as values has therefore to be taken into account, beforehand, during production.*

(Marx 1970b: 78)

9 "The intensity of exchange, its extent and structure, are determined by the development and structure of production … A definite production thus determines a definite consumption, distribution and exchange as well as *definite relations between these different moments*" (Marx 1973: 99).

10 This leads to placing major importance on exchange in precapitalist societies, since the conditions for its full development have been implicitly assumed. Commenting on this, Marx writes, "[I]t is simply wrong to place exchange at the center of a communal society as the original, constituent element" (Marx 1973: 103).

11 One portion of the surplus labor of the peasants, who work under the least favorable conditions, is bestowed gratis upon society and does not at all enter into the regulation of price of production or into the creation of value in general.

(Marx 1971a: 806)

12 [T]he product wholly assumes the form of a commodity only – as a result of the fact that the entire product has to be transformed into exchange value and that also all the ingredients necessary for its product enter it as commodities – in other *words it wholly becomes a commodity only with the development and on the basis of capitalist production.*

(Marx, 1971b: 74, emphasis added)

13 On the work of Bailey, Marx writes:

> Their "mind" [of buyers and sellers], their consciousness, may be completely ignorant of, unaware of the existence of, what in fact determines the value of their products or their products as values. They [buyers and sellers] are placed in relationships which determine their thinking, but they may not know it ... Economic categories are reflected in the mind in a very distorted fashion. He [Bailey] transfers the problem into the sphere of consciousness, because his theory has got struck.
>
> (Marx 1971b: 163)

14 Marx criticizes Smith and Ricardo for such anachronistic arguments:

> Although Adam Smith determines the value of commodities by the labor time contained in them, he then nevertheless transfers this determination of value in actual fact to pre-Smithian times ... [Ricardo] slips into the anachronism of allowing the primitive fisherman and hunter to calculate the value of implements.
>
> (Marx 1970a: 60)

15 Colletti states this well, "In conclusion: the law of value which is indeed a law of exchange of *equivalents*, as soon as it is realized and becomes *dominant*, reveals its true nature as the law of *surplus value* and capitalist appropriation" (1979: 95).

16 "Marx's theory of value is identical to his *theory of fetishism* and it is precisely by virtue of this element ... that Marx's theory differs in principle from the whole of classical political economy" (Colletti 1979: 77).

17 Marx subsequently writes of his discussion in Chapter 1 of Volume I, "At first the rights of property seemed to us to be based on a man's own labor. At least, some such *assumption* was necessary since only commodity owners with equal rights confronted each other" (1970b: 547, emphasis added).

18 This notation differs from that normally used, which is C-M-C rather than C→M→C. The latter is used because the first creates an ambiguity when one wants symbolic form for C minus M (C−M). The arrow symbol is used to mean "leads to" or "results in". When the "<" symbol has the standard meaning "greater than", and "<" is "less than".

19 The symbol ">" means "greater than". See Note 18.

20 This is the first time I have used the phrase "Marx's method", two words about which there is an enormous and contentious literature. Late in life, Marx wrote:

> I do not proceed from "concepts", hence neither from the "concept of value" ... What I proceed from is the simplest social form in which the product of labor presents itself in contemporary society, and this is the "*commodity*". This I analyze, initially in the *form in which it appears*. Here I find that on the one hand in its natural form it is a *thing for use*, alias a *use value*; on the other hand, a *bearer of exchange value*, and from this point of view it is itself an "exchange value". Further analysis of the latter shows me that exchange value is merely a "*form* of appearance", an independent way of presenting the *value* contained in the commodity, and then I start on the analysis of the latter ... I do not divide *value* into use value and exchange value as opposites into which the abstraction "value" splits up, but the *concrete social form* of the product of labor, the "*commodity*", is on the one hand, use value and on the other, "value", not exchange value, since the mere *form* of appearance is not its own *content*.
>
> (1881)

21 In Ricardian value theory labor is a source of expanded value, though some of his followers are of the opinion that it is not necessarily the only source. See Sraffa (1960), which while short is heavy going. The neoclassical value theory of value is based on marginal productivity analysis. There are many presentations of neoclassical value

theory. Relatively non-technical is the summary in Wikipedia, online, available at: http://en.wikipedia.org/wiki/Neoclassical_economics.

22 We abstract from the transformation of values into prices of production, which does not affect the argument.

23 Marx summarizes this contradiction between appearance and reality as follows:

> Production based on exchange value and the community based on the exchange of these exchange values – even though they seem ... to posit property as the outcome of *labor* alone, and to posit private property over the product of one's own labor as condition – and labor as general condition of wealth, *all presuppose and produce the separation of labor from its objective conditions.* This exchange of equivalents proceeds; it is only the *surface layer* [emphasis added] of a production which rests on the appropriation of alien labor *without exchange*, but with the *semblance of exchange.* This system of exchange rests on *capital* as its foundation, and when it is regarded in isolation from capital, then it is a mere illusion, but a necessary illusion. Thus there is no longer any ground for astonishment that the system of exchange values – exchange *of equivalents through* labor – turns into, or rather *reveals as its hidden* background, complete separation of labor and property.
>
> (Marx 1973: 509, emphasis added)

24 "The so-called primitive accumulation, therefore, is nothing *else* than the historical process of divorcing the producer from the means of production" (Marx 1970b: 668).

25 Political Economy confuses on principle two very different kinds of private property, of which one rests on the producer's own labor, the other on the employment of the labor of others. It forgets that the latter not only is the direct antithesis of the former, but absolutely grows on its death only.

> (*Capital*, Volume I: 716)

26 "[A]ccording to Marx, what makes this relation of equality *formal* and conceals real inequality is the fact that the property at the disposal of the worker (his own laboring *capacity*) is only property in *appearance*" (Colletti 1979: 94).

27 Marx called the increase in size of workplaces the concentration of capital, and the reduction in the number of competitors through takeovers and mergers the centralization of capital. We shall use these terms as Marx did, though in the non-Marxist literature the first is used to mean the second.

28 Engels' presupposition of a surplus product is also made by Meek, but more explicitly: "I assume that [a surplus product] is in fact produced, but that at first it is consumed by the direct producers" (1977: 133).

29 In a textual criticism of Robert Torrens, Marx took Torrens' phrase, "in that early period of society", and wrote, "that is, precisely when exchange value in general, the product as a commodity, is hardly developed at all, and consequently *when there is no law of value either*" (1971b: 73).

30 The chapter titles are: "Expropriation of the Agricultural Population from the Land" (Chapter 27); and "Bloody Legislation against the Expropriated, from the End of the 15th Century, Forcing down of Wages by Acts of Parliament" (Chapter 28). In his review and summary of Volume I of *Capital*, Engels does not refer to these chapters.

31 Some writers contemporary with Marx explicitly referred to a social contract agreement, and he criticized them for their benign view of capitalism,

> How then, in old Europe, was the expropriation of the laborer from his conditions of labor, i.e., the coexistence of capital and labor, brought about? By a social contract of a quite original kind. "Mankind have adopted a simple contrivance for promoting the accumulation of capital," which, of course, since the time of Adam, floated in their imagination ... "[T]hey have divided themselves into owners of

capital and owners of labor. This division was the result of concert and combination".

(Marx, 1970b: 718)

The quoted passages are from E.G. Wakefield, a British politician of the first half of the nineteen century.

3 Exploitation and surplus value

1 "[T]here is no way to reduce observable concrete labor to social abstract labor in advance, outside of the market which actually effects the reduction" (Gerstein 1976: 8).

2 It is a well-known empirical generalization for industrial capitalist countries that the variance in wage rates among industries increases in periods of low unemployment and decreases when accumulation slows or becomes negative.

3 See Weeks (1989: Chapter 8) on full employment in the neoclassical model.

4 May Day celebrates a mass mobilization of American workers in Chicago demonstrating for the eight-hour day in the 1880s.

5 When the 1981 version of this book was written, the workers' movements in both the United Kingdom and the United States were under severe political attack by the governments of Margaret Thatcher and Ronald Reagan. I confess to not seriously considering the possibility that those attacks would be so successful that capitalism in these two countries would revert to the raising of surplus value absolutely.

6

> Hence it is that in the history of capitalist production, the determination of what is a working day, presents itself as the result of a struggle, a struggle between collective capital, i.e., the class of capitalists, and collective labor, i.e., the working class.
>
> (Marx 1970b: 225)

7 This ignores the production of luxury commodities, defined as commodities that are not bought by workers nor are they inputs into the commodities workers buy.

8 The clearest analytical discussion of the rate of exploitation (surplus value) and the rate of profit is found in Saad-Filho: "Surplus value is the difference between the newly produced value and the value of labor-power, and profit is the difference between the value of the product and the value of the constant and variable capital" (2002: 82).

9 In its simplest manifestation, neoclassical production theory has two inputs or factors of production, labor and capital, which produce value added (see Weeks 1989: Chapters 2 and 10). "Capital" in the neoclassical sense is conceptually elusive. The simplest definition is means of production that lasts longer than one time period, though this is not without ambiguity.

10 Marx called this ratio the "average rate of profit", which is somewhat misleading, at least in English, because one typically thinks of an average as the summary of the parts. This is the opposite of what Marx intended by the term. In terms of algebra there are various ways to define the profit rate. I use the formula in *Capital*, Volume III.

11 The terms are: SV = surplus value, VC = variable capital, CC = constant capital, s′ = rate of surplus value, p = rate of profit:

$$s' = \frac{SV}{VC}$$

$$p = \frac{SV}{CC + VC}$$

$$p = \frac{s'}{(CC/VC) + 1}$$

The term CC/VC is the composition of capital.

12 This conclusion follows directly from the previous section, where the rate of surplus value was established as a society-wide phenomenon. As before, I abstract from differences in skills among workers.
13 The transformation of values into prices of production is a topic in the economics of Marx that has generated a literature far in excess of its importance. The near fixation on finding a technical solution to the transformation is ideological. Critics of Marx have for generations been under the misinterpretation that if they can demonstrate that no ideal solution exists, they have refuted Marx. Too many defenders of Marx have approached the transformation sharing the same misinterpretation. As a result, what appears as an obscure and arcane exercise in algebra epitomizes an ideological debate. The best treatment is by Fine *et al.* (1999).
14 In neoclassical terminology, technical efficiency refers to using the minimum inputs to produce an output. Economic efficiency refers to using the inputs in a combination that minimizes the cost of production. The distinction does not arise in Marx's analysis.
15 One might attempt to salvage the allocative efficiency argument by suggesting that differences in profit rates across industries which are the result of differences in the ratio of constant to variable capital indicate that the proportion in which commodities are produced is incorrect, and that the equalization of the rate of profit establishes "correct" proportions. This is an untenable argument, for Sraffa, among many others, demonstrated that the equalization of the rate of profit across industries is independent of the composition of output. See Sraffa (1960: Chapter 5).
16 I shall not deal with the details of the transformation process. See Gerstein (1976) and Fine *et al.* (1999).

4 Circuit of capital

1 A version of this chapter first appeared in *Science and Society* (Weeks 1983).
2 See, for example, Dornbusch and Fischer (1994: Chapters 8 and 9).
3 The standard model can be expressed as follows, with C representing all personal consumption (by workers and capitalists), I investment in fixed means of production and Y the money value of the net product:

$$Y = C + I$$

$$Y = bY$$

$$Y = bY + I$$

$$Y = I/(1 - b)$$

Investment in fixed means of production can be rendered endogenous (determined by the level or changes in the level of the net product). If so, the solution to the model is potentially unstable.
4 The analysis of circulation in Marx does not deny the existence of a multiplier process. It treats circulation in a manner in which this process does not appear.
5 Marx's treatment of fixed means of production anticipated the criticisms of neoclassical production theory by the Neo-Keynesians and Neo-Ricardians in what is called the "Cambridge Controversy". See Harcourt (1973).
6 Marx defines capital in Chapter 4 of Volume I of *Capital*, "The General Formula for Capital".
7 The term is frequently used in Volume II of *Capital*. See for example, Marx (1967: 62).
8 Because all of the elements of production are capital, including labor power, the term "capital-intensity of production", however measured, has no meaning within Marx's analysis. The "capital-intensity" of capitalist production is always unity for all production processes. To quote from Marx,

> The following general proposition applies to capital production: All products reach the market as commodities and therefore circulate for the capitalist as the commodity-form of his capital, regardless of whether these products must or can function in their bodily form, in accordance with their use values, as elements of production and therefore fixed or circulating elements of productive capital; or whether they can serve only as means of individual, not of productive, consumption.
>
> (1967: 213)

9 The expansion of capital, which is the expansion of value, appears as the expansion of money capital. The repetitive process of the circuit of capital promoted Marx to characterize capital as "self-expanding value", and "value in motion". See Marx (1970b: Chapter 4).

10

> For our present purpose this process of reproduction must be studied from the point of view of the replacement of the value as well as the substance of the individual component parts of C′ (commodity-capital). We cannot rest content any longer ... with the assumption that the individual capitalist can first convert the component parts of his capital into money by the sale of his commodities, and then reconvert them into productive capital ... In as much as these elements of production are by their nature material, they represent as much a constituent of the social capital as the individual finished product.
>
> (Marx 1967: 397)

11 Marx wrote: "Even on the basis of simple reproduction there takes place not merely a production of wages (variable capital) and surplus value, but direct production of new constant capital-value" (1967: 373).

12 See the appendix to this chapter where this point is demonstrated in detail.

13 The point was made by Marx in Chapter 21 of Volume II of *Capital.* Paul Sweezy (1966: 164) also demonstrated it, and Tarbuck showed it in a numerical example (1972: 271–4).

14 There are places in *The General Theory* that suggest that Keynes realized this limitation on his analysis. See the discussion in Weeks (1988).

15 "Now Adam Smith's first mistake consists in equating the *value* of the annual *product* to *the newly produced annual value*" (Marx 1967: 383, emphasis in original).

16 Commenting on Adam Smith's reduction of the total product to the net product, Marx wrote,

> His proof consists simply in the repetition of the same assertion. He admits, for instance, that the price of corn does not only consist of V+S [wages plus surplus value], but also of the price of the means of production consumed in the production of corn, hence of a capital-value not invested in labor-power by the farmer. But, he says, the prices of all these means of production resolve themselves into V+S, the same as the price of corn ... He refers us from one branch of production to another, and from that to a third. The contention that the entire price of commodities resolves itself "immediately" or "ultimately" into V+S would not be a hollow subterfuge only if he were able to demonstrate that the commodities whose price resolves itself immediately into C (price of consumed means of production)+V+S, are ultimately compensated by commodities which completely replace those "consumed means of production, and which are themselves produced by the mere outlay of variable-capital.
>
> (1967: 378)

17 Marx comments:

> Although the social capital is only equal to the sum of the individual capitals and for this reason the annual commodity-product (or commodity-capital) of society is

> equal to the sum of commodity-products of these individual capitals; and although therefore the analysis of value for *every individual commodity-capital must also be valid for the commodity-capital for all society – and actually proves valid in the end* [emphasis added] – the form of appearance which these component parts assume in the aggregate social process of reproduction is *different*.
>
> (1967: 373, emphasis in original)

18 A technical explanation of the theories of Malthus, Sismondi and other early writers can be found online, available at: http://homepage.newschool.edu/het//essays/classic/glut.htm.

19 An excellent analytical summary of these criticisms is found in Shaikh (1978), and more recent, Saad-Filho (2002: 100–2).

20 The clearest and most theoretically sophisticated presentation of the profit squeeze theory is Itoh (1978), which is critiqued in Weeks (1979).

21 The example is based on the following parameters. Define one unit of each sector's output as what one worker produces in one day. Let X denote the value of a unit of output:

$$X_1 = 0.6X_1 + 1;\ X_2 = 0.4X_1 + 1$$

Therefore, X_1,=2.5 labor days and X,=2.00 labor days. Let each worker consume 0.3 units of the consumption commodity per day. The value of labor power is 0.60 labor days, and the surplus value is (1 – 0.6) labor days per worker.

22 This aggregation, known as the "reduction problem", and of great concern to neo-Ricardian writers (e.g., Steedman 1977), is a reduction to homogeneous *concrete* labor.

23 This term is used by Himmelweit and Mohun (1978).

24 "[B]y exchange we equate as values our different products, by that very act we also equate, as human labour, the different kinds of labour expended upon them. We are not aware of this, nevertheless we do it" (Marx 1970b: 78–9).

25 As before, we assume that all income payments are distributed as wages and capitalist income.

26 It becomes the Marxian equivalent of the mainstream concept of full employment output.

27 This limited role of production is manifested in one of the influential post-war books on the labor process by a Marxist, in which the term surplus value appears on seven of 450 pages of text (Bravermann (1974).

28 These are his famous "reproduction schemes", Chapter 20 on simple reproduction and Chapter 21 on expanded reproduction. In these he abstracts from all qualitative changes which would make these accumulation schemes rather than reproduction schemes. The difference between reproduction and accumulation is treated in Chapters 8 and 9.

29 In the first edition of this book, all non-Marxian theories with the exception of Ricardian ones were placed in the category, "bourgeois economics". I discard this term for several reasons. First, its meaning is unclear, suggesting by implication that there exists "proletarian economics". If the terms "bourgeois economics" and "proletarian economics" have meaning, they must imply that there exists an economics purely in the interest of capital and other purely in the interest of labor. This is a dogmatic approach I once endorsed but now do not. Second, important differences exist among non-Marxist approaches to economics, and to include them all under "bourgeois economics" is to lose sight of analytically progressive and methodologically important insights in them. The somewhat vague and awkward term "mainstream" is used to avoid such a clear ideological and pejorative term.

30 This is explained in Weeks (1989: Chapter 1).

31 The term "neoclassical" refers to what was alleged to be a synthesis of the theory of

Keynes and of his opponents (whom he called "classicals"). In effect it involved almost completely abandoning the insights of Keynes. This was the dominant approach to theory after the mid-1970s. I use "Keynesian" to refer to those economists who sought to maintain the most important contributions of Keynes, which involved demonstrating the inherent instability of a capitalist economy. See Weeks (1989: Chapters 8–10).

32 This is not a minor problem. In 2004 estimated depreciation of fixed capital accounted for about 11 percent of the gross national product of the United States. This estimate derived from rules on taxation of business profits (Council of Economic Advisors 2006: 300).

33 This point is developed in greater detail in Weeks (1989: Chapter 1; and Weeks 1983).

34 Assuming the same level of employment is more than a convenience of presentation. It focuses the analysis on the production of surplus value, as discussed below (see Saad-Filho 2002: Chapter 7).

35 The table corresponding to the values underlying the exchange values in Table 4.a.3 is:

Sector	*CC*	*VC*	*SV*	*TV*
1 MP	150	50	50	250
2 MC	100	50	50	200

MP is means of production, MC is means of consumption and TV is total value.

36 The term "money units" is used instead of specifying a currency.

37 The rate of profit is calculated as $r=\pi/(CC+VC)$. This is the formula used by Marx. The principle of equalization of the profit rate and the distribution of surplus value as profit is unaffected by the specific formula one uses.

5 Commodity money

1 For important recent contributions to the understanding of money in capitalist society in the Marxian tradition see Lapavitsas (2003), Lapavitsas and Itoh (1999), Saad-Filho (2002) and Toporowski (2005). The most famous work is *Das Finanzkapital* (*Finance Capital*) by Rudolf Hilferding, published in 1919 and not translated to English until the end of century.

2 From the 1920s through the 1960s the government of the United States guaranteed the price of gold in the sense that it legally committed itself to purchase gold of a standard quality at a fixed price (US$23 until 1933, then US$35 per ounce). The government of Richard Nixon abandoned this legal obligation in 1970.

3 DeBrunhoff (1976) argued that the theory of money could and should be developed for all historical periods when money appears.

4 Marx rejected the "logical-historical" method explicitly:

> It would therefore be unfeasible and wrong to let the economic categories follow one another in the same sequence as that in which they were historically decisive. Their sequence is determined, rather, by their relation to one another in modern bourgeois society, which is precisely the opposite of that which seems to be their natural order or which corresponds to historical development.
>
> (Marx 1973: 107)

Elsewhere Marx wrote

> From the development of the law that price determines the mass of money in circulation, it follows that presuppositions are here involved which by no means

> apply to all stages of society: it is absurd, therefore, to take, for instance, the influx of money from Asia to Rome and its influence on Roman prices, and simply to put it beside modern commercial conditions.
>
> (Marx and Engels 1965: 106, emphasis added)

One can contrast this to Engels' view, "[T]he introduction of metallic money brought into operation a series of laws which remain valid for all countries and historical epochs in which metallic money is a medium of exchange" (1976: 187).

5
> The body of the commodity that serves as the equivalent, figures as the materialization of human labour in the abstract, and is at the same time the product of some specifically useful concrete labour. The concrete labour becomes, therefore, *the* medium for expressing abstract human labour.
>
> (Marx 1970b: 64)

6 "Hence, the second peculiarity of the equivalent form is, that concrete labour becomes the form under which its opposite, abstract human labour, manifests itself" (Marx 1970b: 64).

7 For uses of gold, see online, available at: http://geology.com/minerals/gold/uses-of-gold.shtml.

8 The absence of a legal link creates a potential instability treated in Chapter 7.

9 In 1941 A.C. Pigou, perhaps the most famous ideological and theoretical opponent of J.M. Keynes, published a book entitled, *The Veil of Money*. The monetary analysis of Keynes and his opponents is treated in Weeks (1989: Chapters 4 and 5).

10 The cost of producing the note is trivial and can be ignored.

11
> But if [exchange] is separated from *the* process [of circulation], the phase C-M [commodities for money] disappears and there remain only two commodities which confront each other, for instance iron and gold, whose exchange is not a distinct part of the cycle but is direct barter.
>
> (Marx 1970a: 90)

12 This abstracts from the transformation of values into prices of production, which does not affect the analysis. The deviation of price from value in order to achieve an equalization of profit rates is considered below.

13
> Because price is not equal to value, therefore the value-determining element, labour time, cannot be the element in which prices are expressed, because labour time would then have to express itself simultaneously as the determining and the non-determining element, as the equivalent and non-equivalent of itself.
>
> (Marx 1973: 140)

Marx makes the same point in *The Poverty of Philosophy.*

14 With this assumption wΛ2 is the systemwide value of labor power.

15 The clearest presentation of the transformation process that considers money is Fine *et al.* (1999).

16 As a superficial generalization, the hypothesis that the quantity of money determines the general level of prices is extremely old. David Hume was the first to state it in a systematically analytical manner in the middle of the eighteenth century in his defense of unregulated international trade (1955). The same argument was developed with greater theoretical rigor by David Ricardo fifty years later (1953).

17 In the quantity theory of money as set out by Hume in the eighteenth century, all money circulated except that held in anticipation of an immediate transaction (transactions demand for money). This simplification characterized non-Marxist monetary analysis for over 150 years until Keynes in the 1930s (Keynes 1936). Subsequently quantity-based money theory included the possibility of idle money determined by the interest rate. Introduction of an amount of idle money that is sensitive to interest rates

does not change the basic argument, which is that money is desired only for its use in exchange and, therefore, would not be held idle by a rational person. See Weeks (1989: Chapters 3, 7–9).

18 The four are (1) medium of exchange or means of circulation, (2) unit of account, (3) standard of deferred payment and (4) store of value. The second is the simple role of calibration. In a typical neoclassical discussion of "standard of deferred payment" one reads, "it is usually the same as the medium of exchange", and for "store of value", that "it would usually be the same as medium of exchange". See online, available at: http://william-king.www.drexel.edu/top/prin/txt/money/funx.html.

19 "As a means of circulation money therefore appears always as a means of purchase, and this obscures the fact that it fulfills different functions in the antithetical phases of the metamorphosis of commodities" (Marx 1970a: p. 98).

20 Recall that "→" means "leads to" or "results in", while ">" means "greater than".

21 The exception is Keynes, who placed stress on money as means of payment or setting debts (Zazzaro 2002).

22 "Purchase" is used to refer to the moment of exchange and "payment" to the money when the seller receives "money", with the latter defined as the general equivalent form of value.

6 Capital and money

1 The neoclassical theory of money is treated in Weeks 1989, Chapters 4 and 8. A revised edition of this book (Weeks 2009) can be found online, available at: http://jweeks.org.

2 This abstraction or simplification is no different in approach from that made in the neoclassical analysis of money, which begins by assuming that there is a money supply which is uniquely determined by what is usually called the "monetary authority". Every economist knows there is no such money supply. Central banks seek to influence the supply of credit created by commercial banks. The link between the actions to influence banks, such as the buying and selling of public debt, and the supply of money is a theory of bank behavior. The neoclassical argument is that the conclusions reached on the basis of the simple abstract of an administratively fixed money supply will not be contradicted in the more complex case that includes private banks. Similarly, assuming the money is gold is not an assertion of fact, but an assertion that the conclusions derived from this assumption will not be contradicted in more complicated cases.

3 To be precise, it is the inverse of the price of production of gold. Moseley (2005), who provides some of the most important insights into Marx's theory of money, calls this parameter "a" the "monetary equivalent of labour time". He abbreviates this as "MELT". He points out that the interpretation of the coefficient depends on whether money is endogenous or exogenous, which is the focus of this chapter.

4 More precisely stated, the abstract necessary labor time objectified in gold determines the price of each commodity, and general price level is the average of all prices weighted by the quantities exchanged at those prices.

5 Shaikh called this the "pure supply effect", uncomplicated by a change in the values of gold or other commodities (1979). Marx wrote,

> Any scholarly investigation of the relation between the volume of means of circulation and movements in commodity prices must assume that the value of the monetary material be given ... It is, of course, quite possible to increase the supply of precious metals while their costs of production remain unchanged. On the other hand a decrease in their value ... will in the first place be attested only by an increase in their supply.
>
> (1970a: 160)

6 "For Ricardo, the regulation of the value of money by its quantity is a particular case in which the adjustment of the market price to the natural price requires a long period of time" (Takenaga 2003: 73). "Natural price" in this context means the price that is determined by the labor time embodied in a commodity. Ricardo stated clearly that the quantity of a money commodity is determined by its value, "The quantity of money that can be employed in a country must depend on its value" (1953: 352).

7 From the point of view of the producers of all but the money commodity, their circuit has three phases ("moments" Marx called them), M→C ... P ... C′→M′. These are capital advanced (M→C), production (P) and realization (C′→M′) The producer of the money commodity has no realization moment, because money *is* realized abstract labor.

8 This was the principle criticism of Keynes of the quantity theory. See Weeks (1989: Chapter 6, section 3). The criticism is central to the analysis of so-called post-Keynesians.

9 Marx, 1970b: 121.

10 "Prices are thus high or low not because more or less money is in circulation, but there is more or less money in circulation because prices are high or low. This is one of the principal economic laws" (Marx 1970a: 105–6).

11 A practical example of the operation of such a rule is the "currency" board monetary regime adopted in several developing countries at the end of the twentieth century and into the twenty-first. An infamous case was Argentina whose government abandoned the regime in 2002 after a disastrous economic performance.

12 The "denationalisation of money" is proposed in Hayek (1978). Banks issued their own valueless money in the United States before the Civil War (1861–1865), resulting in such monetary chaos that the federal government established a monopoly over fiat money. See brief discussion online, available at: http://www.journalofantiques.com/June04/coinsjune04.htm.

13 The advance of money as constant capital realizes the means of production, and the variable capital, through the hands of the working class, realizes the articles of consumption. See discussion in *Capital*, Volume II, Chapters 20 and 21 (Marx 1967).

14 Marx treats this in *Capital*, Volume II, Chapter 27 (1967).

15
> The movement and changing forms of the circulating commodities thus appear as the movement of money mediating the exchange of commodities ... The movement of the circulation process is therefore represented by the movement of money, i.e., by the *circulation of money.*
>
> (Marx 1970a: 100–1)

16
> The circulation process will, on the other hand, absorb or as it were digest any number of paper notes, since irrespective of the gold title borne by the token of value when entering circulation, it is compressed to a token of the quantity of gold which could circulate instead.
>
> (Marx 1970a: 121)

17 I abstract from the division of capital into money capital and productive capital, which implies the functional division between money capitalists and industrial capitalists. The expansion and contraction of symbols of money can affect the division of surplus value between the two. This is considered in the following chapter, with interest-bearing capital.

18 The price-deflated wage falls, leaving the level of employment suboptimal. Whether one considers the pure quantity theory, when the money supply has no effect on savings and investment, or more complicated variations is of no analytical consequence, except in the case of the liquidity trap. In both cases, increases in the money in circulation stimulate increases in output. Perhaps the major difference between the monetary analysis of Keynes and that of the quantity theory was his analysis of why valueless money would be held idle. See Weeks (1989: Chapter 6).

19 Marx repeatedly refers to the process of competition causing relationships to appear as their opposite (see, for example, Marx 1973: 657).

20 From "A Scandal in Bohemia".

21 Ricardo might be interpreted as unsuccessfully attempting to have a commodity-based monetary analysis that incorporated a quantity element. Ricardo stated clearly that the quantity of a money commodity is determined by its value, "The quantity of money that can be employed in a country must depend on its value" (1953: 352). His use of a monetary mechanism in the analysis of trade ("comparative advantage" theory) is discussed in Shaikh (1979).

22 In the analysis of the circuit of capital in Volume II of *Capital*, the turnover rate of money is one. This is not an assumption, but results from Marx's choice of analytical time, the production period.

23 Walras' analysis of general equilibrium (1926) is discussed in Weeks (1989: Chapters 3 and 11). Keynes explicitly argued for including all transactions in the appendix on "User Cost" in *The General Theory* (1936), and is treated in detail in Weeks (1989: Annex to Part I). The input–output distinction is irrelevant for the general equilibrium analysis of Walras because buyers and sellers appear in the market with commodities previously produced. The theoretical inconsistencies that result from treating the circulation of capital as the circulation of value added are treated in Chapter 4 and the appendix to that chapter.

24 By making this assumption one avoids two complications. The more immediately important is that associated with establishing the neutrality of money; i.e., that at full utilization of resources the relationship between changes in the quantity of the means of circulation and changes each commodity price is strictly proportional (Weeks 1989: Chapter 8). Of more profound methodological significance is that assuming one commodity eliminates means of production, so that the total price of the only commodity is P=[wages]+[profit], as discussed in the appendix to Chapter 4.

25 The composite commodity is, in effect, value added which in the simple case is national income See appendix to Chapter 4.

26 This proportionality is an extremely important analytical outcome in neoclassical analysis, "the neutrality of money", but proves very difficult to establish theoretically. Its importance lies in its reactionary implications for policy. For example, if changes in the quantity of money have no impact of relative prices, then full employment is consistent with any price level, even a lower one achieved by a deflationary process. Even with one commodity, neutrality does not hold if the financial system includes bonds (Weeks 1989: Chapters 7 and 8).

27 This possibility was central to the critique by Keynes of the monetary theory of his time, a theory which changed very little as a result of that critique.

28 A full explanation of this complication is beyond the scope of this appendix. To state the problem concisely, the neoclassical money market adjustment process implied by PY=vM is inconsistent with the aggregate demand adjustment process implied by the necessity to equate consumption plus investment to the supply of the single commodity. This inconsistency is summarized in the term the "False Dichotomy". "Dichotomy" refers to the analytical separation of the two markets. Resolving this contradiction within neoclassical monetary theory requires introduction of at least one variable that mediates between the money market and the commodity market. The contradiction was pointed out in a rigorous manner by the neoclassical Pigou (1941).

29 Developing in detail the neoclassical analysis of the money supply is unnecessary for this chapter. The process is one in which the monetary authority (central bank) determines the money base, which is sometimes called "high powered money". From this monetary base, banks create credit in a multiple determined by the amount of the money base that banks must hold as assets (the reserve ratio). This process is based on several restrictive assumptions, including that bank maximizing behavior implies

that reserves will not be held idle. The issue of banks and idle money is considered in a famous article by the Keynesian James Tobin (1958).

30 Graziani provides a clear and concise explanation for why the neoclassicals are unable to account for the existence of money (2003: Introduction). This theoretical impasse provides perhaps the clearest demonstration of the analytical failings of mainstream monetary theory: people use money in all aspects of life, it takes many forms and neoclassical analysis struggles to account for its existence.

31 Two neoclassical proposals to account for money further indicate the theoretical quandary, that money is used because many commodities are not adequately divisible, and because a seller may be unable to find a buyer that wants to trade the commodity she/he seeks. Both problems imply market failure, which opens the door not only to money but to public intervention also.

7 Credit, crises and capital

1 "Insofar as actual payments have to be made, money does not serve as a circulating medium, but as the individual incarnation of social labor, as the independent form of existence of exchange value, as the universal commodity" (Marx 1970b: 137).

2 A detailed treatment of credit is found in Lapavitsas (2003: Chapters 3 and 4).

3 "This contradiction comes to head in those phases of individual and commercial crises which are known as monetary crises" (Marx 1970b: 137).

4

> The capital relation during the process of production arises only because it is inherent in the act of circulation, in the different fundamental economic conditions in which buyer and seller confront each other, in their class relation. It is not money which by its nature creates this wealth; it is rather the existence of this relation which permits of the transformation of a mere money function into a capital-function.
>
> (Marx 1967: 32)

5 As shown in quotations cited later in this chapter, Marx used the term "money capitalists" for those providing credit. This usage can cause confusion due to the use of "money capital" specifically for capital advanced. The term "financial capital" avoids this duplication in usage, though it carries connotations of its own. Lenin referred to "finance capital" as the "highest stage" of capitalist development, using it synonymously with "imperialism". Here and for the rest of this book, financial capital refers to the institutions of the financial sector of capitalist economies and to the forms the capital in that sector take, so-called financial products.

6

> [H]oarding takes place in the simple circulation of commodities long before this is based on capitalist production. The quantity of money existing in society is always greater than the part of it in actual circulation … We find [in capitalism] here again the same hoards and the same formation of hoards, but now as an element immanent in the capitalist process of production.
>
> (Marx 1967: 497)

7 Claims of ownership are "stocks" and the payments to them are "dividends". Mandel provides a summary of Marx's writing on stock companies (1983). The debt that companies issue, bonds, carries no claim on ownership.

8 Among non-Marxist economists, Keynes was one of the first to recognize explicitly this general law of capitalist causality. His most famous example was the "paradox of thrift". If all people attempt to save more there will be no change (or a decline) at the aggregate level because of the resulting lack of demand that causes income to fall. The paradox of thrift is a fallacy of composition.

9 See Marx's discussion of usury (1971a: Chapter XXXVI).

10 See the discussion in Hilton's introduction (Hilton 1976), and in Polanyi's famous

chapter, "The Fictitious Commodities: Land, Labor and Capital" (Polanyi 1944). Insightful on non-capitalist exchange is the discussion of "gifts" in Lapavitsas (2003).

11 We ignore merchant's capital and fictitious capital before the capitalist epoch. This was relevant to a very limited portion of hoarded wealth and is part of an analysis of the historical role of merchant's capital not productive capital (Marx 1971a: Chapter 20).

12 As explained in previous chapters, for capital as a whole C′→M′ and M→C are the same step. The sale of means of production is the realization moment for some capitals and simultaneously the conversion of money capital into productive capital for others. For the consumption commodities the process is more complex because they are directly bought by workers.

13

> Whereas the surplus product directly produced and appropriated by the capitalists is the real basis of the accumulation of capital ... although it does not actually function in this capacity until it reaches the hands of [industrial capitalists], it is on the contrary absolutely unproductive in its chrysalis stare of money, as a hoard and virtual money capital in process of gradual formation, runs parallel the process of production in this form, but lies outside of it. It is a dead weight of capitalist production.
>
> (Marx 1967: 502)

14 This redistribution is not related to the transformation of surplus value into profit, which was described in a previous chapter.

15

> With the absolute increase of the value of the annually reproduced virtual money-capital its segmentation also becomes easier, so that it is more rapidly invested in any particular business, either in the hands of the same capitalist or in those of others ... By segmentation of money capital is meant here that it is wholly detached from the parent stock in order to be invested as new money capital in a new and independent business.
>
> (Marx 1967: 502)

16 In the 1990s and 2000s the term "social capital" was trivialized by its use in mainstream social science writings, where it was defined as individual or group networking. This use of the term is dissected in Fine (2001).

17 In the late twentieth century mainstream social science trivialized the term "social capital" by using it to mean a person's links to other people.

18 This passage indicates that "managerial capitalism", described by institutional economists in the 1930s, was anticipated by Marx over half a century before (Berle and Means 1932).

19 The ascendancy may take the specific form of ownership of industry by banking interests, as Lenin suggested in *Imperialism* (1974).

20

> With the development of social production the means of production cease to be means of private production and products of private production, and can thereafter be only means of production in the hands of associated producers ... [T]his expropriation appears within the capitalist system in a contradictory form, as appropriation of social property by a few.
>
> (Marx 1971a: 440)

21 "The use value of the loaned capital lies in its being able to serve as capital and, as such, to produce the average profit under average conditions" (Marx 1971a: 352).

22 The distinction between circulating capital, advanced for labor power and intermediate commodities, and fixed capital, advanced for machinery and buildings, is treated in Chapter 10.

23 "In the case of other commodities the use value is ultimately consumed.... In contrast, the commodity capital is peculiar in that its value and use value nor only remain intact but also increase, through consumption of it" (Marx 1971a: 352).

24 CDOs are financial assets backed by other financial assets, which can be bonds, loans and a bewildering array of less familiar forms of representations of wealth such as over-the-counter securities (OTCs). For definitions, see online, available at: http://financial-dictionary.thefreedictionary.com/CDO.

25 > Interest, signifying the price of capital, is from the outset quite an irrational expression. The commodity in question has a double value, first a value, and then a price different from its value, while price represents the expression of value in money.
>
> (Marx 1971a: 334)

26 A full treatment of neoclassical theories of interest is beyond the scope of this book. An excellent survey of neoclassical and non-neoclassical theories is found in Toporowski (2005). A Marxian treatment is in Lapavitsas (2003). The inconsistencies arising in short term macroeconomic models (equivalent to Marx's simple reproduction) are explained in Weeks (1989: Chapters 5–7). To state the neoclassical theory simply, interest is the payment to induce people to save, or in more obscure words, the rate of time preference. A useful summary that minimizes jargon is online, available at: http://homepages.uel.ac.uk/K.Bain/interest.html.

27 If a capitalist borrows at 5 percent, and the price of what he or she sells rises by more than 5 percent, the real rate of interest is negative. Nominal interest rates can be zero, as in Japan in the early 2000s, See online, available at: http://news.bbc.co.uk/1/hi/business/1228152.stm.

28 > It is indeed only the separation of capitalists into money-capitalists and industrial capitalists that transforms a portion of the profit into interest, that generally creates the category of interest; and it is only the competition between these two kinds of capitalists which creates the rate of interest ... If all capital were in the hands of the industrial capitalists there would be no such thing as interest and rate of interest.
>
> (Marx 1971a: 370, 379)

29 If rent, the payment to owners of land, is included, there are four categories. The definitive treatment of Marx's theory of rent is in Fine (1979).

30 > If we inquire further as to why the limits of a mean rate of interest cannot be deduced from general laws, we find the answer lies simply in the nature of interest. It is merely a part of the average profit. The same capital appears in two roles – as loanable capital in the lender's hands and as industrial or commercial capital in the hands of the functioning capitalist. But it functions just once and produces profit just once. In the production process itself the nature of capital as loanable capital plays no role ... Two entirely different elements – labor power and capital – act as determinants in the division between surplus value and wages ... these are functions of two independent variables which limit one another, and it is their qualitative difference that is the source of the quantitative division of the produced value ... Nothing of the kind occurs in the case of interest. Here the qualitative differentiation ... proceeds rather from the purely quantitative division of the same sum of surplus value.
>
> (Marx 1971a: 364)

31 Marx's terms were "average" for capital as a whole, and "general" when referring to many sectors. This is not normal English usage, but the specific words are not important. The fundamental point is that the rate for capital as a whole is analytically and socially prior to the rate in each sector.

32 "The general rate of profit, however, appears only as the lower limit of profit, not as an empirical, directly-visible form of the actual rate of profit" (Marx 1971a: 367).

33 "Interest-bearing capital is capital as property as distinct from capital as a function" (Marx 1971a: 379).

34 In relation to [the industrial capitalist] interest appears, therefore, as the mere fruit of owning capital, of capital as such abstracted from the reproduction process of capital ... while profit of enterprise appears to him as the exclusive fruit of the functions which he performs with the capital ... a performance which appears to him as his own activity ... This qualitative distinction is by no means merely a subjective notion of the money-capitalist, on the one hand, and the industrial capitalist, on the other. It rests upon an objective fact, for interest flows to the money-capitalist ... who is the mere owner of capital.

(Marx 1971a: 378)

35 Just as these mutual advances of producers and merchants make up the real foundation of credit, so does the instrument of their circulation, the bill of exchange, form the basis of credit-money paper ... These do not rest upon the circulation of money, be it metallic or government-issued paper money.

(Marx 1971a: 400–1)

36 This limit is set by the inputs produced in previous periods, not by the available labor except in rare cases. A debate over whether the availability of labor is important in setting the limit to the expansion of capital, see Itoh (1978) and Weeks (1979).

37 In times of stringency, the demand for loan capital is a demand for means of payment and nothing else: it is by no means a demand for money as a means of purchase. At the same time, the rate of interest may rise very high, regardless whether real capital, i.e., productive and commodity capital, exists in abundance or is scarce. The demand for means of payment is mere demand for convertibility into money.

(Marx 1971a: 515)

38 The quotation is from Warren Buffet, one of the world's richest men, who also called them "time bombs", online, available at: http://www.fintools.com/docs/Warren%20Buffet%20on%20Derivatives.pdf.

39 [W]e must proceed from the assumption that the money capitalist and the industrial capitalist really confront one another not just as legally different persons, but as persons playing entirely different roles in the reproduction process ... The one merely loans [capital], the other employs it productively.

(Marx 1971a: 372)

40 In a system of production, where the entire continuity of the reproduction process rests upon credit, a crisis must obviously occur – a tremendous rush for means of payment – when credit suddenly ceases and only cash payments have validity. At first glance, therefore, the whole crisis seems to be merely a credit and money crisis.

(Marx 1971a: 490)

41 In times of a squeeze, when credit contracts or ceases entirely, money suddenly stands as the only means of payment and true existence of value in absolute opposition to all other commodities. Hence, the universal depreciation of commodities, the difficulty or even impossibility of transforming them into money, i.e., their own purely fantastic form. Secondly, credit-money itself is only money to the extent that it absolutely takes the place of actual money to the amount of its nominal value. With a drain on gold its convertibility, i.e., its identity with actual gold, becomes problematic. Hence coercive measures, raising the rate of interest, etc., for the purpose of safeguarding the condition of this convertibility.

(Marx 1971a: 517)

42 The complete passage is:

A depreciation of credit-money ... would unsettle all existing relations. Therefore, the value of commodities is sacrificed for the purpose of safeguarding the fantastic

> and independent existence of this value in money ... In former modes of production, this does not occur because, on the narrow basis upon which they stand, neither credit nor credit-money can develop greatly.
>
> (Marx 1971a: 517)

43 In one of his rare theoretical references to the state, Marx wrote,

> [Social capital] is the abolition of the capitalist mode of production within the capitalist mode of production and hence a self-dissolving contradiction, which *prima facie* represents a mere phase of transition to a new form of production. It manifests itself as such a contradiction in its effects. It establishes a monopoly in certain spheres and thereby requires state interference.
>
> (Marx 1971a: 438)

This passage is also one of the few times in his later works when he alludes to the development of a post-capitalist society.

8 Competition among capitals

1 An attempt to adapt the Baran and Sweezy (1967) analysis of monopoly capitalism to the context of globalization is found in Bellamy Foster (2002).
2 Smith wrote, "In general, if any branch of trade, or any division of labor, be advantageous to the public, the freer and more general the competition, it will always be the more so" (1776: Book II: Chapter 2, p. 329, paragraph 106).
3 The following part of the chapter draws on the first chapter of Weeks (2009).
4 Though never refuted, textbooks rarely mention the theory of the second best. The ideological nature of neoclassical economics is demonstrated in the profession's practice of discarding what is inconvenient for the theory.
5 The more sophisticated neoclassical approach stressed the potential for new competitors in a sector (Kenen 1994: 132). This does not alter the basic argument that competition derives from the number of competitors.
6 The absence of an analysis of price competition in neoclassical theory is treated by Rothschild, whose 1947 article in the *Economic Journal* is in my opinion the most insightful discussion of capitalist competition by any non-Marxist.
7 The contradiction between the neoclassical definition of competition and the forms of competition has been treated insightfully in Clifton (1977).
8 Definition does not imply existence. Unicorns come to mind: one can define them as four-legged horse-like creatures with a single horn, and elaborate the anatomical characteristics in some detail. Following neoclassical logic, one would conclude that study of the non-existent unicorn provides powerful insights into the nature of horses.
9 This argument is valid only if the capitalists in each product line use a production process that has a minimum cost point. For example, if unit costs of production were constant, producing more would always increase profit, which would imply that one producer could supply an entire market. A minimum cost point requires that the unit cost of production function be governed by a specific form of the "law of diminishing returns", in which unit costs first fall, then rise as output increases (the function is U-shaped). Diminishing returns requires "factor substitution", in the analysis of which there is an input designated as "capital" which is fixed in amount. The critique of this theory of production lies beyond the scope of this book (for critiques, see Harcourt 1973; Fine 1980).
10 A market-by-market approach is called "partial equilibrium analysis".
11 Inversion of fact and fantasy is enshrined in official neoclassical terminology. Following the proposal of Hicks in the 1930s, exchanges that result in excess demands and excess supplies are called "false trading", with the implication that what happens in the imaginary market is "true". Here one has entered into a quasi-religious realm, in

which the observed world is false, and the world of the imagination is true. Faced with the intractable problem of clearing markets even in theory, Hamlet's famous lament comes to mind, "O cursed spite, That I was ever born to set it right" (*Hamlet*, Act I, scene 2).

12 This example involves invalid simplifications: first, in a Walrasian market, farmers are price-takers, so it is against the rules for them to offer any prices; and, second, the argument is partial equilibrium, not general equilibrium. It is possible that notional excess supply of potatoes at a "false trading" price set might transubstantiate into a cleared market for potatoes at a higher price in the general equilibrium price set.

13 There are others who did not treat competition as a harmonious process, such as Josef Schumpeter and his concept of the "creative destruction" of competition, and Gunnar Myrdal in his argument for "cumulative causation". While interesting, these contributions did not achieve a coherent alternative analysis of competition.

14 Baran and Sweezy wrote "the Marxian analysis of capitalism still rests in the final analysis on the assumption of a competitive economy". They continue, "[Marx] never attempted to investigate what would at the time have been a hypothetical system characterised by the prevalence of large-scale monopoly" (1967: 405).

15 "[In competition] all determinants appear in a position which is the *inverse* of their position in capital in general. Here price is determined by labour, here labour is determined by price, *etc., etc.*" (Marx 1973: 657).

16 The so-called utopian socialists, Sismondi and Proudhon being the most famous, looked back to a pre-monopolistic competitive era. Marx did not believe that there had once existed, or could ever exist, a society of free producers, each small and independent, each pursuing his or her interests. Marx scorned such ideas as illusion. He argued that this view of capitalism and of competition was an idealized description of the historical conditions that freed capital from feudal constraints to its self-expansion presented as natural law. A similarly critical position was taken by Lenin (1972).

17 Marx wrote:

> Because competition appears as the dissolution of compulsory guild membership, government regulation, internal tariffs and the like within a country ... [I]n short, as the negation of the limits and barriers peculiar to the stages of production proceeding capital ... it has [therefore] never been examined even for this merely negative side, this, its merely historical side, and this had led at the same time to the even greater absurdity of regarding it as the collision of unfettered individuals who are determined only by their own interests ... and hence as the absolute mode of existence of free individuality in the sphere of consumption and of exchange. Nothing can be more mistaken.
>
> (1973: 649)

18 "Competition between capitals is predicated upon the circuit of capital-in-general ... for without the relations between *capital and labour* encompassed by these simple circuits competition *between capitals* cannot exist" (Fine and Harris 1979: 14).

19 Marx's discussion of the subsumption of labour to capital was included in Volume I of *Capital* as an appendix to the 1976 Penguin addition.

20 Commenting on Adam Smith's description of competition as the absence of extra-economic constraints to the pursuit of self-interest, Marx wrote: "But competition is very far from having only this historical significance, or merely being *this negative* force. Free competition is the relation of capital to itself as another capital, i.e., the real conduct of capital as capital" (1973: 650).

21 Marx criticized Ricardo on this issue:

> Ricardo presuppose[d] the absolute predominance of free competition in order to be able to study and to formulate the adequate laws of capital ... What Ricardo has thereby admitted, despite himself, is the *historic nature* of capital, and the

> limited character of free competition, which is first the free movement of capital and nothing else.
>
> (1973: 651)

22 In *The Poverty of Philosophy*, Marx gives the following quotation from Prouhdon: "Monopoly is the inevitable doom of competition, which engenders it by continual negation of itself ... Monopoly is the natural opposite of competition." (Marx and Engels 1976: 194).

23 This quotation suggests that Marx anticipated more developed forms of capital, such as the so-called monopoly capitalism.

24 Marx used the term "average rate of profit" to refer to capital as a whole, and the "general rate of profit" for that rate generalized to each industry. This terminology is potentially confusing, because one thinks of an average as determined by its parts. In this case the "average" exists independently of its parts. For that reason I use "aggregate rate of profit" for Marx's "average rate of profit". I use "general rate of profit" as Marx did, the manifestation of the aggregate rate of profit in each sector and enterprise.

25 Neoclassical economics explicitly excludes uneven development within sectors by the "representative firm" assumption. This assumption, combined with another, that technical change is a "long run" phenomenon, trivializes competition. In the "short run" all enterprises are identical, and in the "long run" they all introduce technical changes simultaneously.

9 Fixed capital and circulation

1 If the forest is sold at a profit due to rising land or timber prices prior to cutting of trees it appears that value is created without any input of human labor. However, forests are not capital in any sense, except a relation of ownership, that they could be sold for money. The fact that seeds grow into trees implies nothing more than that labor is not the source of all wealth, as Marx pointed out in his critique of the Gotha program.

2 "Fixed constant capital does not circulate in use value form, but it is merely its value that circulates, and this takes place gradually, piecemeal, in proportion as it passes from it to the product, which circulates as a commodity" (Marx 1967: 161).

3

> In the performance of its function that part of the value of an instrument of labor which exists in its bodily form constantly decreases, while that which is transformed into money constantly increases until the instrument of labor is at last exhausted and its entire value, detached from the corpse, is converted into money. Here the particularity in the turnover of this element of productive capital becomes apparent. The transformation of its value into money keeps pace with the pupation into money of the commodity which is the carrier of its value. But its conversion from the money-form into a use value proceeds separately from the re-conversion of the commodities into other elements of their production and is determined by its own period of reproduction, that is, by the time during which the instrument of labor wears out.
>
> (Marx 1967: 161)

4 A portion of the value of fixed means of production "is continuously circulated and converted into money as a part of the value of the commodities without being re-converted into its original bodily form" (Marx 1967: 161).

5 The income distribution argument is the simplest: the larger the income share of the rich the more probable is it that the rich will not spend it all, with the result that commodities go unsold. This explanation played an important role in non-Marxist treatments of imperialism (Hobson 1902). In more analytical explanations the level of

investment is viewed as unstable, determined by profit expectations rendered volatile by uncertainty (Gordon 1986).

6 In this discussion I ignore those "innovations" by capitalists whose purpose is to render existing means of production useless, so-called planned obsolescence. This is a tool of capitalist competition, especially for commodities sold to households, but does not affect the current discussion.

7 This difference in the behavior of the elements of productive capital in the labor-process forms however only the point of departure of the difference between fixed and non-fixed capital, not this difference itself. That follows from the fact alone that this different behavior [material lifespan] exists in equal measure under all modes of production, capitalist and non-capitalist. To this different behavior of material elements corresponds however the transmission of value to the product, and to this in turn corresponds the replacement of value by the sale of the product ... Hence capital is not called fixed capital because it is fixed in the instruments of labor, but because a part of its value laid out in instruments of labor remains fixed in them, while the other part circulates as a component part of the value of the product.

(Marx 1967: 201–2)

8 In all these cases the point of issue is *how* a given value, laid out in the process of production of commodities, whether it be wages, the price of raw materials, or that of instruments of labor, is transferred to the product, hence is circulated by the product and returned to its starting-point by the sale of the product, or is replaced [through circulation].

(Marx 1967: 230)

9 [C]ompetition compels the replacement of the old instruments of labor by new ones before the expiration of their material life, especially when decisive changes occur. Such premature renewals of factory equipment on a rather large social scale are mainly enforced by catastrophes or crises.

(Marx 1967: 174)

10 This does not make the economics of Keynes "wrong". On the contrary, Keynes provided the analytical basis for the analysis and policy management of short term fluctuations of capitalist economies. However, his explanation of what cause those fluctuations was not correct.

11 The minimal limit of the selling price of a commodity is its cost price. If it is sold under its cost price, the expended constituent elements of productive capital cannot be fully replaced out of the selling price. If this process continues, the value of the advanced capital disappears. From this point of view alone, the capitalist is inclined to regard the cost price as the true inner value of the commodity, because it is the price required for the hare conservation of his capital.

(Marx 1967: 38)

12 This way in which surplus value is transformed into the form of profit by way of the rate of profit is, however, a further development of the inversion of subject and object that takes place already in the process of production.

(Marx 1967: 45)

13 Smith used the example of a pin factory to show how the division of labor increases productivity. The passage in which Smith describes his visit to a pin factory can be read online, available at: http://www.divisionoflabour.com/archives/000006.php.

14 The mathematical proof of this is found in Okishio (1961). Another way to put the general principle is that the requirement for introducing an innovation, that the cost price falls, ensures that the profit rate will rise both for the individual capitalist and for capital as a whole when the innovation is generally adopted.

15 Whereas the development of fixed capital extends the length of this [material] life on the one hand, it is shortened on the other by the continuous revolution in the means of production, which likewise incessantly gains momentum with the development of the capitalist mode of production.

(Marx 1967: 188)

16 See Appendix to Chapter 4 for discussion of "final demand" and "final goods".
17 In a net product framework consumption is a function of income, which is determined by exogenous expenditures, one of which is investment. Consumption could be an independent source of insufficient demand only on the basis of a judgment that the propensity to consume out of income is too low. The existence of saving (non-expenditure) is not in itself a source of demand failure. If one makes the typical assumption that workers spend all their incomes and only capitalists save, the explanation for insufficient demand would be why capitalists do not invest more.
18 All the solutions are a variation on the so-called real balance effect. The real balance effect is also designed to rescue neoclassical full employment from two famous Keynesian adjustment difficulties, the "liquidity trap" and the "inconsistency between saving and investment". See Weeks (1989: Chapters 6, 7 and 8).
19 See section on Liejonhufvud in Chapter 11, Weeks (1989).
20 The secular stagnation hypothesis was further developed by Hansen (1938).
21 Smith argued that the competition among enterprises drives profits to zero in the long run. This explanation has the obvious mistake of lacking a theory of value and profit. Ricardo believed that the productivity of land could not keep pace with the growth of the industrial labor force, leading to a secularly rising relative price of food. This would redistribute profit to agricultural rent: if, as he assumed that rentiers do not invest, growth comes to an end when all profit has been redistributed to rent. This analysis has many mistakes, not least of which are the arbitrary assumptions about technical change in agriculture and landlord behavior.
22 Found in Samuelson (1939), which is not a theory or even an analysis, but an algebraic curiosity.
23 The discussion is in Mill (1867: 512ff.). Toporowski provides a clear analysis of Mill and other nineteenth century English writers (2005: Chapter 2). See also Forget (1990).
24 The most important of these are treated in Toporowski (2005).

10 Accumulation and crises

1 For a discussion of why Adam Smith did not deal with the problem of general overproduction, see Marx (1968: 484ff.).
2 As surprising as it may be, almost no non-Marxist economists consider capitalism to be fundamentally different from previous societies in which exchange was common. A rare exception is the Keynesian Liejonhufvud:

> [T]he dynamic properties of an economic system depend upon what I will call its "transaction structure". That labor services are sold for money and that households obtain their consumption goods in exchange for money is one aspect of the transaction structure in Keynes' system. In an economy of self-employed artisans [the problem of] unemployment cannot appear.
>
> (1968: 90)

3 Shaikh (1978) provides a brief survey of crisis theories, Marxist and non-Marxist.
4 Shaikh (1978) explains the analytical function of expanded reproduction in his discussion of underconsumption theories.
5 In neoclassical theory, the short run is the period over which the enterprise cannot change its plant and equipment. The long run is the period during which fixed means of production can be changed. Whatever the analytical usefulness of this distinction,

it is irrelevant to the actual passage of time, as neoclassical theorists stress. The long run exists only as a concept, which is why "long run cost curves" are often called "planning curves". I treat the role of theoretical and chronological time in macroeconomic theory in Weeks (1989: Chapter 3).

6 Neo-Ricardians argue that in such a situation it is not possible to define the value of a commodity, and, given their definition of value, they are correct. When there are many techniques of production, the labor embodied in a commodity is conceptually indeterminate. Steedman (1977).

7 [S]ince the circulation process of capital is not completed in one day, but extends over a fairly long period until the capital returns to it original form, since this period coincides with the period within which market prices equalize with [prices of production], great upheavals and changes take place in the productivity of labor and therefore also in the *real value* of commodities.

(Marx 1968: 445)

In the original, Marx wrote "cost prices" where I have inserted "prices of production". Cost price does not include profit, so it is obvious that he meant "prices of production".

8 "The *comparison* of value in one period with the value or the same commodities in a later period is no scholastic illusion ... but rather forms the fundamental principle of the circulation process of capital" (Marx 1968: 495).

9 A decline in the value of the commodities workers buy need not cheapen variable capital if the standard of living of the working class rises. These are two separate processes, one the adjustment of unit values (competition among capitalist enterprises), the other adjustment of the standard of living (competition between labor and capital). Their relationship to each other is extremely complex. See Weeks (1979).

10 The contradiction, to put it in a very general way, consists in that the capitalist mode of production involves a tendency towards absolute development of the productive forces, regardless of the social conditions under which capitalist production takes place, while, on the other hand, its aim is to preserve the value of the existing capital and promote its self-expansion to the highest limit (i.e., to promote an ever more rapid growth of this value).

(Marx 1971a: 294)

11 "This is in every respect the most important law of modern political economy, and the most essential for understanding the most difficult relations. It is the most important law from the historical standpoint" (Marx 1973: 748).

12 The mere (direct) *production* process of capital in itself cannot add anything new in this context [crises] ... But [crisis] cannot be shown when dealing with the production process itself, for the latter is not concerned with the *realization* either or the produced value or the surplus value. This can only emerge in the *circulation process* which is in itself also a *process of reproduction.*

(Marx 1968: 313)

13 After referring to the value and material relationships, Marx wrote:

I call the former the value-composition, the latter the *technical composition* of capital. Between the two there is a strict correlation. To express this, I call the value-composition of capital, in so far as it is determined by its technical composition and mirrors the changes of the latter, the *organic composition* of capital.

(Marx 1970b: 574)

14 This conclusion follows even if fixed capital is ignored. The aggregate rate of profit is:

$$\pi = (SV)/(CC + VC)$$

Divide numerator and denominator by VC:

$$\pi = (SV/VC)/[(CC/VC)+1]$$

If CC/VC, the organic composition of capital, rises and SV/VC, the rate of surplus value, is constant, π must fall.

15 Over any specific time period whether profit rates fall is an empirical question. A rigorous empirical investigation requires careful specification of the definition of profit and its relationship to available data. Most of the empirical work on profit rates by radicals suffers from a lack of theoretical clarity, which leads to empirical results that are ambiguous. A major exception is Moseley (1992) in which the empirical work is based on clearly stated theoretical analysis.

16 See Hodgson (1974), and the same is in Sweezy (1966). Some followers of Marx have accepted this definition of the debate (Yaffe 1973). Critics typically present the issue in the form of the following question: can it be demonstrated, given the standard of living of the working class and the length of the working day, that as a result of technical change one can move from one static equilibrium state with a given rate of profit to another static equilibrium state in which the rate of profit is lower? By "static equilibrium" is meant that all commodities circulate at values implied by the most advanced production technique. This question implies a corollary: is there a set of available technical changes that capitalists would choose, which when generally adopted would result in a lower rate of profit? Both questions are irrelevant to the tendency of the rate of profit to fall, though much ink has been spilled debating the answers. The answers can be summarized briefly. If one assumes that all constant capital turns over in one production period, then the answer to both questions is "no". If one allows for fixed constant capital, then the answer depends upon the assumption made about the ratio of fixed to circulating constant capital over time.

17 In the three chapters on the law and its operation (Marx 1971a: Chapters 13–15), the terminology is not always precise, because Marx did not live to revise these chapters. He did not even set the order of Volume III, which was the work of Engels. However, from the existing text it is clear that Marx used the organic/value distinction he had specified in Volume I.

18

> In reproduction, just as in the accumulation of capita, it is not only a question of replacing, the same quantity of use values of which capital consists on the former scale or an enlarged scale … but of replacing the *value* of the capital advance along with the usual rate of profit (surplus-value).
>
> (Marx 1968: 494)

19

> The *possibility of* crisis, which became apparent in the *simple metamorphosis* of the commodity, is once more demonstrated, and further developed, by the disjunction between the (direct) process of production and the process of circulation. As soon as these processes do not merge smoothly into one another but become independent of one another, the crisis is there.
>
> (Marx 1968: 507)

20 "The *most abstract form of* crisis (and therefore the formal possibility *of* crisis) is thus the *metamorphosis* commodity itself: the contradiction of exchange value and use value, and furthermore of money and commodity" (Marx 1968: 508).

21 "The factors which turn this possibility of crisis into [an actual] crisis are not contained in this form itself; it only implies that the framework for a crisis exists" (Marx 1968: 508).

22 "The crisis in its second form is the function of money as means of payment, in which money has two different functions and figures in two different phases, divided from each other in time" (Marx 1968: 5010).

23

> At a given moment the supply of all commodities can be greater than the demand for all commodities, since the demand for the *general commodity*, money,

exchange value, is greater than the demand for all particular commodities; in other words the motive to turn the commodity into money, to realize its exchange value, prevails over the motive to transform the commodity into use value.

(Marx 1968: 507)

24 The emphasis and first two bracketed inserts are in the original text.

25 The specific feature about [capitalist accumulation] is that it uses the existing value of capital as a means of increasing this value to the utmost. The methods by which it accomplishes this include the fall of the rate of profit, depreciation of existing capital, and the development of the productive forces of labor at the expense of already created productive forces.

(Marx 1971a: 249)

26 The periodic depreciation of existing capital, one of the means immanent in capitalist production to check the fall of the rate of profit and hasten accumulation of capital-value through formation of new capital, disturbs the given conditions, within which the process of circulation and reproduction takes place, and is therefore accompanied by sudden stoppages and crises in the production process.

(Marx 1971a: 249)

27 [A] sudden general increase in the forces of production would relatively devalue all the grocer values which labor objectifies at the lower stage of the productive forces, and hence would destroy present capital as well as present laboring capacity. The other side of the crisis resolves itself into a real decrease in production, in living labor, in order to restore the correct relation between necessary and surplus labor, on which in the last analysis, everything rests.

(Marx 1973: 446)

28 The analysis of accumulation itself provides no reason to predict or expect a "final crisis" that because of its severity or specific nature will alone result in the collapse of the capitalist system.

11 First crisis of the twenty-first century

1 Marx explicitly rejected the argument that forms of finance might protect capitalism from crises:

> Can the existing relations of production and the relations of distribution which correspond to them be revolutionized by a change in the instrument of circulation, in the organization of circulation? ... Various forms of money may correspond better to social production at various stages; one form may remedy evils against which another is powerless; but none of them, as long as they remain forms of money, and as long as money remains an essential relation of production, is capable of overcoming the contradictions inherent in the money relation, and can instead only hope to reproduce these contradictions in one or another form.
>
> (1973: 122–3)

This passage is quoted in the excellent discussion of monetary crises in Toporowski (2009).

2 Notable exceptions are Rogoff (2006) and Izurieta and Godley (2002).

3 Perhaps the best known is the sixteenth century occultist, Phillippus Aureolus Theophrastus Bombastus von Hohenheim, born in what is now Austria.

4 Keynes, who was not beyond speculation himself, passed the following withering judgment on the pursuit of personal wealth,

> When the accumulation of wealth is no longer of high social importance, there will be great changes in the code of morals. We shall be able to rid ourselves of

> many of the pseudo-moral principles which have hag-ridden us for two hundred years, by which we have exalted some of the most distasteful of human qualities into the position of the highest virtues. We shall ... dare to assess the money-motive at its true value. The love of money as a possession ... will be recognized for what it is, a somewhat disgusting morbidity, one of those semi-criminal, semi-pathological propensities which one hands over with a shudder to the specialists in mental disease.
>
> (1972: 329–30)

5 A financial website found it necessary to explain why it was wise to hold stocks that do pay a dividend:

> In the 1950s investors used to own stocks mainly for their dividends. They looked for companies that paid consistent dividends out of profits. If the stock appreciated in price that was an added incentive. However all that changed in the recent years when many investors started investing purely for price appreciation.
>
> (http://topforeignstocks.com/2009/11/28/why-should-you-own-dividend-paying-stocks/)

6 Collections of stocks have different names whose meaning can vary across countries. The terms "unit trust" and "mutual funds" are common.

7 Berle and Means (1932), though their conclusion was that the separation resulted in a weakening of the profit motive, because managers sought to maximize sales.

8 A straightforward explanation of derivatives is given by Stulz (2005).

9 The claims for a "new economy" were journalistically summarized in *Newsweek*, January 2001. Alan Greenspan, head of the US Federal Reserve Bank infamously endorsed the concept. In testimony before the US Congress in October 2008 he would recant.

10 "Risk [is the danger] that a firm will be unable to meet its financial obligations. This risk is primarily a function of the relative amount of debt that the firm uses to finance its assets". See online, available at: http://financial-dictionary.thefreedictionary.com/financial+risk.

11 The Banking Act of 1933 (the Glass-Steagall Act) introduced the separation of finance into commercial and investment banking. It also created the Federal Deposit Insurance Corporation to insure bank deposits. Repeal of the provisions of the law was completed in 1999.

12 See the discussion of equity sales in Toporowski (2005:147ff.; and Toporowski 2000).

13

> The social character of capital is first promoted and wholly realized through the full development of the credit and the banking system ... The distribution of capital as a special business, a social function, is taken out of the hands of the private capitalists and usurers. But at the same time, banking and credit thus become the most potent means of driving capitalist production beyond its own limits, and one of the most effective vehicles of crises and swindle.
>
> (Marx 1971a: 607)

14 This is frequently treated in the context of "corporate responsibility". See the analysis online, available at: http://www.progressivereform.org/perspcorp_behav.cfm.

15 If we assume that productivity change was the same across all commodities, then the increase in the constant price market value of output should be close to the increase for fixed means of production.

16 This business cliché is defined online, available at: http://www.investopedia.com/terms/f/flighttoquality.asp.

17 In descending order, with GDP for 2008 in parenthesis in trillions of US dollars: the United States (12.3), Japan (4.1), Germany (2.8), the United Kingdom (2.3) and

France (2.1). China with a GDP of 3.3 trillion ranked third in size. Statistics online, available at: http://www.oecd.org.

18 The "golden age of capitalism" is the title of Marglin and Schor (1991). In their introduction, Marglin wrote, "Full employment and high growth can be restored, but only on the condition that policymakers face up to the need for a profound restructuring of the system of production, the macroeconomic structure, and the international order" (p. 37).

19 The four elements are much the same as those in the program of the British Labor Party in 1945, which was more radical than what was implemented during 1945–1951. See online, available at: http://www.unionhistory.info/timeline/1945_1960.php.

20 A journalist account of the Swedish nationalization is given by Carter Dougherty, "Stopping a Financial Crisis, the Swedish Way", *New York Times*, September 22, 2008. The nationalization was implemented by the short-lived right wing government, not the Social Democrats. Once banks recovered they were privatized.

21 This principle appears online, available at: http://www.ilo.org/ilolex/english/iloconst.htm.

22 A universal guaranteed income scheme would be paid to the employed as well as the unemployed. The possible specifications for such programs are explained in detail online, available at: http://www.basicincome.org/bien/.

References

Baran, P.A. and Paul Sweezy (1968) *Monopoly Capital*, New York: Monthly Review Press.

Baumol, William J. (1961) *Economic Theory and Operations Analysis*, Engelwood Cliffs, NJ: Prentice Hall.

Berle, A.A. and Gardner Means (1932) *The Modern Corporation and Private Property*, New York: Macmillan.

Bravermann, H. (1974) *Labor and Monopoly Capital*, New York: Monthly Review Press.

Byres, T.J. (1996) *Capitalism from Above and Capitalism from Below: An Essay in Comparative Political Economy*, London: Palgrave.

Clifton, A. (1977) "Competition and the Evolution of the Capitalist Mode of Production", *Cambridge Journal of Economics*, 1, 2: 137–51.

Colletti, Lucio (1979) *From Rousseau to Lenin*, New York: Monthly Review Press.

Council of Economic Advisors (2006) *Economic Report to the President 2006*, Washington, DC: United States Government Printing Office.

Council of Economic Advisors (2009) *Economic Report to the President 2009*, Washington, DC: United States Government Printing Office.

Council of Economic Advisors (2010) *Economic Report to the President 2010*, Washington, DC: United States Government Printing Office.

DeBrunhoff, Suzanne (1976) *Marx on Money*, New York: Urizen Books.

Dornbusch, Rudiger and Stanley Fischer (1994) *Macroeconomics*, 6th edn, New York: McGraw-Hill.

Engels, Friedrich (1971) "Law of Value and Rate of Profit", in *Capital*, Volume III (cited as Marx 1971a).

Engels, Fredrich (1972) *On Marx's Capital*, Moscow: Progress Publishers.

Engels, Friedrich (1976) *Anti-Duhring*, Peking: Foreign Languages Press.

Fine, Ben (1979) "On Marx's Theory of Agricultural Rent", *Economy and Society*, 8, 3: 241–78.

Fine, Ben (1980) *Economic Theory and Ideology*, London: Edward Arnold.

Fine, Ben (2001) *Social Capital versus Social Theory: Political Economy and Social Science at the Turn of the Millennium*, London: Routledge.

Fine, Ben and Laurence Harris (1979) *Re-reading Capital*, New York: Columbia University Press.

Fine, Ben, Costas Lapavitsas and Alfredo Saad-Fihlo (1999) "Transforming the Transformation Problem: Why the 'New Interpretation' is a wrong turning", *Review of Radical Political Economics*, 36, 1: 3–19.

Foley, Duncan (1982) "The Value of Money, the Value of Labour Power and the Marxian Transformation Problem", *Review of Radical Political Economics*, 14, 2: 37–47.

Foley, Duncan (1983) "On Marx's Theory of Money", *Social Concept*, 1, 1: 5–19.

Forget, Evelyn L. (1990) "John Stuart Mill's Business Cycle", *History of Political Economy*, 22, 4: 629–42.

Foster, John Bellamy (2002) "Monopoly Capital and the New Globalization", *Monthly Review*, January: 1–5.

Gerstein, Ira (1976) "Production, Circulation and Value", *Economy and Society*, 5, 3: 254–71.

Gordon, Robert J. (ed.) (1986) *The American Business Cycle: Continuity and Change*, New York: NBER.

Graziani, Augusto (2003) *Monetary Theory of Production*, Cambridge: Cambridge University Press.

Hansen, Alvin B. (1938) *Stagnation or full Recovery?* New York: W.W. Norton and Company.

Harcourt, Geoffrey (1973) *Some Cambridge Controversies in the Theory of Capital*, Cambridge: Cambridge University Press.

Hayek, Friedrich (1978) *Denationalization of Money*, London: IEA, online, available at: http://www.gold-speculator.com/quotes/1805-friedrich-von-hayek-denationalization-money.html.

Hilton, Rodney (ed.) (1976) *The Transition from Feudalism to Capitalism*, London: New Left Books.

Himmelweit, Susan and Simon Mohun (1978) "The Anomalies of Capital", *Cambridge Journal of Economics*, Autumn: 23–36.

Hobson, J.A. (1902) *Imperialism*, New York: James Pott and Co.

Hodgson, Geoffrey (1974) "The Theory of the Falling Rate of Profit", *New Left Review*, 84, March–April: 55–82.

Hume, David (1955) *Writings on Economics* (edited by Eugene Rotwein), London: Nelson.

International Monetary Fund (2010) *World Economic Outlook 2010*, Washington, DC: IMF.

Itoh, M. (1978) "The Formation of Marx's Theory of Crisis", *Science and Society*, XLII, 2: 129–55.

Izurieta, Alex and W. Godley (2002) "Scenarios for the U.S: A New Dilemma", *Strategic Analysis Series*, CERF, Cambridge Endowment for Research in Finance, November.

Johnson, Harry G. (1972) *Essays in Monetary Economics*, London: George Allen & Unwin.

Kautsky, Karl (1914) "Imperialism and the War", *International Socialist Review*, 15: 107–8.

Kenen, Peter B. (1994) *The International Economy* (3rd edn), Cambridge: Cambridge University Press.

Keynes, John Maynard (1936) *The General Theory of Employment, Interest and Money*, London: Macmillan.

Keynes, John Maynard (1972) *The Collected Writings of John Maynard Keynes*, Volume IX, New York: St Martin's Press.

Lapavitsas, Costas (2003) *Social Foundations of Markets, Money and Credit*, London: Routledge.

Lapavitsas, Costas and Makoto Itoh (1999) *Political Economy of Money and Finance*, London, Basingstoke: Macmillan.

Leijonhufvud, Axel (1968) *Keynesian Economics and the Economics of Keynes*, Oxford: Oxford University Press.

Lenin, V.I. (1972) "On the So-called Market Question", in *Collected Works*, Vol. 1, Moscow: Progress Publishers, pp. 75–128.
Lenin, V.I. (1974) *Imperialism, the Highest Stage of Capitalism*, in *Collected Works*, Vol. 22, Moscow: Progress Publishers, pp. 187–298.
Lenin, V.I. (2000) "Imperialism and the Split in Socialism", *Sbornik Sotsial-Demokrata* No. 2, online, available at: http://www.marxists.org/archive/lenin/works/1916/oct/x01.htm.
Lipsey, R.G. and Kelvin Lancaster (1956–57) "The General Theory of Second Best", *Review of Economic Studies*, 24, 1: 11–32.
Mandel, Ernest (1983) "Joint-stock Companies", in T.M. Bottomore (ed.), *A Dictionary of Marxist Thought*, Oxford: Basil Blackwell, pp. 241–4.
Marglin, Stephen A. and Juliet B. Schor (1991) *The Golden Age of Capitalism: Reinterpreting the Post-war Experience*, Oxford: Clarendon.
Marx, Karl (1881) "Notes on Adolph Wagner's 'Lehrbuch der politischen Ökonomie'", online, available at: http://www.marxists.org/archive/marx/works/1881/01/wagner.htm.
Marx, Karl (1955) *The Poverty of Philosophy*, Moscow: Progress Publishers.
Marx, Karl (1967) *Capital, A Critique of Political Economy, Volume II: The Process of Circulation of Capital*, Moscow: Progress Publishers.
Marx, Karl (1968) *Theories of Surplus Value, Part II*, Moscow: Progress Publishers.
Marx, Karl (1970a) *A Contribution to the Critique of Political Economy*, Moscow: Progress Publishers.
Marx, Karl (1970b) *Capital, A Critique of Political Economy, Volume I: A Critical Analysis of Capitalist Production*, Moscow: Progress Publishers.
Marx, Karl (1971a) *Capital, A Critique of Political Economy, Volume III: The Process of Capitalist Production as a Whole*, Progress Publishers.
Marx, Karl (1971b) *Theories of Surplus Value, Part III*, Moscow: Progress Publishers.
Marx, Karl (1973) *Grundrisse*, New York: Vintage.
Marx, Karl (1974) *The First International and After*, New York: Vintage.
Marx, Karl and Friedrich Engels (1965) *Selected Correspondence*, Moscow: Progress Publishers.
Marx, Karl and Friedrich Engels (1972) *The German Ideology*, New York: International Publishers.
Marx, Karl and Friedrich Engels (1976) *Collected Works, Volume VI*, New York: International Publishers.
Meek, Ronald (1977) *Smith, Marx and After*, London: Chapman and Hall.
Mill, John Stuart (1867) *Principles of Political Economy with Some of Their Applications to Social Philosophy*, London: Longmans, Green, Reader and Dyer.
Morishima, Michio (1972) *Marx's Economics*, Cambridge: Cambridge University Press.
Morishima, Michio and George Catephores (1975) "Is There a 'Historical Transformation Problem'?" *Economic Journal*, 85: 309–28.
Morishima, Michio and George Catephores (1978) *Value, Exploitation and Growth*, New York: McGraw-Hill.
Moseley, Fred (1992) *The Falling Rate of Profit in the Postwar United States Economy*, New York: St Martins Press.
Moseley, Fred (ed.) (2005) *Marx's Theory of Money*, London: Palgrave Macmillan.
Okishio, Nobuo (1961) "Technical Changes and the Rate of Profit", *Kobe University Economic Review*, 7: 85–99.
Pigou, A.C. (1941) *The Veil of Money*, London: Macmillan.
Polanyi, Karl (1944) *The Great Transformation*, Boston, MA: Beacon Press.

Prouhdon, Pierre-Joseph (1847) *Philosophy of Poverty*, online, available at: http://www.marxists.org/reference/subject/economics/proudhon/philosophy/index.htm.

Ricardo, David (1953 [1817]) *Principles of Political Economy and Taxation*, Cambridge: Cambridge University Press.

Rogoff, Kenneth (2006) "Will Emerging Markets Escape the Next Big Systemic Financial Crisis?" Online, available at: http://www.allbusiness.com/public-administration/4077148–1.html.

Rothschild, K.W. (1947) "Price Theory and Oligopoly", *Economic Journal*, 57, 227: 299–320.

Rubin, I.I. (n.d.) *Essays on Marx's Theory* of *Value*, Detroit, MI: Black and Red.

Saad-Filho, Alfredo (2002) *The Value of Marx*, London, Routledge.

Samuelson, P.A. (1939) "Interactions between the Multiplier Analysis and the Principle of Acceleration", *Review of Economic Statistics*, 21: 75–8.

Shaikh, Anwar (1978) "An Introduction to the History of Crisis Theories", in Economics Education Project, *U.S. Capitalism in Crisis*, New York: URPE.

Shaikh, Anwar (1979) "On the Laws of International Exchange", *Science and Society*, 43, Fall: 214–25.

Shiller, Robert (2000) *Irrational Exuberance*, Princeton, NJ: Princeton University Press.

Sismondi, Jean Charles Léonard de (1819) *Nouveaux principes d'economie politique, ou de la Richesse dans ses rapports avec la population*, Paris: Perspectives de l'economie, Les Fondateurs.

Smith, Adam (1776) *An Inquiry into the Nature and Causes of the Wealth of Nations*, online, available at: http://www.bibliomania.com/2/1/65/112/frameset.html.

Sraffa, Piero (1960) *Production of Commodities by Means of Commodities*, Cambridge: Cambridge University Press.

Steedman, Ian (1977) *Marx after Sraffa*, London: New Left Books.

Stulz, René M. (2005) "Demystifying Financial Derivatives", *Milkin Institute Review*. Online, available at: http://www.cob.ohio-state.edu/fin/faculty/stulz/publishedpapers/financial%20derivatives-Lessons%20from%20the%20subprime%20crisis.pdf.

Sweezy, Paul (1966) *Theory of Capitalist Development*, New York: Monthly Review Press.

Takenaga, Susumu (2003) "Theory of Money of David Ricardo: Quantity Theory and Theory of Value", *Lecturas de Economia*, Universidad de Antioquia, Departamento de Economía, 59, Julio–Diciembre: 73–126.

Tarbuck, Kenneth J. (ed.) (1972) *The Accumulation of Capital: An Anti-Critique*, and *Imperialism and the Accumulation of Capital* by Rosa Luxemburg and Nikolai I. Bukharin, New York: Monthly Review Press.

Toporowski, Jan (2000) *The End of Finance: The Theory of Capital Market Inflation, Financial Derivatives and Pension Fund Capitalism*, London: Routledge.

Toporowski, Jan (2005) *Theories of Financial Disturbance: An Examination of Critical Theories of Finance from Adam Smith to the Present Day*, London: Edward Elgar.

Toporowski, Jan (2009) *Marx's Grundrisse and the Monetary Business Cycle*, London: SOAS and the University of Amsterdam.

Walras, Marie-Esprit-Léon (1926) *Éléments d'économie politique pure, ou théorie de la richesse sociale*, Amsterdam: North-Holland.

Weeks, John (1979) "The Process of Accumulation and the 'Profit Squeeze' Hypothesis", *Science and Society*, 43, 3: 259–80.

Weeks, John (1981) *Capital and Exploitation*, Princeton, NJ: Princeton University Press.

Weeks, John (1982) "Equilibrium, Uneven Development and the Tendency of the Rate of Profit to Fall", *Capital and Class*, 6, 1: 62–77.

Weeks, John (1983) "On the Issue of Capitalist Circulation and the Concepts Appropriate to its Analysis", *Science and Society*, 48, 2: 214–25.

Weeks, John (1988) "Value and Production in The General Theory", in John Hillard (ed.), *J M Keynes in Retrospect*, Aldershot: Edward Elgar.

Weeks, John (1989) *A Critique of Neoclassical Macroeconomics*, London and New York: Macmillan and St Martin's Press.

Weeks, John (1990) "Abstract Labor and Commodity Production", *Research in Political Economy*, 12, 3: 3–19.

Weeks, John (2009) *Teoria de la competencia en los neoclasicos y en Marx*, Madrid: Maia Ediciones.

Weeks, John (2010) *False Paradigm: The Internal Inconsistencies of Neoclassical Macroeconomics*, London: manuscript. Online, available at: http://jweeks.org.

Yaffe, David (1973) "The Marxian Theory of Crisis, Capital and the State", *Economy and Society*, 2, 2: 184–232.

Wray, L.R. (1994) "The Political Economy of the Current U.S. Financial Crisis", *International Papers in Political Economy*, 1, 3: 1–51.

Zazzaro, Alberto (2002) "How Heterodox is the Heterodoxy of the Monetary Circuit Theory? The Nature of Money and the Microeconomy of the Circuit", Universita' Politecnica delle Marche (I), Dipartimento di Economia, Working Paper 163.

Index